Reactive Programming in Kotlin

Design and build non-blocking, asynchronous Kotlin applications with RXKotlin, Reactor-Kotlin, Android, and Spring

Rivu Chakraborty

BIRMINGHAM - MUMBAI

Reactive Programming in Kotlin

First published: December 2017

Production reference: 1011217

Published by Packt Publishing Ltd.
Livery Place
35 Livery Street
Birmingham
B3 2PB, UK.

ISBN 978-1-78847-302-6

www.packtpub.com

Credits

Author
Rivu Chakraborty

Reviewers
Alexander Hanschke
Ravindra Kumar

Commissioning Editor
Richa Tripathi

Acquisition Editor
Sandeep Mishra

Content Development Editor
Akshada Iyer

Technical Editor
Supriya Thabe

Copy Editor
Zainab Bootwala

Project Coordinator
Prajakta Naik

Proofreader
Safis Editing

Indexer
Francy Puthiry

Graphics
Jason Monteiro

Production Coordinator
Nilesh Mohite

About the Author

Rivu Chakraborty is a Google-certified Android developer and a senior tech member at the Institute of Engineers (India), and also has certifications in Scrum. With over 5 years of experience, he is currently working as a senior software engineer (Android) at Indus Net Technologies Pvt. Ltd.

He considers himself a Kotlin and Android enthusiast and a Kotlin evangelist. He has been using Kotlin since December 2015, so he has around 2 years of experience in Kotlin at the time of publishing this book. As a part of his mission to spread the use and knowledge of the Kotlin language as much as possible, he created the KotlinKolkata user group—one of the most active Kotlin user groups throughout the world, and he is the Founder Organizer of KotlinKolkata. He is also an active member of GDG Kolkata and gives talks at the GDG Kolkata meetups.

As Rivu believes that knowledge increases by sharing, he writes a lot of tutorials on JavaCodeGeeks, AndroidHive, and his own site (`http://www.rivuchk.com`), which you can visit to read his tutorials and learn more about him.

I would like to thank my wife, parents and whole family (including inlaws) for being with me while I was writing this book.

I would like to thank my college teachers, Avik Dey and Nandan Banerjee—they have always encouraged and helped me learn and strive to become a better developer from the beginning of my engineering course till date. I always feel more encouraged whenever I speak to them.

Also, this book wouldn't have been completed without the continuous guidance and support of the Packt team, especially by the CDE of this book, Akshada—her encouraging comments meant a lot to me.

About the Reviewers

Alexander Hanschke is CTO at techdev Solutions GmbH, a technology company located in Berlin. He worked on various Java-based projects in the financial industry for 8 years, before turning to Kotlin in 2016. Since then, he has been applying Kotlin to all kinds of projects, including Alexa skills, blockchain clients, and Spring-based applications. He frequently speaks at technology meetups and occasionally writes articles about various aspects of the Kotlin programming language.

Ravindra Kumar is an Android developer and Computer Polyglot from Bengaluru, India. He is an Android + WEB lover, speaker, start-up geek, and open source junkie.

He is working as an Android developer at Fueled. Previously, he used to work with Cleartrip, as the lead developer of Cleartrip.com's Android App. He likes open source projects. He is a huge fan of fancy Android libraries out there, and he contributes to bug reporting, fixing, and feedbacks. He has given talks at DroidCon, TiConf, and JSFOO.

Ravindra started as a web engineer who used to write lots of JavaScript, but, after some time, looking for his real passion, he started his journey in mobile app development through Titanium, where, later, he discovered the Android world. After getting some experience on such an awesome platform, he started a new adventure at a mobile company, where he led several projects for important Indian companies.

He has a strong interest in code quality, testing, and automation—preferably all three together. Combining technical skills with soft skills, he also ventures into the realms of mentoring and article writing. He hates doing things manually and hates to see `src/test/java` directories with Empty Example classes. He believes that by working with legacy code, and improving it, he can make the world a better place. To his disappointment, the world does not seem to care all that much about his efforts.

He is a pretty normal person—a husband and father of one who loves cricket. Follow him on Twitter at `@ravidsrk` or email him at `ravidsrk@gmail.com`.

www.PacktPub.com

For support files and downloads related to your book, please visit www.PacktPub.com.

Did you know that Packt offers eBook versions of every book published, with PDF and ePub files available? You can upgrade to the eBook version at www.PacktPub.com and as a print book customer, you are entitled to a discount on the eBook copy. Get in touch with us at service@packtpub.com for more details.

At www.PacktPub.com, you can also read a collection of free technical articles, sign up for a range of free newsletters and receive exclusive discounts and offers on Packt books and eBooks.

https://www.packtpub.com/mapt

Get the most in-demand software skills with Mapt. Mapt gives you full access to all Packt books and video courses, as well as industry-leading tools to help you plan your personal development and advance your career.

Why subscribe?

- Fully searchable across every book published by Packt
- Copy and paste, print, and bookmark content
- On demand and accessible via a web browser

Customer Feedback

Thanks for purchasing this Packt book. At Packt, quality is at the heart of our editorial process. To help us improve, please leave us an honest review on this book's Amazon page at https://www.amazon.com/dp/1788473027.

If you'd like to join our team of regular reviewers, you can e-mail us at customerreviews@packtpub.com. We award our regular reviewers with free eBooks and videos in exchange for their valuable feedback. Help us be relentless in improving our products!

I would like to dedicate this book to my wife - Esha, and my to be born child (yes, my wife is expecting at the time of writing this whole book), and my parents for supporting and encouraging me while I was writing this book.

Table of Contents

Preface

Is our world just a collection of states? No. Then why do all the programming paradigms represent our world as a series of states? Can't we reflect objects that are real, moving, and continuously changing state in programming? These are the questions that have interested me ever since I first learned programming.

When I started working as an Android developer, these questions continued to plague me, but got some friends as well. Why do we need so many loops in an application? Isn't there anything to replace the iterators? Also, for Android applications, we must keep a lot of things in mind, as the processors and RAM in a mobile device are not as powerful as those in your PC. There is often an Out of Memory Exception if you do not structure your projects well. So, if we could have less iterators in our program, the UX will significantly improve, but, how do we do it? How do we replace iterators, and with what?

One fine day, I read a blog post about reactive programming and the ReactiveX Framework, (most probably by Thomas Nield, thanks to him), and it gave me a glimpse of the answers to all my questions. So, I started learning reactive programming.

I found out that the learning curve of reactive programming is very much complex, and many developers out there leave it part way through. Reactive programming is considered an advanced topic in most places. However, I continued my journey toward learning reactive programming, and as a reward for my patience and consistency, I got answers to my questions. RxJava (and all other ReactiveX libraries) represents models just like our real-time world, and, unlike states, they model behavior with moving and continuously changing states. Unlike an iterator pattern, it believes on push mechanism, which will push data/event to the subscriber/observer as it comes, making the programming a lot more easier and a lot more like the human world.

On the other hand, around 2 years ago (in December 2015), when I read a Jetbrains blog (yes, I do read a lot, and write as well) about a new language that will work in JVM, my first thought was, why a new language? So, I started exploring Kotlin, and I fell in love with it. The sole purpose of the language is making programming a lot easier. Whenever someone speaks about the benefits of Kotlin, they talk about handling null pointer exceptions so easily, but there are a lot more advantages; the list is never-ending and continues to grow.

The best thing that can happen to a programmer is combining the Kotlin and ReactiveX Frameworks; Mario Arias did this awesome job for the sake of the Developers Community and started RxKotlin on October 2013.

The only thing that RxKotlin lacks is documentation; I personally believe that the main reason behind the complex learning curve of ReactiveX libraries is a lack of documentation and, mostly, a lack of awareness. I've seen a lot of developers, even with more than 6-8 years of experience who have not heard of reactive programming; I believe this book will have a bigger role in changing this scenario. This book is also a part of my mission (also the mission of Kotlin Kolkata User Group) to spread the use and knowledge of Kotlin as much as possible.

As per as my knowledge, this is the first book that helps you learn reactive programming in Kotlin, covering RxKotlin (precisely RxKotlin 2.0) and the Reactor-Kotlin Framework. It is a step-by-step guide to learn RxKotlin and Reactor-Kotlin with added coverage on Spring and Android. I hope this book will help you find the benefits of Kotlin and reactive programming altogether, and, with the help of this book, you will be able to successfully apply reactive programming to all your Kotlin projects.

If you have any concerns, feedback, or comments, you can contact me through my site `http://www.rivuchk.com`, or drop an email to `rivu@rivuchk.com`. Make sure to mention Book Query - Reactive Programming in Kotlin in the subject of the email.

What this book covers

Chapter 1, *A Short Introduction to Reactive Programming*, helps you understand the context, thinking pattern, and principles of reactive programming.

Chapter 2, *Functional Programming with Kotlin and RxKotlin*, chapter walks you through the essential concepts of functional programming paradigms and their possible implementations on Kotlin so that you can understand functional reactive programming easily.

Chapter 3, *Observables, Observers, and Subjects*, enables you to gain a grip on the base of RxKotlin—Observables, Observers, and Subjects lay at the core of RxKotlin.

Chapter 4, *Introduction to Backpressure and Flowables*, introduces you to Flowables, which enable you to use Backpressure—a technique in RxKotlin that prevents producers from outpacing consumers.

Chapter 5, *Asynchronous Data Operators and Transformations*, introduces you to operators in RxKotlin.

Chapter 6, *More on Operators and Error Handling*, gets your grip stronger on operators, and introduces how to combine producers and how to filter them with operators. This chapter will also help you handle errors more efficiently in RxKotlin.

Chapter 7, *Concurrency and Parallel Processing in RxKotlin with Schedulers*, enables you to leverage the benefits of Schedulers to achieve concurrent programming.

Chapter 8, *Testing RxKotlin Applications*, walks you through the most crucial part of application development—testing—which is a bit different in RxKotlin as reactive programming defines behaviors instead of states. This chapter starts with the basics of testing, enabling you to learn testing from scratch.

Chapter 9, *Resource Management and Extending RxKotlin*, helps you learn how to manage resources in Kotlin—resources could be database instances, files, HTTP accesses, or anything that needs to be closed. You will also learn how to create your own custom operators in RxKotlin in this chapter.

Chapter 10, *Introduction to Web Programming with Spring for Kotlin Developers*, gets you started with Spring and Hibernate so that you can leverage its benefits while writing APIs in Kotlin.

Chapter 11, *REST APIs with Spring JPA and Hibernate*, introduces you to the Reactor framework, the reactor-kotlin extension, so that you can apply reactive programming with Spring in Kotlin.

Chapter 12, *Reactive Kotlin and Android*, the last chapter of this book, gets you started with reactive programming in Android with Kotlin.

What you need for this book

We will be using Java 8 and Kotlin 1.1.50 for the programs in this book, so Oracle's JDK 1.8 along with Kotlin 1.1.50 (this can be skipped downloading if you're using IntelliJ IDEA) will be required. You will need an environment to write and compile your Kotlin code (I strongly recommend Intellij IDEA, but you can use anything of your choice), and preferably a build automation system such as Gradle or Maven. Later in this book, we will use Android Studio (2.3.3 or 3.0). Everything you need in this book should be free to use and not require commercial or personal licensing (we are using the IntelliJ IDEA Community Edition).

Who this book is for

This book is for Kotlin developers who would like to build fault-tolerant, scalable, and distributed systems. A basic knowledge of Kotlin is required; however, no prior knowledge of reactive programming is assumed.

Conventions

In this book, you will find a number of text styles that distinguish between different kinds of information. Here are some examples of these styles and an explanation of their meaning.

Code words in text, database table names, folder names, filenames, file extensions, pathnames, dummy URLs, user input, and Twitter handles are shown as follows: "Let's first take a look at the init block of the ReactiveCalculator class"

A block of code is set as follows:

```
async(CommonPool) {
    Observable.range(1, 10)
      .subscribeOn(Schedulers.trampoline())//(1)
      .subscribe {
          runBlocking { delay(200) }
          println("Observable1 Item Received $it")
      }
```

When we wish to draw your attention to a particular part of a code block, the relevant lines or items are set in bold:

```
abstract class BaseActivity : AppCompatActivity() {
    final override fun onCreate(savedInstanceState: Bundle?) {
      super.onCreate(savedInstanceState)
      onCreateBaseActivity(savedInstanceState)
    }
    abstract fun onCreateBaseActivity(savedInstanceState: Bundle?)
}
```

Any command-line input or output is written as follows. The input command might be broken into several lines to aid readability, but needs to be entered as one continuous line in the prompt:

```
$ git clone https://github.com/ReactiveX/RxKotlin.git
$ cd RxKotlin/
$ ./gradlew build
```

New terms and **important words** are shown in bold. Words that you see on the screen, for example, in menus or dialog boxes, appear in the text like this: "Go to **Android Studio | Settings | Plugins**."

Warnings or important notes appear like this.

Tips and tricks appear like this.

Reader feedback

Feedback from our readers is always welcome. Let us know what you think about this book—what you liked or disliked. Reader feedback is important for us as it helps us develop titles that you will really get the most out of.

To send us general feedback, simply e-mail feedback@packtpub.com, and mention the book's title in the subject of your message.

If there is a topic that you have expertise in and you are interested in either writing or contributing to a book, see our author guide at www.packtpub.com/authors.

Customer support

Now that you are the proud owner of a Packt book, we have a number of things to help you to get the most from your purchase.

Downloading the example code

You can download the example code files for this book from your account at http://www.packtpub.com. If you purchased this book elsewhere, you can visit http://www.packtpub.com/support and register to have the files e-mailed directly to you.

You can download the code files by following these steps:

1. Log in or register to our website using your e-mail address and password.
2. Hover the mouse pointer on the **SUPPORT** tab at the top.
3. Click on **Code Downloads & Errata**.
4. Enter the name of the book in the **Search** box.
5. Select the book for which you're looking to download the code files.
6. Choose from the drop-down menu where you purchased this book from.
7. Click on **Code Download**.

Once the file is downloaded, please make sure that you unzip or extract the folder using the latest version of:

- WinRAR / 7-Zip for Windows
- Zipeg / iZip / UnRarX for Mac
- 7-Zip / PeaZip for Linux

The code bundle for the book is also hosted on GitHub at `https://github.com/PacktPublishing/Reactive-Programming-in-Kotlin`. We also have other code bundles from our rich catalog of books and videos available at `https://github.com/PacktPublishing/`. Check them out!

Downloading the color images of this book

We also provide you with a PDF file that has color images of the screenshots/diagrams used in this book. The color images will help you better understand the changes in the output. You can download this file from `https://www.packtpub.com/sites/default/files/downloads/ReactiveProgramminginKotlin_ColorImages.pdf`.

Errata

Although we have taken every care to ensure the accuracy of our content, mistakes do happen. If you find a mistake in one of our books—maybe a mistake in the text or the code—we would be grateful if you could report this to us. By doing so, you can save other readers from frustration and help us improve subsequent versions of this book. If you find any errata, please report them by visiting `http://www.packtpub.com/submit-errata`, selecting your book, clicking on the **Errata Submission Form** link, and entering the details of your errata. Once your errata are verified, your submission will be accepted and the errata will be uploaded to our website or added to any list of existing errata under the Errata section of that title.

To view the previously submitted errata, go to `https://www.packtpub.com/books/content/support` and enter the name of the book in the search field. The required information will appear under the **Errata section.**

Piracy

Piracy of copyrighted material on the Internet is an ongoing problem across all media. At Packt, we take the protection of our copyright and licenses very seriously. If you come across any illegal copies of our works in any form on the Internet, please provide us with the location address or website name immediately so that we can pursue a remedy.

Please contact us at `copyright@packtpub.com` with a link to the suspected pirated material.

We appreciate your help in protecting our authors and our ability to bring you valuable content.

Questions

If you have a problem with any aspect of this book, you can contact us at `questions@packtpub.com`, and we will do our best to address the problem.

1
A Short Introduction to Reactive Programming

The term **reactive** got famous recently. Not only did it get trending, but it has started ruling the software development sector with new blog posts articles every day, and presentations, emerging frameworks and libraries, and more. Even the big IT companies that are often referred to as market giants, such as Google, Facebook, Amazon, Microsoft, and Netflix, are not only supporting and using reactive programming themselves, but they've even started releasing new frameworks for the same.

So, as a programmer, we are wondering about reactive programming. Why is everyone getting crazy about it? What does *reactive programming* exactly mean? What are the benefits of reactive programming? And, finally, should we learn it? If yes, then how?

On the other hand, **Kotlin** is also the newest programming language you've heard of (we're guessing you've heard of Kotlin, as this book assumes that you've a little understanding of the language). Kotlin, as a language, solves many important problems in Java. The best part is its interoperability with Java. If you carefully watch the trends, then you would know that Kotlin has created not a strong wind but a storm to blow things around it. Even the Google at *Google IO/17* declared its official support for Kotlin as an official programming language for Android application development, noting that it is the first time since the perception of the Android Framework that Google has added another language to the Android family other than Java. Soon after, Spring also expressed their support for Kotlin.

To say it in simple words, Kotlin is powerful enough to create a great application, but if you combine reactive programming style with Kotlin, it would be super easy to build great apps better.

This book will present reactive programming in Kotlin with RxKotlin and Reactor, along with their implementations in Spring, Hibernate, and Android.

In this chapter, we will cover the following topics:

- What is reactive programming?
- Reasons to adapt functional reactive programming
- Reactive Manifesto
- Comparison between the `observer` (reactive) pattern and familiar patterns
- Getting started with RxKotlin

What is reactive programming?

Reactive programming is an asynchronous programming paradigm that revolves around data streams and the propagation of change. In simpler words, those programs which propagate all the changes that affected its data/data streams to all the interested parties (such as end users, components and sub-parts, and other programs that are somehow related) are called **reactive programs**.

For example, take any spreadsheet (say the Google Sheet), put any number in the A1 cell, and in the B1 cell, write the `=ISEVEN(A1)` function; it'll show `TRUE` or `FALSE`, depending on whether you've entered an even or odd number. Now, if you modify the number in A1, the value of B1 will also get changed automatically; such behavior is called **reactive**.

Not clear enough? Let's look at a coding example and then try to understand it again. The following is a normal Kotlin code block to determine if a number is even or odd:

```
fun main(args: Array<String>) {
  var number = 4
  var isEven = isEven(number)
  println("The number is " + (if (isEven) "Even" else "Odd"))
  number = 9
  println("The number is " + (if (isEven) "Even" else "Odd"))
}

fun isEven(n:Int):Boolean = ((n % 2) == 0)
```

If you check the output of the program, then you'll see that, although the number is assigned a new value, isEven is still true; however, if isEven was made to track changes of the number, then it would automatically become false. A reactive program would just do the same.

Reasons to adapt functional reactive programming

So, let's first discuss the reasons to adapt functional reactive programming. There's no point in changing the whole way you code unless it gets you some really significant benefits, right? Yes, functional reactive programming gets you a set of mind-blowing benefits, as listed here:

- **Get rid of the callback hell**:
  A callback is a method that gets called when a predefined event occurs. The mechanism of passing interfaces with callback methods is called **callback mechanism**. This mechanism involves a hell of a lot of code, including the interfaces, their implementations, and more. Hence, it is referred to as **callback hell**.

- **Standard mechanism for error handling**:
  Generally, while working with complex tasks and HTTP calls, handling errors are a major concern, especially in the absence of any standard mechanism, it becomes a headache.

- **It's a lot simpler than regular threading**:
  Though Kotlin makes it easier to work with threading as compared to Java, it's still complicated enough. Reactive programming helps to make it easier.

- **Straightforward way for async operations**:
  Threading and asynchronous operations are interrelated. As threading got easier, so did the async operations.

- **One for everything, the same API for every operations**:
  Reactive programming, especially RxKotlin, offers you a simple and straightforward API. You can use it for anything and everything, be it network call, database access, computation, or UI operations.

- **The functional way**:
  Reactive programming leads you to write readable declarative code as, here, things are more functional.

- **Maintainable and testable code**:
  The most important point-by following reactive programming properly, your program becomes more maintainable and testable.

Reactive Manifesto

So, what is the Reactive Manifesto? The Reactive Manifesto (`http://www.reactivemanifesto.org`) is a document defining the four reactive principles. You can think of it as the map to the treasure of reactive programming, or like the bible for the programmers of the reactive programming religion.

Everyone starting with reactive programming should have a read of the manifesto to understand what reactive programming is all about and what its principles are.

So, the following is the gist of four principles that Reactive Manifesto defines:

- **Responsive**:
  The system responds in a timely manner. Responsive systems focus on providing rapid and consistent response times, so they deliver a consistent quality of service.
- **Resilient**:
  In case the system faces any failure, it stays responsive. Resilience is achieved by replication, containment, isolation, and delegation. Failures are contained within each component, isolating components from each other, so when failure has occurred in a component, it will not affect the other components or the system as a whole.
- **Elastic**:
  Reactive systems can react to changes and stay responsive under varying workload. They achieve elasticity in a cost effective way on commodity hardware and software platforms.
- **Message driven**:
  In order to establish the resilient principle, reactive systems need to establish a boundary between components by relying on asynchronous message passing.

By implementing all four preceding principles, the system becomes reliable and responsive thus, reactive.

Reactive Streams standard specifications

Along with the Reactive Manifesto, we also have a standard specification on Reactive Streams. Everything in the reactive world is accomplished with the help of Reactive Streams. In 2013, Netflix, Pivotal, and Lightbend (previously known as Typesafe) felt a need for a standards specification for Reactive Streams as the reactive programming was beginning to spread and more frameworks for reactive programming were starting to emerge, so they started the initiative that resulted in Reactive Streams standard specification, which is now getting implemented across various frameworks and platforms.

You can take a look at the Reactive Streams standard specification at—http://www.reactive-streams.org/.

Reactive Frameworks for Kotlin

To write Reactive programs, we need a library or a specific programming language; we can't refer to Kotlin as a reactive language (basically, I don't know any such language that is reactive by itself) as it is a powerful and flexible programming language for modern multiplatform applications, fully interoperable with Java and Android. However, there are reactive libraries out there to help us with these. So, let's take a look at the available list:

- RxKotlin
- Reactor-Kotlin
- Redux-Kotlin
- FunKTionale
- RxJava and other Reactive Java Frameworks can also be used with Kotlin (as Kotlin is 100% interoperable with Java-bidirectional)

 In this book, we will focus on RxJava and Reactor-kotlin (in the later chapters, on Spring).

Getting started with RxKotlin

RxKotlin is a specific implementation of reactive programming for Kotlin, which is influenced by functional programming. It favors function composition, avoidance of global state, and side effects. It relies on the `observer` pattern of producer/consumer, with a lot of operators that allow composing, scheduling, throttling, transforming, error handling, and lifecycle management.

Whereas Reactor-Kotlin is also based on functional programming, and it is widely accepted and backed by the Spring Framework.

Downloading and setting up RxKotlin

You can download and build RxKotlin from GitHub (`https://github.com/ReactiveX/RxKotlin`). I do not require any other dependencies. The documentation on the GitHub wiki page is well structured. Here's how you can check out the project from GitHub and run the build:

```
$ git clone https://github.com/ReactiveX/RxKotlin.git
$ cd RxKotlin/
$ ./gradlew build
```

You can also use Maven and Gradle, as instructed on the page.

For Gradle, use the following compile dependency:

```
compile 'io.reactivex.rxjava2:rxkotlin:2.x.y'
```

For Maven, use this dependency:

```
<dependency>
  <groupId>io.reactivex.rxjava2</groupId>
  <artifactId>rxkotlin</artifactId>
  <version>2.x.y</version>
</dependency>
```

This book targets RxKotlin 2.x, so remember to use `io.reactive.rxjava2` instead of `io.reactivex.rxkotlin`, as the latter one is for RxKotlin 1.x.

 Note that we are using RxKotlin version 2.1.0 for this book.

Now, let's take a look at what RxKotlin is all about. We will begin with something well-known and, gradually, we will get into the secrets of the library.

Comparing the pull mechanism with the RxJava push mechanism

RxKotlin revolves around the observable type that represents a system of data/events intended for push mechanism (instead of the pull mechanism of the `iterator` pattern of traditional programs), thus it is lazy and can be used synchronously and asynchronously.

It will be easier for us to understand if we start with a simple example that works with a list of data. So, here is the code:

```
fun main(args: Array<String>) {
  var list:List<Any> = listOf("One", 2, "Three", "Four", 4.5,
  "Five", 6.0f) // 1
  var iterator = list.iterator() // 2
  while (iterator.hasNext()) { // 3
    println(iterator.next()) // Prints each element 4
  }
}
```

The following screenshot is the output:

```
"C:\Program Files\Java\jdk1.8.0_131\bin\java" ...
One
2
Three
Four
4.5
Five
6.0

Process finished with exit code 0
```

So, let's go through the program line by line to understand how it works.

At comment 1, we're creating a list of seven items (the list contains data of mixed data types with the help of any class). On comment 2, we are creating `iterator` from the list, so that we can iterate over the data. In comment 3, we have created a `while` loop to pull data from the list with the help of `iterator`, and then, in 4, we're printing it.

The thing to notice is that we're pulling data from the list while the current thread is blocked until the data is received and ready. For example, think of getting that data from a network call/database query instead of just `List` and, in that case, how long the thread will be blocked. You can obviously create a separate thread for those operations, but then also, it will increase complexity.

Just give a thought; which one is a better approach? Making the program wait for data or pushing data to the program whenever it's available?

The building blocks of the ReactiveX Framework (be it RxKotlin or RxJava) are the observables. The `observable` class is just the opposite of `iterator` interface. It has an underlying collection or computation that produces values that can be consumed by a consumer. However, the difference is that the consumer doesn't *pull* these values from the producer, like in the `iterator` pattern; instead, the producer *pushes* the values as notifications to the consumer.

So, let's take the same example again, this time with `observable`:

```kotlin
fun main(args: Array<String>) {
    var list:List<Any> = listOf("One", 2, "Three",
    "Four", 4.5, "Five", 6.0f) // 1
    var observable: Observable<Any> = list.toObservable();

    observable.subscribeBy( // named arguments for
    lambda Subscribers
      onNext = { println(it) },
      onError =  { it.printStackTrace() },
      onComplete = { println("Done!") }
    )
}
```

This program output is the same as the previous one—it prints all the items in the list. The difference is in the approach. So, let's see how it actually works:

1. Create a list (just the same as the previous one).
2. An `observable` instance is created with that list.
3. We're subscribing to the `observer` instance (we're using named arguments for `lambda` and covering it in detail later).

As we subscribe to `observable`, each data will be pushed to `onNext`, and, as it gets ready, it will call `onComplete` when all data is pushed and `onError` if any error occurs.

So, you learned to use the `observable` instances, and they are quite similar to the `iterator` instances, which is something we're very familiar with. We can use these `observable` instances to build asynchronous streams and push data updates to their subscribers (even to multiple subscribers).This was a simple implementation of the reactive programming paradigm. The data is being propagated to all the interested parties—the subscribers.

The ReactiveEvenOdd program

So, now that we are somewhat familiar with `observables`, let's modify the even-odd program in a reactive way. Here is the code for doing so:

```
fun main(args: Array<String>) {
    var subject:Subject<Int> = PublishSubject.create()

    subject.map({ isEven(it) }).subscribe({println
    ("The number is ${(if (it) "Even" else "Odd")}" )})

    subject.onNext(4)
    subject.onNext(9)
}
```

Here is the output:

```
"C:\Program Files\Java\jdk1.8.0_131\bin\java" ...
The number is Even
The number is Odd

Process finished with exit code 0
```

In this program, we have used `subject` and `map`, which we will cover in the later chapters. Here, it is just to show how easy it is in reactive programming to notify the changes. If you look at the program closely, then you'll also find that the code is modular and functional. When we notify `subject` with a number, it calls the method in `map`, then it calls the method in `subscribe` with the return value of the `map` method. The `map` method checks if the number is even and returns true or false accordingly; in the `subscribe` method, we are receiving that value and printing even or odd accordingly. The `subject.onNext` method is the way through which we message the new value to the subject, so it can process it.

The ReactiveCalculator project

So, let's start with an event with the user input. Go through the following example:

```kotlin
fun main(args: Array<String>) {
  println("Initial Out put with a = 15, b = 10")
  var calculator:ReactiveCalculator = ReactiveCalculator(15,10)
  println("Enter a = <number> or b = <number> in separate
  lines\nexit to exit the program")
  var line:String?
  do {
    line = readLine();
    calculator.handleInput(line)
  } while (line!= null && !line.toLowerCase().contains("exit"))
}
```

If you run the code, you'll get the following output:

```
"C:\Program Files\Java\jdk1.8.0_131\bin\java" ...
Initial Out put with a = 15, b = 10
Add = 25
Substract = 5
Multiply = 150
Divide = 1.5
Enter a = <number> or b = <number> in separate lines
exit to exit the program

Add = 31
Substract = 11
Multiply = 210
Divide = 2.1

Add = 61
Substract = -19
Multiply = 840
Divide = 0.525


Process finished with exit code 0
```

In the `main` method, we are not doing much operation except for just listening to the input and passing it to the `ReactiveCalculator` class, and doing all other operations in the class itself, thus it is modular. In the later chapters, we will create a separate `observable` for the input process, and we will process all user inputs there. We have followed the pull mechanism on the user input for the sake of simplicity, which you will learn to remove in the next chapters. So, let's now take a look at the following `ReactiveCalculator` class:

```
class ReactiveCalculator(a:Int, b:Int) {
    internal val subjectAdd: Subject<Pair<Int,Int>> =
      PublishSubject.create()
    internal val subjectSub: Subject<Pair<Int,Int>> =
      PublishSubject.create()
    internal val subjectMult: Subject<Pair<Int,Int>> =
      PublishSubject.create()
    internal val subjectDiv: Subject<Pair<Int,Int>> =
      PublishSubject.create()

    internal val subjectCalc:Subject<ReactiveCalculator> =
      PublishSubject.create()

    internal var nums:Pair<Int,Int> = Pair(0,0)

    init{
      nums = Pair(a,b)

      subjectAdd.map({ it.first+it.second }).subscribe
      ({println("Add = $it")} )
      subjectSub.map({ it.first-it.second }).subscribe
      ({println("Substract = $it")} )
      subjectMult.map({ it.first*it.second }).subscribe
      ({println("Multiply = $it")} )
      subjectDiv.map({ it.first/(it.second*1.0) }).subscribe
      ({println("Divide = $it")} )

      subjectCalc.subscribe({
        with(it) {
          calculateAddition()
          calculateSubstraction()
          calculateMultiplication()
          calculateDivision()
        }
      })

      subjectCalc.onNext(this)
    }

    fun calculateAddition() {
```

```
      subjectAdd.onNext(nums)
  }

  fun calculateSubstraction() {
    subjectSub.onNext(nums)
  }

  fun calculateMultiplication() {
    subjectMult.onNext(nums)
  }

  fun calculateDivision() {
    subjectDiv.onNext(nums)
  }

  fun modifyNumbers (a:Int = nums.first, b: Int = nums.second) {
    nums = Pair(a,b)
    subjectCalc.onNext(this)
  }

  fun handleInput(inputLine:String?) {
   if(!inputLine.equals("exit")) {
      val pattern: Pattern = Pattern.compile
      ("([a|b])(?:\\s)?=(?:\\s)?(\\d*)");

      var a: Int? = null
      var b: Int? = null

      val matcher: Matcher = pattern.matcher(inputLine)

      if (matcher.matches() && matcher.group(1) != null
      &&  matcher.group(2) != null) {
        if(matcher.group(1).toLowerCase().equals("a")){
          a = matcher.group(2).toInt()
        } else if(matcher.group(1).toLowerCase().equals("b")){
          b = matcher.group(2).toInt()
        }
      }

      when {
        a != null && b != null -> modifyNumbers(a, b)
        a != null -> modifyNumbers(a = a)
        b != null -> modifyNumbers(b = b)
        else -> println("Invalid Input")
      }
    }
  }
}
```

In this program, we have push mechanism (`observable` pattern) only to the data, not the event (user input). While the initial chapters in this book will show you how to observe on data changes; RxJava also allows you to `observer` events (such as user input), we will get them covered during the end of the book while discussing RxJava on Android. So, now, let's understand how this code works.

First, we created a `ReactiveCalculator` class, which observes on its data and even on itself; so, whenever its property is modified, it calls all its `calculate` methods.

We used `Pair` to pair two variables and created four `subject` on the `Pair` to observe changes on it and then process it; we need four `subject` as there are four separate operations. You will also learn to optimize it with just one method in the later chapters.

On the `calculate` methods, we are just notifying the subject to process the `Pair` and print the new result.

If you focus on the `map` methods in both the programs, then you will learn that the `map` method takes the value that we passed with `onNext` and processes it to come up with a resultant value; that resultant value can be of any data type, and this resultant value is passed to the subscriber to process further and/or show the output.

Summary

In this chapter, we learned about what reactive programming is and the reasons we should learn it. We also started with coding. The reactive coding pattern may seem new or somehow uncommon, but it is not that hard; while using it, you just need to declare a few more things.

We learned about `observable` and its use. We also got introduced to `subject` and `map`, which we will learn in depth in the later chapters.

We will continue with `ReactiveCalculator` example in the later chapters and see how we can optimize and enhance this program.

The three examples presented in this chapter may seem a bit confusing and complex at first, but they're really simple, and they will become familiar to you as you proceed with this book.

In the next chapter, we will learn more about functional programming and functional interfaces in RxKotlin.

2
Functional Programming with Kotlin and RxKotlin

Functional programming paradigms are slightly different than that of **Object-oriented programming** (**OOP**). It focuses on the use of declarative and expressive programs and immutable data rather than on statements. The definition of functional programming says *functional programming is a programming system that relies on structuring the program as the evaluation of mathematical functions with immutable data, and it avoids state-change*. It is a declarative programming paradigm that suggests use of small, reusable declarative functions.

We have seen the definition of functional programming; now, don't you want to delve into its definition and see what it exactly means? Do all languages support functional programming? If not, then which languages does and what about Kotlin? What exactly does reactive programming have to do with functional programming? And, finally, what do we need to learn, for functional programming?

In this chapter, we will cover the following topics:

- Getting started with functional programming
- Relationship of functional programming with reactive programming
- The path breaking feature of Kotlin–coroutines

Introducing functional programming

So, functional programming wants you to distribute your programming logic into small pieces of reusable declarative small and pure functions. Distributing your logic into small pieces of code will make the code modular and non-complex, thus you will be able to refactor/change any module/part of the code at any given point without any effects to other modules.

Functional programming requires some interfaces and support from the language, thus we can't say any language is functional unless it gives some sort of support to implement functional programming. However, functional programming isn't something new; it is actually quite an old concept and has several languages supporting it. We call those languages functional programming languages, and the following is a list of some of the most popular functional programming languages:

- Lisp
- Clojure
- Wolfram
- Erlang
- OCaml
- Haskell
- Scala
- F#

Lisp and Haskell are some of the oldest languages and are still used today in academia and industry. While talking about Kotlin, it has excellent support for functional programming from its first stable release in contrast to Java, which doesn't have any support for functional programming before Java 8. You can use Kotlin in both object-oriented and functional-programming style or even in a mix of two, which is really a great benefit for us. With a first-class support for features, such as higher-order functions, function types, and lambdas, Kotlin is a great choice if you're doing or exploring functional programming.

The concept of **functional reactive programming** (FRP) is actually a product of mixing reactive programming with functional programming. The main objective of writing functional programming is to implement modular programming; this modular programming is really helpful, or sometimes a necessity to implement reactive programming or rather to implement the four principles of the Reactive Manifesto.

Fundamentals of functional programming

Functional programming consists of few new concepts such as lambdas, pure functions, high-order functions, function types, and inline functions, which we will be learning. Quite interesting, isn't it?

 Note that, although in many programmers word, pure functions and lambdas are the same, they are actually not. In the following part of this chapter, we will learn more about them.

Lambda expressions

Lambda or lambda expressions generally mean *anonymous functions*, that is, functions without names. You can also say a lambda expression is a function, but not every function is a lambda expression. Not every programming language provides support for lambda expressions, for instance, Java didn't have it until Java 8. The implementations of lambda expressions are also different in respect to languages. Kotlin has good support for lambda expressions and implementing them in Kotlin is quite easy and natural. Let's now take a look at how lambda expressions work in Kotlin:

```
fun main(args: Array<String>) {
  val sum = { x: Int, y: Int -> x + y } // (1)
  println("Sum ${sum(12,14)}")// (2)
  val anonymousMult = {x: Int -> (Random().nextInt(15)+1) * x}
  // (3)
  println("random output ${anonymousMult(2)}")// (4)
}
```

In the preceding program, in comment (1), we declare a lambda expression that will add two numbers and return the sum as result; in comment (2), we call that function and print it; in comment (3), we declare another lambda that will multiply a random number bound to 15 with the value x passed to it and return the result; in comment (4), we, again, print it. Both the lambda expressions are actually functions, but without any function name; thus they are also referred to as an anonymous function. If you compare with Java, Java has a feature of anonymous class, but included lambda/anonymous functions only after Java 8.

If you are curious about the output, then refer to the following screenshot:

```
"C:\Program Files\Java\jdk1.8.0_131\bin\java" ...
Sum 26
random output 24

Process finished with exit code 0
```

Pure function

The definition of pure function says that *if the return value of a function is completely dependent on its arguments/parameters, then this function may be referred to as a pure function.* So, if we declare a function as fun func1(x:Int):Int, then its return value will be strictly dependent on its argument x; say, if you call func1 with a value of 3 twice, then, for both the times, its return value will be the same. A pure function can be a lambda or a named function as well. In the previous example, the first lambda expression was a pure function but not the second one, as for the second one, its return value can be different at different times with the same value passed to it. Let's look at the following example to understand it better:

```
fun square(n:Int):Int {// (1)
  return n*n
}

fun main(args: Array<String>) {
  println("named pure func square = ${square(3)}")
  val qube = {n:Int -> n*n*n}// (2)
  println("lambda pure func qube = ${qube(3)}")
}
```

Both the functions, (1) and (2), here are pure functions—one is named, while the other is lambda. If you pass the value 3 to any of the functions n times, their return value will be the same for each time. Pure functions don't have side effects.

 Side effects: A function or expression is said to have a side effect if it modifies some state outside its scope or has an observable interaction with its calling functions or the outside world besides returning a value. Source–Wikipedia https://en.wikipedia.org/wiki/Side_effect_(computer_science).

It is to note that, as we said earlier, pure functions have nothing to do with lambda expressions, their definitions are completely different.

The following is the output:

```
named pure func square = 9
lambda pure func qube = 27
```

High-order functions

Those functions that take another function as an argument or return a function as result are called **high-order functions**. Consider the following example to understand it better:

```
fun highOrderFunc(a:Int, validityCheckFunc:(a:Int)->Boolean) {//(1)
  if(validityCheckFunc(a)) {//(2)
    println("a $a is Valid")
  } else {
    println("a $a is Invalid")
  }
}

fun main(args: Array<String>) {
  highOrderFun(12,{ a:Int -> a.isEven()})//(3)
  highOrderFunc(19,{ a:Int -> a.isEven()})
}
```

In this program, we've declared a `highOrderFunc` function, which will take an `Int` and a `validityCheckFunc`**(Int)** function. We are calling the `validityCheckFunc` function inside the `highOrderFunc` function, to check whether the value was valid or not. However, we are defining the `validityCheckFunc` function at runtime, while we are calling the `highOrderFunc` function inside the `main` function.

 Note that the `isEven` function in this program is an extension function that has been defined inside the `project` files you got with the book.

Here is the output:

```
a 12 is Valid
a 19 is Invalid
```

Inline functions

While functions are a great way to write modular code, it may sometimes increase program execution time and reduce memory optimization due to function stack maintenance and overhead. Inline functions are a great way to avoid those hurdles in functional programming. For example, see the following code snippet:

```
fun doSomeStuff(a:Int = 0) = a+(a*a)

fun main(args: Array<String>) {
  for (i in 1..10) {
    println("$i Output ${doSomeStuff(i)}")
  }
}
```

Let's recite the definition of inline function; it says that *inline functions are an enhancement feature to improve the performance and memory optimization of a program*. Functions can be instructed to the compiler to make them inline so that the compiler can replace those function definitions wherever those are being called. Compiler replaces the definition of inline functions at compile time instead of referring function definition at runtime; thus, no extra memory is needed for a function call, stack maintenance, and more, and getting the benefits of functions as well.

The preceding program declares a function that adds two numbers and returns the result, and we will call the function in the loop. Instead of declaring a function for this, we can write the addition code right in the place where we will call the function, but declaring a function gives us freedom to modify the addition logic anytime without any effect on the remaining code, for example, if we want to modify the addition with multiplication or something else. If we declare a function as inline, then the code inside that function will replace all the function calls, thus improving performance while keeping our freedom intact. Consider the following code snippet as an example:

```
inline fun doSomeStuff(a:Int = 0) = a+(a*a)

fun main(args: Array<String>) {
  for (i in 1..10) {
    println("$i Output ${doSomeStuff(i)}")
  }
}
```

Here is the output of the program:

```
"C:\Program Files\Java\jdk1.8.0_131\bin\java" ...
1 Output 2
2 Output 6
3 Output 12
4 Output 20
5 Output 30
6 Output 42
7 Output 56
8 Output 72
9 Output 90
10 Output 110

Process finished with exit code 0
```

There is one more feature Kotlin provides with inline functions–if you declare a high-order function as `inline`, then the `inline` keyword affects both the function itself and the lambda passed to it. Let's modify the high-order function code with `inline`:

```kotlin
inline fun highOrderFuncInline(a:Int, validityCheckFunc:(a:Int)-
>Boolean) {
  if(validityCheckFunc(a)) {
     println("a $a is Valid")
  } else {
    println("a $a is Invalid")
  }
}

fun main(args: Array<String>) {
  highOrderFuncInline(12,{ a:Int -> a.isEven()})
  highOrderFuncInline(19,{ a:Int -> a.isEven()})
}
```

The compiler will replace all calls to `validityCheckFunc` with its lambda, as it would do with `highOrderFuncInline` with its definition. As you can see, there's not much modification of the code, just a small change of adding `inline` before a function declaration can improve performance.

Applying functional programming to the ReactiveCalculator class

So, now, after trying to understand the ReactiveCalculator class from the previous chapter, we will try to optimize the code as well. Let's first take a look at the init block of the ReactiveCalculator class:

```
init{
  nums = Pair(a,b)

  subjectAdd.map({ it.first+it.second }).subscribe({println
  ("Add = $it")} )//1
  subjectSub.map({ it.first-it.second }).subscribe({println
  ("Substract = $it")} )
  subjectMult.map({ it.first*it.second }).subscribe
  ({println("Multiply = $it")} )
  subjectDiv.map({ it.first/(it.second*1.0) }).subscribe
  ({println("Divide = $it")} )

  subjectCalc.subscribe({
    with(it) {
      calculateAddition()
      calculateSubstraction()
      calculateMultiplication()
      calculateDivision()
    }
  })

  subjectCalc.onNext(this)
}
```

So, now, with the knowledge of functional programming, we can easily say that the map and subscribe methods are high-order functions that take function as parameter. However, do you really think that many subject and subscriber are required? Shouldn't subscriber on the class be sufficient to accomplish the job itself? Let's try to modify and optimize the following piece of code:

```
class ReactiveCalculator(a:Int, b:Int) {
  val subjectCalc: io.reactivex.subjects.Subject
  <ReactiveCalculator>    =
  io.reactivex.subjects.PublishSubject.create()

  var nums:Pair<Int,Int> = Pair(0,0)

  init{
```

```kotlin
    nums = Pair(a,b)

    subjectCalc.subscribe({
      with(it) {
        calculateAddition()
        calculateSubstraction()
        calculateMultiplication()
        calculateDivision()
      }
    })

    subjectCalc.onNext(this)
  }

  inline fun calculateAddition():Int {
    val result = nums.first + nums.second
    println("Add = $result")
    return result
  }

  inline fun calculateSubstraction():Int {
    val result = nums.first - nums.second
    println("Substract = $result")
    return result
  }

inline fun calculateMultiplication():Int {
  val result = nums.first * nums.second
  println("Multiply = $result")
  return result
}

inline fun calculateDivision():Double {
  val result = (nums.first*1.0) / (nums.second*1.0)
  println("Multiply = $result")
  return result
}

inline fun modifyNumbers (a:Int = nums.first, b:
Int = nums.second) {
  nums = Pair(a,b)
  subjectCalc.onNext(this)
}

fun handleInput(inputLine:String?) {
  if(!inputLine.equals("exit")) {
      val pattern: java.util.regex.Pattern =
      java.util.regex.Pattern.compile
```

```
                ("([a|b])(?:\\s)?=(?:\\s)?(\\d*)");

                var a: Int? = null
                var b: Int? = null

                val matcher: java.util.regex.Matcher =
                pattern.matcher(inputLine)

                if (matcher.matches() && matcher.group(1) != null &&
                matcher.group(2) != null) {
                    if(matcher.group(1).toLowerCase().equals("a")){
                        a = matcher.group(2).toInt()
                    } else if(matcher.group(1).toLowerCase().equals("b")){
                        b = matcher.group(2).toInt()
                    }
                }

                when {
                    a != null && b != null -> modifyNumbers(a, b)
                    a != null -> modifyNumbers(a = a)
                    b != null -> modifyNumbers(b = b)
                    else -> println("Invalid Input")

                }
            }
        }

    }
```

So, we have removed all other `subscriber` and are doing the job with only one. And here's the output:

```
Initial Output with a = 15, b = 10
Add = 25
Substract = 5
Multiply = 150
Multiply = 1.5
Enter a = <number> or b = <number> in separate lines
exit to exit the program
a = 6
Add = 16
Substract = -4
Multiply = 60
Multiply = 0.6
b=4
Add = 10
Substract = 2
Multiply = 24
```

```
Multiply = 1.5
exit
```

We subscribe to the class object itself; so, whenever its variables get changed, we get notified, and we perform all the tasks right there in the `subscribe` method. Moreover, as we have made the functions inline, they'll also help in the optimization of performance.

Coroutines

Path breaking and, probably, the most exciting feature in Kotlin are coroutines. They are a new way to write asynchronous, non-blocking code somewhere like the threads, but way more simple, efficient, and lightweight. Coroutines were added in Kotlin 1.1 and are still experimental, so think before using it in production.

In the later chapters of this book, you'll learn about Schedulers in RxKotlin, which encapsulates the complexities of threading, but you can use it only in RxKotlin chain, while you can use coroutines anywhere and everywhere. That is indeed a path-breaking feature of Kotlin. They provide a great abstraction on threads, making context changes and concurrency easier.

Keep in mind that RxKotlin does not use coroutines yet; the reason is quite simple–both coroutines and Schedulers in RxKotlin share nearly the same internal architecture; while coroutines are new, Schedulers have been there for a long time with RxJava, RxJs, RxSwift, and more.

Coroutines are the best fit for developers to implement concurrency when they're not using/can't use RxKotlin Schedulers.

So, let's start by adding it to our project. If you are using Gradle, follow these steps (`apply plugin` could be `'kotlin'` or `'kotlin-android'`, depending on whether you use it for JVM or Android):

```
apply plugin: 'kotlin'

kotlin {
  experimental {
    coroutines 'enable'
  }
}
```

And then, we have to add the following dependency:

```
repositories {
  ...
  jcenter()
}
dependencies {
  ...
  compile "org.jetbrains.kotlinx:kotlinx-coroutines-core:0.16"
}
```

If you are using Maven, then add the following code block in the pom.xml file:

```
<plugin>
  <groupId>org.jetbrains.kotlin</groupId>
  <artifactId>kotlin-maven-plugin</artifactId>
  ...
  <configuration>
    <args>
        <arg>-Xcoroutines=enable</arg>
    </args>
  </configuration>
</plugin>
<repositories>
  ...
  <repository>
    <id>central</id>
    <url>http://jcenter.bintray.com</url>
  </repository>
</repositories>
<dependencies>
  ...
  <dependency>
    <groupId>org.jetbrains.kotlin</groupId>
    <artifactId>kotlinx-coroutines-core</artifactId>
    <version>0.16</version>
  </dependency>
</dependencies>
```

 Apache Maven is a software project management and comprehension tool. Based on the concept of a **Project Object Model** (**POM**), Maven can manage a project's build, reporting, and documentation from a central piece of information. Please refer to the following URL for more information–https://maven.apache.org/.

So, what exactly is a coroutine? While developing applications, we often come into situations where we need to perform long running or time taking operations, such as network call, database operations, or some complex computations. The only option in Java is to use a thread to handle such situations, which is very complex itself. Whenever we face those situations, we feel the need for a simple yet powerful API to handle such cases. Developers from the .NET domain, especially those who used C# before, are familiar with the `async/await` operators; this is somehow the closest to Kotlin coroutines.

Getting started with coroutines

So, let's take the following example into consideration:

```
suspend fun longRunningTsk():Long {//(1)
  val time = measureTimeMillis {//(2)
    println("Please wait")
    delay(2,TimeUnit.SECONDS)//(3)
    println("Delay Over")
  }
  return time
}

fun main(args: Array<String>) {
  runBlocking {//(4)
    val exeTime = longRunningTsk()//(5)
    println("Execution Time is $exeTime")
  }
}
```

We will inspect through the code, but let's first see the output:

```
Please wait
Delay Over
Execution Time is 2018
```

So, now, let's understand the code. On comment (1), while declaring the function, we mark the function with the `suspend` keyword, which is used to mark a function as suspending, that is, while executing the function the program should wait for its result; therefore, execution of suspending a function in main thread is not allowed (giving you a clear barrier between main thread and suspending functions). On comment (2), we started a block with `measureTimeMillis` and assigned its value to the (val) `time` variable. The job of `measureInMillis` is quite simple–it executes the block passed to it while measuring its execution time, and returns the same. We will use the `delay` function on comment (3) to intentionally delay the program execution by 2 seconds. The `runBlocking` block in the `main` function on comment (4) makes the program wait until the called `longRunningTsk` function on comment (5) completes. So, this was a quite simple example; however, we are making the main thread wait here. Sometimes, you will not want this; instead, you will want to do asynchronous operations. So, let's try to achieve this as well:

```
fun main(args: Array<String>) {
    val time = async(CommonPool) { longRunningTsk() }// (1)
    println("Print after async ")
    runBlocking { println("printing time ${time.await()}") }// (2)
}
```

Here, we kept `longRunningTsk` same, just modified the `main` function. On comment (1), we assigned the `time` variable to the value of `longRunningTsk` inside the `async` block. The `async` block is quite interesting; it executes the code inside its block asynchronously on the coroutine context passed to it.

 There are basically three types of coroutine contexts. `Unconfined` means it'll run on the main thread, `CommonPool` runs on the common thread pool, or you can create a new coroutine context as well.

On comment (2) we run a blocking code that will make the `main` function wait until the value of the `time` variable is available; the `await` function helps us accomplish this task–it tells the `runBlocking` block to wait until the `async` block completes execution to make the value of `time` available.

Building sequences

As I mentioned earlier, Kotlin coroutines are something more than threads in Java and `async`/`await` in C#. Here is a feature that, after learning, you will be pissed that it was not there while you were learning to code. To add icing on the cake, this feature is application level, it is even shipped with `kotlin-stdlib`, so you can use it right there without doing anything or even using coroutines explicitly.

Before learning what I am talking about, let's do some old school code, say the fibonacci series? Consider the following piece of code as an example:

```kotlin
fun main(args: Array<String>) {
  var a = 0
  var b = 1
  print("$a, ")
  print("$b, ")

  for(i in 2..9) {
    val c = a+b
    print("$c, ")
    a=b
    b=c
  }
}
```

So, this is the old-school fibonacci series program in Kotlin. This code becomes more problematic when you plan to take the user input for how many numbers to print. What if I say Kotlin has a `buildSequence` function that can do this task for you, that too pretty naturally and in a simpler way? So, let's modify the code now:

```kotlin
fun main(args: Array<String>) {
  val fibonacciSeries = buildSequence {//(1)
    var a = 0
    var b = 1
    yield(a)//(2)
    yield(b)

    while (true) {
        val c = a+b
        yield(c)//(3)
        a=b
        b=c
    }
  }

  println(fibonacciSeries.take(10) join "," )//(4)
```

```
}
```

The following is the output for both the programs:

```
0, 1, 1, 2, 3, 5, 8, 13, 21, 34
```

Now, let's understand the program. On comment (1), we declare `val fibonacciSeries` to be filled up by the `buildSequence` block. Whenever we have computed some value to output to the sequence/series, we will yield that value (in comment 2 and 3). On comment 4, we call `fibonacciSeries` to compute up to the 10th variable and join elements of the sequence with a comma (,).

So, you learned coroutine; now, let's implement it into our program.

The ReactiveCalculator class with coroutines

So far, in the `ReactiveCalculator` program, we were performing everything on the same thread; don't you think we should rather do the things asynchronously? So, let's do it:

```
class ReactiveCalculator(a:Int, b:Int) {
  val subjectCalc:
  io.reactivex.subjects.Subject<ReactiveCalculator> =
  io.reactivex.subjects.PublishSubject.create()

  var nums:Pair<Int,Int> = Pair(0,0)

  init{
    nums = Pair(a,b)

    subjectCalc.subscribe({
        with(it) {
            calculateAddition()
            calculateSubstraction()
            calculateMultiplication()
            calculateDivision()
        }
    })

    subjectCalc.onNext(this)
  }

  inline fun calculateAddition():Int {
    val result = nums.first + nums.second
    println("Add = $result")
    return result
```

```
    }

    inline fun calculateSubstraction():Int {
      val result = nums.first - nums.second
      println("Substract = $result")
      return result
    }

    inline fun calculateMultiplication():Int {
      val result = nums.first * nums.second
      println("Multiply = $result")
      return result
    }

    inline fun calculateDivision():Double {
      val result = (nums.first*1.0) / (nums.second*1.0)
      println("Division = $result")
      return result
    }

    inline fun modifyNumbers (a:Int = nums.first, b:
    Int = nums.second) {
      nums = Pair(a,b)
      subjectCalc.onNext(this)

    }

    suspend fun handleInput(inputLine:String?) {//1
      if(!inputLine.equals("exit")) {
        val pattern: java.util.regex.Pattern =
        java.util.regex.Pattern.compile
        ("([a|b])(?:\\s)?=(?:\\s)?(\\d*)");

        var a: Int? = null
        var b: Int? = null

        val matcher: java.util.regex.Matcher =
        pattern.matcher(inputLine)

        if (matcher.matches() && matcher.group(1) != null &&
        matcher.group(2) != null) {
          if(matcher.group(1).toLowerCase().equals("a")){
            a = matcher.group(2).toInt()
          } else if(matcher.group(1).toLowerCase().equals("b")){
            b = matcher.group(2).toInt()
          }
        }
```

```
                when {
                    a != null && b != null -> modifyNumbers(a, b)
                    a != null -> modifyNumbers(a = a)
                    b != null -> modifyNumbers(b = b)
                    else -> println("Invalid Input")

                }
            }
        }
    }

    fun main(args: Array<String>) {
    println("Initial Out put with a = 15, b = 10")
    var calculator: ReactiveCalculator = ReactiveCalculator(15, 10)

    println("Enter a = <number> or b = <number> in separate lines\nexit
    to exit the program")
    var line:String?
    do {
        line = readLine();
        async(CommonPool) {//2
            calculator.handleInput(line)
        }
    } while (line!= null && !line.toLowerCase().contains("exit"))
    }
```

On comment (1), we will declare the handleInput function as suspending, which tells the
JVM that this function is supposed to take longer, and the execution of the context calling
this function should wait for it to complete. As I already mentioned earlier, suspending
functions cannot be called in the main context; so, on comment (2), we created an async
block to call the function.

Functional programming – monads

Functional programming is incomplete without monads. If you are into functional
programming, then you know it very well; otherwise, you are hearing it for the first time.
So, what is a monad? Let's learn about it. The concept of monad is quite abstract; the
definition says *monad is a structure that creates a new type by encapsulating a value and adding
some extra functionalities to it*. So, let's start by using a monad; take a look at the following
program:

```
fun main(args: Array<String>) {
    val maybeValue: Maybe<Int> = Maybe.just(14)//1
```

```
      maybeValue.subscribeBy(//2
        onComplete = {println("Completed Empty")},
        onError = {println("Error $it")},
        onSuccess = { println("Completed with value $it")}
      )
    val maybeEmpty:Maybe<Int> = Maybe.empty()//3
    maybeEmpty.subscribeBy(
        onComplete = {println("Completed Empty")},
        onError = {println("Error $it")},
        onSuccess = { println("Completed with value $it")}
      )
  }
```

Here, `Maybe` is a monad that encapsulates an `Int` value with some added functionalities. The `Maybe` monad says it may or may not contain a value, and it completes with or without a value or with an error. So, if there's an error, then it would obviously call `onError`; if there are no errors, and if it has a value, it will call `onSuccess` with the value; and, if it doesn't have a value and no error as well, it will call `onComplete`. The thing to note is that all three methods here, `onError`, `onComplete`, and `onSuccess`, are terminal methods, meaning either one of these three will get called by a `Maybe` monad, and others will never be called.

Let's go through the program to understand the monads better. On comment (1), we will declare a `Maybe` monad and assign a value of 14 to it. On comment (2), we will subscribe to the monad. On comment (3), we will again declare a `Maybe` monad, this time with an empty value. The subscription takes three lambdas as parameter–when the monad contains a value, `onSuccess` gets called; when it doesn't contain any value, `onComplete` gets called; and if any error occurs, then `onError` gets called. Let's see the output now:

```
Completed with value 14
Completed Empty
```

So, as we can see, for `maybeValue`, `onSuccess` gets called, but for `maybeEmpty` , the `onComplete` method gets called.

Single monad

`Maybe` is just another type of monad, there are a lot more; we will cover a few of the most important ones in later chapters, and combine them with reactive programming as well.

Summary

In this chapter, we learned about functional programming. If you grasped the concept of functional programming well enough, the puzzles for reactive programming will automatically get solved for you. We also learned the meaning of functional reactive programming.

By learning functional programming, we also got a clear idea on the constraints from the previous chapter.

We also got our hands on the introduction to coroutines, which is a path breaking new feature of the Kotlin language.

We have modified our `ReactiveCalculator` class with coroutine and a few new concepts of functional programming and optimized it.

3
Observables, Observers, and Subjects

Observables and subscribers are at the base of reactive programming. We can say that they are the building blocks of reactive programming. In the previous two chapters, you already got a glimpse of Observables and subject. We observed on data with observable/subject instances; but that's not all we want; instead, we want to get all the actions and data changes reactively into the observable instances, making the application completely reactive. Also, while reading the previous chapters, you may have wondered how exactly does it operate? In this chapter, let's have a foundation of the pillars of reactive programming—Observables, Observers, and subjects:

- We will look into details of transforming various data sources to observable instances
- You will learn about various types of Observables
- How to use Observer instances and subscriptions, and, lastly, subjects and their various implementations

We will also learn about various factory methods of Observable.

There's a lot to understand in this chapter, so let's start with understanding Observables first.

Observables

As we discussed earlier, in reactive programming, Observable has an underlying computation that produces values that can be consumed by a consumer (Observer). The most important thing here is that the consumer (Observer) doesn't pull values here; rather, Observable pushes the value to the consumer. So, we may say, an Observable is a push-based, composable iterator that emits its items through a series of operators to the final Observer, which finally consumes the items. Let's now break things sequentially to understand it better:

- Observer subscribes to Observable
- Observable starts emitting items that it has in it
- Observer reacts to whatever item Observable emits

So, let's delve into how an Observable works through its events/methods, namely, onNext, onComplete, and onError.

How Observable works

As we stated earlier, an Observable has three most important events/methods; let's discuss them one by one:

- onNext: Observable passes all items one by one to this method.
- onComplete: When all items have gone through the onNext method, Observable calls the onComplete method.
- onError: When Observable faces any error, it calls the onError method to deal with the error, if defined. Note that both onError and onComplete are terminal events, and if onError is called, then it would never call onComplete and vice versa.

 One thing to note here, the item in Observable that we are talking about can be anything; it is defined as Observable<T>, where T can be any class; even an array/list can be assigned as an Observable.

Let's look at the following image:

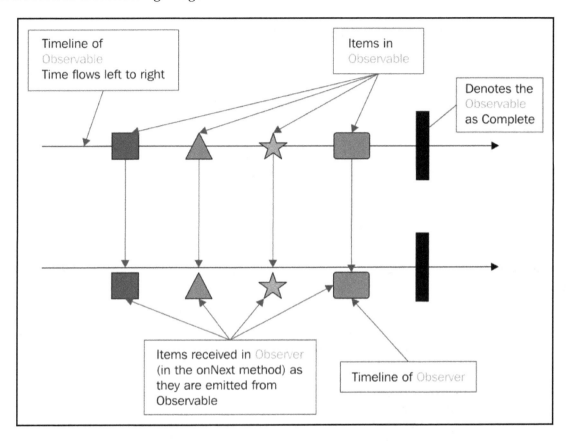

Let's look at this code example to understand it better:

```
fun main(args: Array<String>) {

    val observer:Observer<Any> = object :Observer<Any>{//1
        override fun onComplete() {//2
            println("All Completed")
        }

        override fun onNext(item: Any) {//3
            println("Next $item")
        }

        override fun onError(e: Throwable) {//4
            println("Error Occured $e")
```

```
        }

        override fun onSubscribe(d: Disposable) {//5
            println("Subscribed to $d")
        }
    }

    val observable: Observable<Any> = listOf
    ("One", 2, "Three", "Four", 4.5, "Five", 6.0f).toObservable() //6

    observable.subscribe(observer)//7

    val observableOnList: Observable<List<Any>> =
    Observable.just(listOf("One", 2, "Three", "Four",
    4.5, "Five", 6.0f),
      listOf("List with Single Item"),
      listOf(1,2,3,4,5,6))//8
      observableOnList.subscribe(observer)//9
}
```

In the preceding example, we declared the observer instance of Any datatype on comment (1).

 Here, we are taking benefit of the Any datatype. In Kotlin, every class is a child class of Any. Also, in Kotlin, everything is class and object; there is no separate primitive datatype.

The observer interface has four methods declared in it. The onComplete() method at comment 2 gets called when Observable is finished with all its items without any error. On comment 3, we defined the onNext(item: Any) function, which will be called by observable for each item it has to emit. In that method, we will print the data to the console. On comment 4, we defined the onError(e: Throwable) method, which will be called in case any error is faced by Observable. On comment 5, the onSubscribe(d: Disposable) method will get called whenever Observer subscribes to Observable. On comment 6, we will create Observable from a list (val observable) and subscribe to observable with observer on comment 7. On comment 8, we will create an observable (val observableOnList) again, this it holds lists as items.

The output of the program is as follows:

```
"C:\Program Files\Java\jdk1.8.0_131\bin\java" ...
Subscribed to io.reactivex.internal.operators.observable.ObservableFromIterable$FromIterableDisposable@504bae78
Next One
Next 2
Next Three
Next Four
Next 4.5
Next Five
Next 6.0
All Completed
Subscribed to io.reactivex.internal.operators.observable.ObservableFromArray$FromArrayDisposable@484b61fc
Next [One, 2, Three, Four, 4.5, Five, 6.0]
Next [List with Single Item]
Next [1, 2, 3, 4, 5, 6]
All Completed

Process finished with exit code 0
```

So, as you can see in the output, for the first subscription (comment 7), when we subscribe to `Observable`, it calls the `onSubscribe` method, and then `Observable` starts emitting items as `Observer` starts receiving them on the `onNext` method and prints them. When all items are emitted from `Observable`, it calls the `onComplete` method to denote that all items have been successfully emitted. Same with the second one, except that, here, each item is a list.

So, as we gained some basis in `Observables`, let's learn various ways to create `Observable`—factory methods for `Observable`.

Understanding the Observable.create method

You can create your own `Observable` with the `Observable.create` method at any time. This method takes an instance of the `ObservableEmitter<T>` interface as a source to observe on. So, let's consider this following example:

```kotlin
fun main(args: Array<String>) {

    val observer: Observer<String> = object : Observer<String> {
        override fun onComplete() {
            println("All Completed")
        }

        override fun onNext(item: String) {
            println("Next $item")
        }
```

```
      override fun onError(e: Throwable) {
        println("Error Occured ${e.message}")
      }

      override fun onSubscribe(d: Disposable) {
        println("New Subscription ")
      }
}//Create Observer

val observable:Observable<String> = Observable.create<String> {//1
    it.onNext("Emit 1")
    it.onNext("Emit 2")
    it.onNext("Emit 3")
    it.onNext("Emit 4")
    it.onComplete()
}

observable.subscribe(observer)

val observable2:Observable<String> = Observable.create<String> {//2
    it.onNext("Emit 1")
    it.onNext("Emit 2")
    it.onNext("Emit 3")
    it.onNext("Emit 4")
    it.onError(Exception("My Custom Exception"))
}

observable2.subscribe(observer)
}
```

First, we created an instance of the `Observer` interface as the previous example. I will not elaborate on `observer`, as we have already seen an overview in the previous example, and we will see it in detail later in this chapter.

On comment 1, we created `Observable` with the `Observable.create` method; we emitted four `string` from `Observable` with the help of the `onNext` method, and then notified it is complete with the `onComplete` method.

On comment 2, we did almost the same, except here instead of calling `onComplete`, we called `onError` with a custom `Exception`.

Here is the output of the program:

```
"C:\Program Files\Java\jdk1.8.0_131\bin\java" ...
New Subscription
Next Emit 1
Next Emit 2
Next Emit 3
Next Emit 4
All Completed
New Subscription
Next Emit 1
Next Emit 2
Next Emit 3
Next Emit 4
Error Occured My Custom Exception

Process finished with exit code 0
```

The `Observable.create` method is useful, especially when you are working with a custom data structure and want to have control over what values are getting emitted. You can also emit values to `Observer` from a different thread.

Note that the `Observable` contract (http://reactivex.io/documentation/contract.html) states that `Observable` must issue notifications to `observers` serially (not in parallel). They may issue these notifications from different threads, but there must be a formal happens—before relationship between the notifications.

Understanding the Observable.from methods

The `Observable.from` methods are comparatively simpler than the `Observable.create` method. You can create `Observable` instances from nearly every Kotlin structure with the help of `from` methods.

Note that in RxKotlin 1, you will have `Observale.from` as a method; however, from RxKotlin 2.0 (as with RxJava2.0), operator overloads have been renamed with a postfix, such as `fromArray`, `fromIterable`, `fromFuture`, and so on.

So, let's take a look at this code:

```kotlin
fun main(args: Array<String>) {

  val observer: Observer<String> = object : Observer<String> {
    override fun onComplete() {
      println("All Completed")
    }

    override fun onNext(item: String) {
      println("Next $item")
    }

    override fun onError(e: Throwable) {
      println("Error Occured ${e.message}")
    }

    override fun onSubscribe(d: Disposable) {
      println("New Subscription ")
    }
  }//Create Observer

  val list = listOf("String 1","String 2","String 3","String 4")
  val observableFromIterable: Observable<String> =
  Observable.fromIterable(list)//1
  observableFromIterable.subscribe(observer)


  val callable = object : Callable<String> {
    override fun call(): String {
      return "From Callable"
    }
  }
  val observableFromCallable:Observable<String> =
  Observable.fromCallable(callable)//2
  observableFromCallable.subscribe(observer)

  val future:Future<String> = object :Future<String> {
    override fun get(): String = "Hello From Future"

    override fun get(timeout: Long, unit: TimeUnit?): String  =
    "Hello From Future"

    override fun isDone(): Boolean = true

    override fun isCancelled(): Boolean = false

    override fun cancel(mayInterruptIfRunning: Boolean):
```

```
        Boolean = false

    }
    val observableFromFuture:Observable<String> =
    Observable.fromFuture(future)//3
    observableFromFuture.subscribe(observer)
}
```

On comment 1, I used the `Observable.fromIterable` method to create `Observable`
from an `Iterable` instance (here, `List`). On comment 2, I called the
`Observable.fromCallable` method to create `Observable` from a `Callable` instance,
and same for comment 3, where I called the `Observable.fromFuture` method to derive
`Observable` from a `Future` instance.

Here is the output:

```
"C:\Program Files\Java\jdk1.8.0_131\bin\java" ...
New Subscription
Next String 1
Next String 2
Next String 3
Next String 4
All Completed
New Subscription
Next From Callable
All Completed
New Subscription
Next Hello From Future
All Completed

Process finished with exit code 0
```

Understanding the toObservable extension function

Thanks to the extension functions of Kotlin, you can turn any `Iterable` instance, such as
`List`, to `Observable` without much effort; we have already used this method in Chapter
1, *A Short Introduction to Reactive Programming*, however, take a look at this:

```
fun main(args: Array<String>) {

    val observer: Observer<String> = object : Observer<String> {
        override fun onComplete() {
            println("All Completed")
        }

        override fun onNext(item: String) {
            println("Next $item")
        }
```

```
    override fun onError(e: Throwable) {
        println("Error Occured ${e.message}")
    }

    override fun onSubscribe(d: Disposable) {
        println("New Subscription ")
    }
}//Create Observer

val list:List<String> = listOf
("String 1","String 2","String 3","String 4")

val observable:Observable<String> = list.toObservable()

observable.subscribe(observer)
}
```

And the following is the output:

```
"C:\Program Files\Java\jdk1.8.0_131\bin\java" ...
New Subscription
Next String 1
Next String 2
Next String 3
Next String 4
All Completed

Process finished with exit code 0
```

So, aren't you curious to look into the toObservable method? Let's do it. You can find this method inside the observable.kt file provided with the RxKotlin package:

```
fun <T : Any> Iterator<T>.toObservable(): Observable<T> =
toIterable().toObservable()
fun <T : Any> Iterable<T>.toObservable(): Observable<T> =
Observable.fromIterable(this)
fun <T : Any> Sequence<T>.toObservable(): Observable<T> =
asIterable().toObservable()

fun <T : Any> Iterable<Observable<out T>>.merge(): Observable<T> =
Observable.merge(this.toObservable())
fun <T : Any> Iterable<Observable<out T>>.mergeDelayError():
Observable<T> = Observable.mergeDelayError(this.toObservable())
```

So, it basically uses the `Observable.from` method internally; thanks again to extension functions of Kotlin.

Understanding the Observable.just method

Another interesting factory method is `Observable.just`; this method creates `Observable` and adds the parameters passed to it as the only items of the `Observable`. Note that if you pass an `Iterable` instance to `Observable.just` as a single parameter, it will take the entire `list` as a single item, unlike `Observable.from`, where it will create items of `Observable` from each item in `Iterable`.

Here is what happens when you call `Observable.just`:

- You call `Observable.just` with parameters
- `Observable.just` will create `Observable`
- It will emit each of its parameters as the `onNext` notification
- When all parameters are emitted successfully, it will emit the `onComplete` notification

Let's look at this code example to understand it better:

```kotlin
fun main(args: Array<String>) {
  val observer: Observer<Any> = object : Observer<Any> {
    override fun onComplete() {
        println("All Completed")
    }

    override fun onNext(item: Any) {
        println("Next $item")
    }

    override fun onError(e: Throwable) {
        println("Error Occured ${e.message}")
    }

    override fun onSubscribe(d: Disposable) {
        println("New Subscription ")
    }
  }//Create Observer

  Observable.just("A String").subscribe(observer)
  Observable.just(54).subscribe(observer)
  Observable.just(listOf("String 1","String 2","String 3",
  "String 4")).subscribe(observer)
```

```
Observable.just(mapOf(Pair("Key 1","Value 1"),Pair
("Key 2","Value 2"),Pair("Key 3","Value
3"))).subscribe(observer)
Observable.just(arrayListOf(1,2,3,4,5,6)).subscribe(observer)
Observable.just("String 1","String 2",
"String 3").subscribe(observer)//1
}
```

And here is the output:

```
"C:\Program Files\Java\jdk1.8.0_131\bin\java" ...
New Subscription
Next A String
All Completed
New Subscription
Next 54
All Completed
New Subscription
Next [String 1, String 2, String 3, String 4]
All Completed
New Subscription
Next {Key 1=Value 1, Key 2=Value 2, Key 3=Value 3}
All Completed
New Subscription
Next [1, 2, 3, 4, 5, 6]
All Completed
New Subscription
Next String 1
Next String 2
Next String 3
All Completed

Process finished with exit code 0
```

As you can see in the output, lists and maps are also treated as a single item, but look at comment 1 in the code where I passed three strings as parameters of the `Observable.just` method. `Observable.just` took each of the parameters as a separate item and emitted them accordingly (see the output).

Other Observable factory methods

Before moving forward with `Observer`, subscribing, unsubscribing, and `Subjects`, let's try our hands on a few other factory methods of `Observable`.

So, let's look at this code first, and then we will try to learn it line by line:

```
fun main(args: Array<String>) {
  val observer: Observer<Any> = object : Observer<Any> {
    override fun onComplete() {
```

```
        println("All Completed")
    }

    override fun onNext(item: Any) {
        println("Next $item")
    }

    override fun onError(e: Throwable) {
        println("Error Occured ${e.message}")
    }

    override fun onSubscribe(d: Disposable) {
        println("New Subscription ")
    }
}//Create Observer

Observable.range(1,10).subscribe(observer)//(1)
Observable.empty<String>().subscribe(observer)//(2)

runBlocking {
  Observable.interval(300,TimeUnit.MILLISECONDS).
  subscribe(observer)//(3)
  delay(900)
  Observable.timer(400,TimeUnit.MILLISECONDS).
  subscribe(observer)//(4)
  delay(450)
}

}
```

On comment (1), we created Observable with the Observable.range() factory method. This method creates an Observable and emits integers with the supplied start parameter until it emits a number of integers as per the count parameter.

On comment (2), we created Observable with the Observable.empty() method. This method creates Observable and emits onComplete() right away, without emitting any items with onNext().

On comment (3) and comment (4), we used two interesting Observable factory methods. The method on comment (3), Observable.interval(), emits numbers sequentially starting from 0, after each specified interval. It will continue emitting until you unsubscribe and until the program runs. Whereas, the method on comment (4), Observable.timer(), will emit only once with 0 after the specified time elapsed.

Here is the output if you are curious:

```
"C:\Program Files\Java\jdk1.8.0_131\bin\java" ...
New Subscription
Next 1
Next 2
Next 3
Next 4
Next 5
Next 6
Next 7
Next 8
Next 9
Next 10
All Completed
New Subscription
All Completed
New Subscription
Next 0
Next 1
Next 2
New Subscription
Next 3
Next 0
All Completed

Process finished with exit code 0
```

Subscribers - the Observer interface

The `Subscriber` from RxKotlin 1.x, essentially became an `Observer` in RxKotlin 2.x. There is an `Observer` interface in RxKotlin 1.x, but `Subscriber` is what you pass to the `subscribe()` method, and it implements `Observer`. However, In RxJava 2.x, `Subscriber` only exists when talking about `Flowables`, which we will cover in `Chapter 4`, *Introduction to Backpressure and Flowables*.

As you can see in the previous examples in this chapter, `Observer` is an interface with four methods in it—`onNext(item:T)`, `onError(error:Throwable)`, `onComplete()`, and `onSubscribe(d:Disposable)`. As stated earlier, when we connect `Observable` to `Observer`, it looks for these four methods in `Observer` and calls them. So, the following is a short description of the four methods:

- `onNext`: `Observable` calls this method of `Observer` to pass each of the items one by one.
- `onComplete`: When `Observable` wants to denote, it's done with passing items to the `onNext` method, and it calls the `onComplete` method of `Observer`.

- onError: When Observable faces any error, it calls the onError method to deal with the error if defined in the Observer, otherwise, it throws the exception.
- onSubscribe: This method is called whenever a new Observable subscribes to the Observer.

Subscribing and disposing

So, we have Observable (the thing that should be observed upon) and we have Observer (that should observe); now what? How to connect them? Observable and Observer are like an input device (be it keyboard or mouse) and the computer, we need something to connect them (even wireless input devices have some connectivity channels, be it Bluetooth or Wi-Fi).

The subscribe operator serves the purpose of the media by connecting an Observable to Observer. We can pass one to three methods (onNext, onComplete, onError) to the subscribe operator, or we can pass an instance of the Observer interface to the subscribe operator to get the Observable connected with an Observer.

So, let's take a look at the following example now:

```kotlin
fun main(args: Array<String>) {
  val observable:Observable<Int> = Observable.range(1,5)//1

  observable.subscribe({//2
    //onNext method
    println("Next $it")
  },{
    //onError Method
    println("Error ${it.message}")
  },{
    //onComplete Method
    println("Done")
  })

  val observer: Observer<Int> = object : Observer<Int> {//3
    override fun onComplete() {
      println("All Completed")
    }

    override fun onNext(item: Int) {
      println("Next $item")
    }

    override fun onError(e: Throwable) {
```

```
      println("Error Occurred ${e.message}")
    }

    override fun onSubscribe(d: Disposable) {
      println("New Subscription ")
    }
  }

  observable.subscribe(observer)
}
```

In this example, we have created `Observable` instance (on comment 1) and used it twice with different overload `subscribe` operators. On comment 2, we have passed three methods as arguments to the `subscribe` method. The first parameter is the `onNext` method, the second one is the `onError` method, and last, `onComplete`. On comment 2, we have passed an instance of the `Observer` interface.

The output can be easily predicted as follows:

```
"C:\Program Files\Java\jdk1.8.0_131\bin\java" ...
Next 1
Next 2
Next 3
Next 4
Next 5
Done
New Subscription
Next 1
Next 2
Next 3
Next 4
Next 5
All Completed

Process finished with exit code 0
```

So, we have got the concepts of subscribing, and we can do it now. What if you want to stop the emissions after some period of subscription? There must be a way, right? So let's inspect this.

Remember the `onSubscribe` method of `Observer`? There was a parameter on that method that we have not talked about yet. While you `subscribe`, if you pass the methods instead of the `Observer` instance, then the `subscribe` operator will return an instance of `Disposable`, or if you use an instance of `Observer`, then you will get the instance of `Disposable` in the parameter of the `onSubscribe` method.

You can use the instance of the `Disposable` interface to stop emissions at any given time. Let's take a look at this example:

```
fun main(args: Array<String>) {
  runBlocking {
    val observale:Observable<Long> =
    Observable.interval(100,TimeUnit.MILLISECONDS)//1
    val observer:Observer<Long> = object : Observer<Long> {
      lateinit var disposable:Disposable//2

      override fun onSubscribe(d: Disposable) {
        disposable = d//3
      }

      override fun onNext(item: Long) {
        println("Received $item")
        if(item>=10 && !disposable.isDisposed) {//4
          disposable.dispose()//5
          println("Disposed")
        }
      }

      override fun onError(e: Throwable) {
        println("Error ${e.message}")
      }

      override fun onComplete() {
        println("Complete")
      }

    }

    observale.subscribe(observer)
    delay(1500)//6
  }
}
```

I hope you remember the `Observable.interval` factory method, from just few pages ago in this chapter. This method takes two parameters describing the interval period and time unit, then, it prints integers sequentially, starting from 0. `Observable` created with interval never completes and never stops until you stop them or the program stops execution. I thought it will be the perfect fit in this scenario, as here we want to stop the `Observable` midway.

So, in this example on comment 1, we created an `Observable` with the `Observable.interval` factory method that will emit an integer after each 100 millisecond interval.

On comment 2, I have declared a `lateinit var disposable` of type `Disposable` (`lateinit` means the variable will get initialized at a later point of time). On comment 3, inside the `onSubscribe` method, we will assign the received parameter value to the `disposable` variable.

We intend to stop the execution after the sequence reaches 10, that is, after 10 is emitted, the emission should be stopped immediately. To achieve that, we placed a check inside the `onNext` method, where we are checking if the value of the emitted item is equal to or greater than 10, and if the emission is not already stopped (disposed), then we will dispose the emission (comment 5).

Here is the output:

```
Received 0
Received 1
Received 2
Received 3
Received 4
Received 5
Received 6
Received 7
Received 8
Received 9
Received 10
Disposed
```

From the output, we can see that no integer got emitted after the `disposable.dispose()` method was called, although the execution waited 500 milliseconds more (100*10=1000 milliseconds to print sequence until 10, and we called the `delay` method with 1500, thus 500 milliseconds after emitting 10).

If you are curious to know the `Disposable` interface, then the following is the definition:

```
interface Disposable {
  /**
  * Dispose the resource, the operation should be idempotent.
  */
  fun dispose()
  /**
  * Returns true if this resource has been disposed.
  * @return true if this resource has been disposed
  */
  val isDisposed:Boolean
}
```

It has one property that denotes if the emission is already notified to stop (`disposed`) and a method to notify the emission to stop (`dispose`).

Hot and Cold Observables

So, as we have a grip on the basic concepts of `Observables` and `Observers` by now, let's move to something more interesting and advanced. The `Observables` that we are talking all about can be categorized into two categories based on their behavior. As the heading suggests, the two categories are `Hot Obervables` and `Cold Observable`. I can bet that, by now, you are craving to know more about `Hot` and `Cold Observables`, aren't you? So, let's dive into it.

Cold Observables

Take a careful look at all the previous examples. In all the examples, if you subscribe to the same `Observable` multiple times, you will get the emissions from the beginning for all the subscriptions. Don't believe it? Take a look at the following example:

```
fun main(args: Array<String>) {
  val observable: Observable<String> = listOf
  ("String 1","String 2","String 3","String 4").toObservable()//1

  observable.subscribe({//2
    println("Received $it")
  },{
    println("Error ${it.message}")
  },{
    println("Done")
```

```
    })

    observable.subscribe({//3
      println("Received $it")
    },{
      println("Error ${it.message}")
    },{
      println("Done")
    })
  }
```

Here is its output:

```
"C:\Program Files\Java\jdk1.8.0_131\bin\java" ...
Received String 1
Received String 2
Received String 3
Received String 4
Done
Received String 1
Received String 2
Received String 3
Received String 4
Done

Process finished with exit code 0
```

The program is quite straightforward. Declared an `Observable` on comment 1, subscribed to the `Observable` twice—on comment 2 and 3. Now, look at the output. For both the subscribe calls, you got the exact same emission from the first one to the last one.

Those `Observables`, which have this particular behavior, that is, emitting items from the beginning for each subscription, are called `Cold Observable`. To be more specific, `Cold Observables` start running upon subscriptions and `Cold Observable` starts pushing items after `subscribe` gets called, and pushes the same sequence of items on each subscription.

All the `Observable` factory methods we have used up until this chapter return `Cold Observables`. `Cold Observables` resemble data. When we are working with data, for example, say, while working with SQLite or Room database in Android, we rely more on `Cold Observables` than `Hot Observables`.

Hot Observables

Cold Observables are passive, they don't emit anything until subscribe is called. Hot Observables are contrary to Cold Observables; it doesn't need subscriptions to start emission. While you can compare Cold Observables to CD/DVD recordings, Hot Observables are like TV channels—they continue broadcasting (emitting) their content, irrespective of whether anyone is watching (Observing) it or not.

Hot Observables resemble events more than data. The events may carry data with them, but there is a time-sensitive component where Observers that subscribed lately can miss out previously emitted data. They are specifically useful for UI events while working with Android/JavaFX/Swing. They are also very useful in resembling server requests.

Introducing the ConnectableObservable object

A great example of Hot Observables is ConnectableObservable. It is one of the most helpful forms of Hot Observables as well. It can turn any Observable, even a Cold Observable, into a Hot Observable. It doesn't start emitting on the subscribe call; instead, it gets activated after you call the connect method. You have to make the subscribe calls before calling connect; any subscribe calls after calling connect will miss the emissions fired previously.

Let's consider the following code snippet:

```
fun main(args: Array<String>) {
  val connectableObservable = listOf
  ("String 1","String 2","String 3","String 4","String
  5").toObservable()
  .publish()//1
  connectableObservable.subscribe({ println
  ("Subscription 1: $it") })//2
  connectableObservable.map(String::reversed)//3
  .subscribe({ println("Subscription 2 $it")})//4
  connectableObservable.connect()//5
  connectableObservable.subscribe({ println
  ("Subscription 3: $it") })//6 //Will not receive emissions
}
```

The main purpose of `ConnectableObservable` is for `Observables` with multiple subscriptions to connect all subscriptions of an `Observable` together so that they can react to a single push; contrary to `Cold Observables` that repeats operations for doing the push, and pushes separately for each subscription, thus repeating the cycle. `ConnectableObservable` connects all `subscriptions` (`Observers`) called before the `connect` method and relays a single push to all `Observers`, `Observers` then react to/process that push.

In the preceding example, we created `Observable` with the `toObservable()` method, then, on comment 1, we used the `publish` operator to convert `Cold Observable` into `ConnectableObservable`.

On comment 2, we subscribed to `connectableObservable`. On comment 3, we used the `map` operator to reverse `String`, and, on comment 4, we subscribed to the mapped `connectableObservable`.

On comment 5, we called `connect` method, and emissions got started to both `Observers`.

 Note that we used the `map` operator in this example on comment 3. We will discuss the `map` operator in detail in `Chapter 5`, *Asynchronous Data Operators and Transformations*. However, here is the definition, if you are curious. The `map` operator applies a function of your choosing to each item emitted by the source `Observable`, and returns an `Observable` that emits the results of these function applications.

Here is the output:

```
"C:\Program Files\Java\jdk1.8.0_131\bin\java" ...
Subscription 1: String 1
Subscription 2 1 gnirtS
Subscription 1: String 2
Subscription 2 2 gnirtS
Subscription 1: String 3
Subscription 2 3 gnirtS
Subscription 1: String 4
Subscription 2 4 gnirtS
Subscription 1: String 5
Subscription 2 5 gnirtS

Process finished with exit code 0
```

Note that, as the output suggests, each emission goes to each `Observer` simultaneously, and they are processing data in an interleaved fashion.

This mechanism of emitting from `Observable` once and then relaying the emission to all `Subscriptions/Observers` is known as **multicasting**.

Also note that the `subscribe` call on comment 6, after `connect`, has not received any emissions, as `ConnectableObservable` is hot, and any new subscriptions occurred after connect will miss out the emissions fired previously (between the call of the `connect` method and the new subscription, remember that, within a few milliseconds, computers can do a lot of tasks); in this case, it missed all the emissions.

The following piece of code is another example to make you understand it better:

```
fun main(args: Array<String>) {
  val connectableObservable =
  Observable.interval(100,TimeUnit.MILLISECONDS)
  .publish()//1
  connectableObservable.
  subscribe({ println("Subscription 1: $it") })//2
  connectableObservable
  .subscribe({ println("Subscription 2 $it")})//3
  connectableObservable.connect()//4
  runBlocking { delay(500) }//5

  connectableObservable.
  subscribe({ println("Subscription 3: $it") })//6
  runBlocking { delay(500) }//7
}
```

This example is almost the same as the previous one, just a few tweaks.

Here, we used the `Observable.interval` method to create `Observable`; the benefit is that, as it takes an interval before each emission, it will give some room to the subscription after connect to get a few emissions.

On comment 1, we converted `Cold Observable` to `ConnectableObservable`, as with the previous one, and did two subscriptions and then connected, as in the previous example (comment 2, 3, 4).

We called delay right after connect on comment 5, then subscribed again on comment 6, and again a delay on comment 7 to allow the 3rd subscription to print some data.

The following output will allow us to understand better:

Go through the output carefully to note that the 3rd subscription received emissions from sequence 5, and missed all previous ones (there were 5 emissions before the 3rd subscription—500 millisecond delay/100 millisecond interval).

Subjects

Another great way to implement Hot Observables is Subject. Basically, it is a combination of Observable and Observer, as it has many common behaviors to both Observables and Observers. Like Hot Observables, it maintains an internal Observer list and relays a single push to every Observer subscribed to it at the time of emission.

So, let's take a look at what Subject has to offer us. And why is it called a combination of Observables and Observers? Please refer to the following points:

- It has all the operators that Observable should have.
- Like Observer, it can listen to any value emitted to it.
- After Subject is completed/errored/unsubscribed, it cannot be reused.
- The most interesting point is that it passes values through itself. As an explanation, if you pass a value with onNext to a Subject (Observer) side, it will come out of the Observable side of it.

So, `Subject` is a combination of `Observable` and `Observer`. You have already seen the use of `Subject` in the previous chapters, but, to make things clearer, let's take a new example:

```
fun main(args: Array<String>) {
  val observable = Observable.interval(100,
  TimeUnit.MILLISECONDS)//1
  val subject = PublishSubject.create<Long>()//2
  observable.subscribe(subject)//3
  subject.subscribe({//4
    println("Received $it")
  })
  runBlocking { delay(1100) }//5
}
```

Let's check the output first, and then we will explain the code:

```
"C:\Program Files\Java\jdk1.8.0_131\bin\java" ...
Received 0
Received 1
Received 2
Received 3
Received 4
Received 5
Received 6
Received 7
Received 8
Received 9
Received 10

Process finished with exit code 0
```

Now, let's understand the code. In this program, we have used the good old `Observable.interval` method. So, on comment 1, we again created an instance of `Observable` with `Observable.interval`, with a 100 millisecond interval.

On comment 2, we created `Subject` with `PublishSubject.create()`.

There are many types of `Subject` available. `PublishSubject` is one of them. `PublishSubject` emits to an `observer` only those items that are emitted by the `Observable` sources subsequent to the time of the subscription.
We will discuss in detail about the various types of `Subject` in the next section in this chapter.

On comment 3, we used the `Subject` instance just like `Observer`, to subscribe to the emissions by the `Observable` instance. On comment 4, we used the `Subject` instance like an `Observable` and subscribed with lambda to listen to the emissions by the `Subject` instance.

You probably got used to it with the code in comment 5; if not, then we used it to make the program wait for `1100` milliseconds so that we can see the outputs made by the interval program. You can think of the `delay` method as similar to the `sleep` method in Java, the only difference here is that you must use `delay` inside a `Coroutine context`, so, in order to use `delay` method, you have to specify and start a `Coroutine context`; this is not quite possible always. The `runBlocking` method is there to help you in that scenario; it mocks a `Coroutine context` inside the calling thread while blocking that thread until `runBlocking` completes executing all its code.

The `Subject` instance listens to the emissions by the `Observable` instance and then broadcasts those emissions to its `Observers`, very likely, to a TV Channel broadcasting a Film (from a CD/DVD recording).

You are probably thinking, what is the benefit of that? When I can directly `subscribe` and `Observer` to `Observable`, why should I use `PublishSubject` in between? To find the answers, let's modify this code a little bit in a way that will help us understand it better:

```
fun main(args: Array<String>) {
  val observable = Observable.interval(100,
  TimeUnit.MILLISECONDS)//1
  val subject = PublishSubject.create<Long>()//2
  observable.subscribe(subject)//3
  subject.subscribe({//4
    println("Subscription 1 Received $it")
  })
  runBlocking { delay(1100) }//5
  subject.subscribe({//6
    println("Subscription 2 Received $it")
  })
  runBlocking { delay(1100) }//7
}
```

Here, the code is almost the same until comment 5 (except on `Subscribe` on comment 3, where I prepended `Subscription 1` to the `String` output).

On comment 6, we again subscribed to subject. As we are subscribing after 1100 milliseconds, it should receive emissions after the first 11 emissions. On comment 7, we are again making the program wait by 1100 milliseconds.

Let's see the output:

```
Subscription 1 Received 0
Subscription 1 Received 1
Subscription 1 Received 2
Subscription 1 Received 3
Subscription 1 Received 4
Subscription 1 Received 5
Subscription 1 Received 6
Subscription 1 Received 7
Subscription 1 Received 8
Subscription 1 Received 9
Subscription 1 Received 10
Subscription 1 Received 11
Subscription 2 Received 11
Subscription 1 Received 12
Subscription 2 Received 12
Subscription 1 Received 13
Subscription 2 Received 13
Subscription 1 Received 14
Subscription 2 Received 14
Subscription 1 Received 15
Subscription 2 Received 15
Subscription 1 Received 16
Subscription 2 Received 16
Subscription 1 Received 17
Subscription 2 Received 17
Subscription 1 Received 18
Subscription 2 Received 18
Subscription 1 Received 19
Subscription 2 Received 19
Subscription 1 Received 20
Subscription 2 Received 20
Subscription 1 Received 21
Subscription 2 Received 21
```

In the output, it is printing the second subscription from the 12th emission (sequence 11). So, Subject doesn't replay the actions such as Cold Observables, it just relays the emission to all Observers, turning a Cold Observable into Hot Oberservale one.

Varieties of Subject

As we mentioned earlier, there are a lot of varieties available for Subjects. As we have gained some grip in Subject, let's now dive into varieties of Subject to understand it better. So, these are some of the most useful and important varieties of Subject, which we will discuss here:

- AsyncSubject
- PublishSubject
- BehaviorSubject
- ReplaySubject

Understanding AsyncSubject

AsyncSubject only emits the last value of the source observable (Observable it listens on), and the last emission only. To say things more clearly, AsyncSubject will emit the last value it got, and will emit it only one time.

This is a marble diagram for AsyncSubject, which has been taken from ReactiveX documentation (http://reactivex.io/documentation/subject.html):

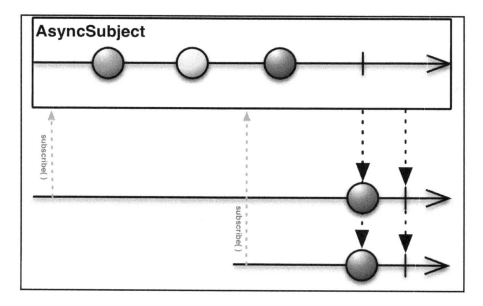

Let's consider the following code example:

```
fun main(args: Array<String>) {
  val observable = Observable.just(1,2,3,4)//1
  val subject = AsyncSubject.create<Int>()//2
  observable.subscribe(subject)//3
  subject.subscribe({//4
    //onNext
    println("Received $it")
  },{
    //onError
    it.printStackTrace()
  },{
    //onComplete
    println("Complete")
  })
  subject.onComplete()//5
}
```

Here is the output:

```
Received 4
Complete
```

In this example, we created an example with `Observable.just`, with 4 integers (on comment 1). Then, on comment 2, we created an `AsyncSubject` example. After that, on comment 3 and 4, like the previous example, we subscribed to the `observable instance` with `subject` and then subscribed to the `Subject` instance with lambda; only this time, we passed all the three methods—`onNext`, `onError`, and `onComplete`.

On comment 6, we called `onComplete`.

As the output suggests, `Subject` only emitted the last value it got, that is, 4.

On `Subject` instances, you can pass values directly with the `onNext` method, without subscribing to any `Observable`. Recall the examples in the previous chapters where we used `Subject` (`PublishSubject`); there, we only used `onNext` to pass the values. You can subscribe to another `Observable` with `Subject`, or pass values with `onNext`. Basically, when you subscribe to `Observable` with `Subject`, `Subject` calls its `onNext` internally upon `Observable`'s value emission.

Have doubts? Let's tweak the code a little. Instead of subscribing to an `Observable`, we will call `onNext` only to pass values, and will have another subscription. Here is the code, to do so:

```
fun main(args: Array<String>) {
  val subject = AsyncSubject.create<Int>()
  subject.onNext(1)
  subject.onNext(2)
  subject.onNext(3)
  subject.onNext(4)
  subject.subscribe({
    //onNext
    println("S1 Received $it")
  },{
    //onError
    it.printStackTrace()
  },{
    //onComplete
    println("S1 Complete")
  })
  subject.onNext(5)
  subject.subscribe({
    //onNext
    println("S2 Received $it")
  },{
    //onError
    it.printStackTrace()
  },{
    //onComplete
    println("S2 Complete")
  })
  subject.onComplete()
}
```

Here is the output:

```
"C:\Program Files\Java\jdk1.8.0_131\bin\java" ...
S1 Received 5
S1 Complete
S2 Received 5
S2 Complete

Process finished with exit code 0
```

Here, we passed all values via `onNext`; it only emitted the last value it got (5) to both of the subscriptions. Look carefully, the 1ˢᵗ subscription was before passing the last value. As `ConnectableObservable` starts emitting on call of `connect`, `AsyncSubject` emits its only value on call of `onComplete` only.

Note that as the outputs suggest, `AsyncSubject` doesn't in an interleave manner, that is, it will replay its action multiple times to emit the value to multiple `Observers`, although it is only one value.

Understanding PublishSubject

`PublishSubject` emits all subsequent values that it got at the time of subscription, whether it got the value via the `onNext` method or through another subscription. We have already seen the application of `PublishSubject`, and it is the most commonly used `Subject` variant.

Here is a graphical representation of `PublishSubject` which has been taken from ReactiveX documentation (`http://reactivex.io/documentation/subject.html`):

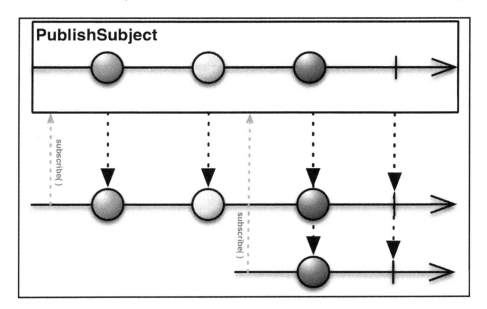

Understanding BehaviorSubject

What if we combine `AsyncSubject` and `PublishSubject`? Or mix the benefits of both? `BehaviorSubject` emits the last item it got before the subscription and all the subsequent items at the time of subscription while working with multicasting, that is, it keeps an internal `list` of `Observers` and relays the same emit to all of its `Observers` without replaying.

Here is the graphical representation which has been taken from ReactiveX documentation (`http://reactivex.io/documentation/subject.html`):

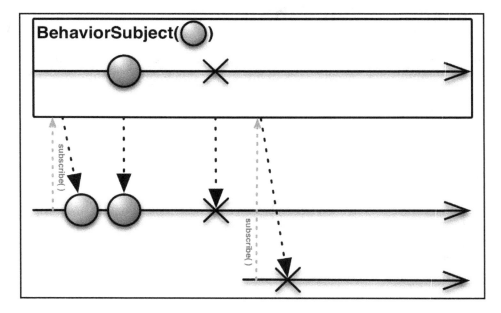

Let's modify the last example with `BehaviorSubject` and see what happens:

```
fun main(args: Array<String>) {
  val subject = BehaviorSubject.create<Int>()
  subject.onNext(1)
  subject.onNext(2)
  subject.onNext(3)
  subject.onNext(4)
  subject.subscribe({
    //onNext
    println("S1 Received $it")
  },{
    //onError
    it.printStackTrace()
```

```
    },{
      //onComplete
      println("S1 Complete")
    })
    subject.onNext(5)
    subject.subscribe({
      //onNext
      println("S2 Received $it")
    },{
      //onError
      it.printStackTrace()
    },{
      //onComplete
      println("S2 Complete")
    })
    subject.onComplete()
  }
```

Here, I took the last example where we worked with `AsyncSubject`, and modified it with `BehaviorSubject`. So, let's see the output and understand `BehaviorSubject`:

```
S1 Received 4
S1 Received 5
S2 Received 5
S1 Complete
S2 Complete
```

While the 1st subscription gets 4 and 5; 4 was emitted before its subscription and 5 after. For the 2nd subscription, it only got 5, which was emitted before its subscription.

Understanding ReplaySubject

It is more like `Cold Observable`; it will replay all the items it got, regardless of when `Observer` subscribes.

Here is the graphical representation:

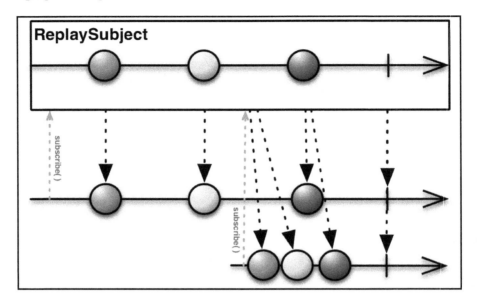

Image credit: http://reactivex.io/documentation/subject.html

Let's modify the previous program with ReplaySubject:

```
fun main(args: Array<String>) {
  val subject = ReplaySubject.create<Int>()
  subject.onNext(1)
  subject.onNext(2)
  subject.onNext(3)
  subject.onNext(4)
  subject.subscribe({
    //onNext
    println("S1 Received $it")
  },{
    //onError
    it.printStackTrace()
  },{
    //onComplete
    println("S1 Complete")
  })
  subject.onNext(5)
  subject.subscribe({
    //onNext
    println("S2 Received $it")
  },{
```

```
    //onError
    it.printStackTrace()
},{
    //onComplete
    println("S2 Complete")
})
subject.onComplete()
}
```

And, here is the output:

```
S1 Received 1
S1 Received 2
S1 Received 3
S1 Received 4
S1 Received 5
S2 Received 1
S2 Received 2
S2 Received 3
S2 Received 4
S2 Received 5
S1 Complete
S2 Complete
```

It emitted all of the items for both the subscriptions.

Summary

In this chapter, we learned about `Observables` and `Observers` and how to use them. We worked with several examples to get our grips strong on them. We learned that there are two categories of `Observables`—Hot `Observables` and Cold `Observables`. We also learned about several `Subject` and its variant. Several `Subject` are basically a combination of `Observables` and many `Observer`.

While `Observables` provide us with great flexibilities and power, it too has some disadvantages, such as backpressure. Curious about it? Want to know more about the disadvantages of `Observables` and how to overcome them? Rush to the fourth chapter then.

4
Introduction to Backpressure and Flowables

So far, we were trying to understand the push-based architecture of reactive programming. By now, we have gained a good understanding of `Observables`. We now understand that an `Observable` emits items to be consumed by an `Observer` for further processing. However, while going through previous chapters, did you ever think of a situation where the `Observable` emits items faster than the `Observer` can consume them? This whole chapter is devoted to this problem. We will start by trying to understand how and when this problem may occur, and then we will try to solve the problem.

So, in this chapter, we will focus on the following topics, and by the end of the chapter we should have a solution to the problem mentioned earlier:

- Understanding backpressure
- Flowables and Subscriber
- Creating Flowables with `Flowable.create()`
- Using Observable and Flowables together
- Backpressure operators
- An `Flowable.generate()` operator

So, now, let's start with backpressure—the problem with Observables.

Understanding backpressure

The only problem with `Observable` is when an `Observer` cannot cope with the pace of an `Observable`. An `Observable`, by default, chains work by pushing items synchronously to the `Observer`, one at a time. However, if the `observer` has to perform some time-consuming computations, this may take longer than the interval of each item emission of `Observable`. Confused? Let's consider this example:

```kotlin
fun main(args: Array<String>) {
    val observable = Observable.just(1,2,3,4,5,6,7,8,9)//(1)
    val subject = BehaviorSubject.create<Int>()
    subject.observeOn(Schedulers.computation())//(2)
        .subscribe({//(3)
            println("Subs 1 Received $it")
            runBlocking { delay(200) }//(4)
        })

    subject.observeOn(Schedulers.computation())//(5)
    .subscribe({//(6)
        println("Subs 2 Received $it")
     })
     observable.subscribe(subject)//(7)
    runBlocking { delay(2000) }//(8)
}
```

The code is quite simple. We created `Observable` on comment (1), then, we created `BehaviorSubject`, and then, on comment (3) and (6), we subscribe to `BehaviorSubject`. On comment (7), after subscribing to `BehaviorSubject`, we will use `BehaviorSubject` to subscribe to the `Observable` so that `Observers` of `BehaviorSubject` should get all the emissions. On comment (4), inside the first subscription, we used the `delay` method to simulate a time-taking subscriber. There is a new code on comment (2) and (6), `subject.observeOn(Schedulers.computation())`; we will discuss this method in detail in the later chapters, but, for now, just keep in mind that this `observeOn` method helps us specify a thread to run the subscription, and `Scheduler.computation()` provides us a with a thread to perform computations. On comment (8), we used the `delay` method to wait for the execution, as the execution will occur in the background.

Based on the knowledge we gathered from previous chapters, we can easily say that subscriptions should print all the numbers from 1-9 in an interleaved manner, or shouldn't they? Let's see the output first:

```
"C:\Program Files\Java\jdk1.8.0_131\bin\java" ...
Subs 1 Received 1
Subs 2 Received 1
Subs 2 Received 2
Subs 2 Received 3
Subs 2 Received 4
Subs 2 Received 5
Subs 2 Received 6
Subs 2 Received 7
Subs 2 Received 8
Subs 2 Received 9
Subs 1 Received 2
Subs 1 Received 3
Subs 1 Received 4
Subs 1 Received 5
Subs 1 Received 6
Subs 1 Received 7
Subs 1 Received 8
Subs 1 Received 9

Process finished with exit code 0
```

Shocked to see the output? Instead of working in an interleaved manner, subscription 2 completes printing all the numbers before subscription 1 prints even the second number, even though it starts printing first. So, why did it break the behavior of `Hot Observables`? Why didn't both the `Observers` work in an interleaved manner? Let's inspect. The program actually didn't break the behavior of `Hot Observables`, the `subject` actually emitted once for both of the `observers`; however, as for the first `observer`, each computation took long, **the emissions got queued**; and this is obviously not any good, as this could lead to a lot of problems, including the `OutOfMemoryError` exceptions.

Still have doubts? Let's look at another example:

```kotlin
fun main(args: Array<String>) {
  val observable = Observable.just(1,2,3,4,5,6,7,8,9)//(1)
  observable
      .map { MyItem(it) }//(2)
      .observeOn(Schedulers.computation())//(3)
      .subscribe({//(4)
        println("Received $it")
        runBlocking { delay(200) }//(5)
      })
      runBlocking { delay(2000) }//(6)
}

data class MyItem (val id:Int) {
  init {
    println("MyItem Created $id")//(7)
  }
}
```

In this example, we eliminated the `Subject` and multiple `Subscribers` to make the program simpler and easier to understand. We have already introduced the `map` operator in the previous chapter that we used on comment `(2)` to convert the `Int` items to the `MyItem` object.

If you forgot the `map` operator from the previous chapter, it takes a source observable, processes items emitted by them on runtime, and creates another observable to observe on. Put simply, the `map` operator sits before subscribe to process each item emitted by `observable` before passing the new generated item to `observer`. We will also take a closer look at the `map` operator in the later chapters.

Here, we used it to keep track of each emission. Whenever an emission will occur, it will be passed instantly to the `map` operator, where we are creating an object of the `MyItem` class. In the `init` block of the `MyItem` class, we are printing the value passed to it; so, as soon as an item is emitted, it will be printed by the `MyItem` class.

Here, the `MyItem` class is a `data class`, that is, it will have the getter of `val id` and `toString` methods by default.

The remaining part of the program is almost the same; let's take a look at the output, then we will continue to discuss:

```
"C:\Program Files\Java\jdk1.8.0_131\bin\java" ...
MyItem Created 1
MyItem Created 2
MyItem Created 3
MyItem Created 4
MyItem Created 5
MyItem Created 6
MyItem Created 7
MyItem Created 8
MyItem Created 9
Received MyItem(id=1)
Received MyItem(id=2)
Received MyItem(id=3)
Received MyItem(id=4)
Received MyItem(id=5)
Received MyItem(id=6)
Received MyItem(id=7)
Received MyItem(id=8)
Received MyItem(id=9)

Process finished with exit code 0
```

As we can see in the output, the creation of many `MyItem`, as known as emissions was quite fast, and completed even before the `Observer` as known as consumer can even start printing.

So, the problem is that the emissions get queued in the consumer, while the consumer is busy processing previous emissions by the producer.

A solution to this problem could be a feedback channel from consumer to producer, through which the consumer can tell the producer to wait until it completes processing the previous emission. This way, consumers or messaging middleware will not become saturated and unresponsive under high load; instead, they may request fewer messages, letting the producer decide how to slow down. This feedback channel is called **backpressure**. Backpressure is not supported in `Observables` and `Observers`, the solution could be using `Flowables` and `Subscribers` instead. Let's learn what those are.

Flowable

We may call Flowables a backpressured version of Observables. Probably, the only difference between Flowables and Observables is that Flowable takes backpressure into consideration. Observable does not. That's it. Flowable hosts the default buffer size of 128 elements for operators, so, when the consumer is taking time, the emitted items may wait in the buffer.

Note that Flowables were added in ReactiveX 2.x (RxKotlin 2.X), and the previous versions don't include them. Instead, in previous versions, Observables was retrofitted to support backpressure that caused many unexpected `MissingBackpressureException`.
Here is the release note if you are interested:
`https://github.com/ReactiveX/RxJava/wiki/What%27s-different-in-2`
`.0#observable-and-flowable`

We had a long discussion so far; let's now try our hands on code. At first, we will try a code with Observable, and then we will do the same with Flowables to see and understand the difference:

```
fun main(args: Array<String>) {
  Observable.range(1,1000)//(1)
    .map { MyItem3(it) }//(2)
    .observeOn(Schedulers.computation())
    .subscribe({//(3)
      print("Received $it;\t")
      runBlocking { delay(50) }//(4)
    },{it.printStackTrace()})
    runBlocking { delay(60000) }//(5)
}
data class MyItem3 (val id:Int) {
init {
  print("MyItem Created $id;\t")
}
}
}
```

A simple code with the `Observable.range()` operator, which should emit numbers from 1 to 1000. On comment (2), we used the `map` operator to create the `MyItem3` object from `Int`. On comment (3), we subscribed to `Observable`. On comment (4), we ran a blocking delay to simulate a long running subscription code. On comment (5), we, again, ran a blocking delay code to wait for the consumer to complete processing of all items before the program stops execution.

The whole output will take some space, so we will put parts of outputs as screenshots here:

```
"C:\Program Files\Java\jdk1.8.0.131\bin\java" ...
MyItem Created 1;    MyItem Created 2;    MyItem Created 3;    MyItem Created 4;    MyItem Created 5;    MyItem Created 6;    MyItem Created 7;    MyItem
Created 8; MyItem Created 9;   MyItem Created 10;   MyItem Created 11;   MyItem Created 12;   MyItem Created 13;   MyItem Created 14;   MyItem Created
15;    MyItem Created 16;   MyItem Created 17;   MyItem Created 18;   MyItem Created 19;   MyItem Created 20;   MyItem Created 21;   MyItem Created
22;    MyItem Created 23;   MyItem Created 24;   MyItem Created 25;   MyItem Created 26;   MyItem Created 27;   MyItem Created 28;   MyItem Created
29;    MyItem Created 30;   MyItem Created 31;   MyItem Created 32;   MyItem Created 33;   MyItem Created 34;   MyItem Created 35;   MyItem Created
36;    MyItem Created 37;   MyItem Created 38;   MyItem Created 39;   MyItem Created 40;   MyItem Created 41;   MyItem Created 42;   MyItem Created
43;    MyItem Created 44;   MyItem Created 45;   MyItem Created 46;   MyItem Created 47;   MyItem Created 48;   MyItem Created 49;   MyItem Created
50;    MyItem Created 51;   MyItem Created 52;   MyItem Created 53;   MyItem Created 54;   MyItem Created 55;   MyItem Created 56;   MyItem Created
57;    MyItem Created 58;   MyItem Created 59;   MyItem Created 60;   MyItem Created 61;   MyItem Created 62;   MyItem Created 63;   MyItem Created
64;    MyItem Created 65;   MyItem Created 66;   MyItem Created 67;   MyItem Created 68;   MyItem Created 69;   MyItem Created 70;   MyItem Created
71;    MyItem Created 72;   MyItem Created 73;   MyItem Created 74;   MyItem Created 75;   MyItem Created 76;   MyItem Created 77;   MyItem Created
78;    MyItem Created 79;   MyItem Created 80;   MyItem Created 81;   MyItem Created 82;   MyItem Created 83;   MyItem Created 84;   MyItem Created
85;    MyItem Created 86;   MyItem Created 87;   MyItem Created 88;   MyItem Created 89;   MyItem Created 90;   MyItem Created 91;   MyItem Created
92;    MyItem Created 93;   MyItem Created 94;   MyItem Created 95;   MyItem Created 96;   MyItem Created 97;   MyItem Created 98;   MyItem Created
99;    MyItem Created 100;  MyItem Created 101;  MyItem Created 102;  MyItem Created 103;  MyItem Created 104;  MyItem Created 105;  MyItem Created
106;   MyItem Created 107;  MyItem Created 108;  MyItem Created 109;  MyItem Created 110;  MyItem Created 111;  MyItem Created 112;  MyItem Created
113;   MyItem Created 114;  MyItem Created 115;  MyItem Created 116;  MyItem Created 117;  MyItem Created 118;  MyItem Created 119;  MyItem Created
120;   MyItem Created 121;  MyItem Created 122;  MyItem Created 123;  MyItem Created 124;  MyItem Created 125;  MyItem Created 126;  MyItem Created
127;   MyItem Created 128;  MyItem Created 129;  MyItem Created 130;  MyItem Created 131;  MyItem Created 132;  MyItem Created 133;  MyItem Created
134;   MyItem Created 135;  MyItem Created 136;  MyItem Created 137;  MyItem Created 138;  MyItem Created 139;  MyItem Created 140;  MyItem Created
141;   MyItem Created 142;  MyItem Created 143;  MyItem Created 144;  MyItem Created 145;  MyItem Created 146;  MyItem Created 147;  MyItem Created
148;   MyItem Created 149;  MyItem Created 150;  MyItem Created 151;  MyItem Created 152;  MyItem Created 153;  MyItem Created 154;  MyItem Created
155;   MyItem Created 156;  MyItem Created 157;  MyItem Created 158;  MyItem Created 159;  MyItem Created 160;  MyItem Created 161;  MyItem Created
162;   MyItem Created 163;  MyItem Created 164;  MyItem Created 165;  MyItem Created 166;  MyItem Created 167;  MyItem Created 168;  MyItem Created
169;   MyItem Created 170;  MyItem Created 171;  MyItem Created 172;  MyItem Created 173;  MyItem Created 174;  MyItem Created 175;  MyItem Created
176;   MyItem Created 177;  MyItem Created 178;  MyItem Created 179;  MyItem Created 180;  MyItem Created 181;  MyItem Created 182;  MyItem Created
183;   MyItem Created 184;  MyItem Created 185;  MyItem Created 186;  MyItem Created 187;  MyItem Created 188;  MyItem Created 189;  MyItem Created

903;   MyItem Created 904;  MyItem Created 905;  MyItem Created 906;  MyItem Created 907;  MyItem Created 908;  MyItem Created 909; MyItem Created
910;   MyItem Created 911;  MyItem Created 912;  MyItem Created 913;  MyItem Created 914;  MyItem Created 915;  MyItem Created 916;  MyItem Created
917;   MyItem Created 918;  MyItem Created 919;  MyItem Created 920;  MyItem Created 921;  MyItem Created 922;  MyItem Created 923; MyItem Created
924;   MyItem Created 925;  MyItem Created 926;  MyItem Created 927;  MyItem Created 928;  MyItem Created 929;  MyItem Created 930;  MyItem Created
931;   MyItem Created 932;  MyItem Created 933;  MyItem Created 934;  MyItem Created 935;  MyItem Created 936;  MyItem Created 937;  MyItem Created
938;   MyItem Created 939;  MyItem Created 940;  MyItem Created 941;  MyItem Created 942;  MyItem Created 943;  MyItem Created 944;  MyItem Created
945;   MyItem Created 946;  MyItem Created 947;  MyItem Created 948;  MyItem Created 949;  MyItem Created 950;  MyItem Created 951;  MyItem Created
952;   MyItem Created 953;  MyItem Created 954;  MyItem Created 955;  MyItem Created 956;  MyItem Created 957;  MyItem Created 958;  MyItem Created
959;   MyItem Created 960;  MyItem Created 961;  MyItem Created 962;  MyItem Created 963;  MyItem Created 964;  MyItem Created 965;  MyItem Created
966;   MyItem Created 967;  MyItem Created 968;  MyItem Created 969;  MyItem Created 970;  MyItem Created 971;  MyItem Created 972; MyItem Created
973;   MyItem Created 974;  MyItem Created 975;  MyItem Created 976;  MyItem Created 977;  MyItem Created 978;  MyItem Created 979;  MyItem Created
980;   MyItem Created 981;  MyItem Created 982;  MyItem Created 983;  MyItem Created 984;  MyItem Created 985;  MyItem Created 986;  MyItem Created
987;   MyItem Created 988;  MyItem Created 989;  MyItem Created 990;  MyItem Created 991;  MyItem Created 992;  MyItem Created 993;  MyItem Created
994;   MyItem Created 995;  MyItem Created 996;  MyItem Created 997;  MyItem Created 998;  MyItem Created 999;  MyItem Created 1000;    Received
MyItem3(id=4); Received MyItem3(id=31); Received MyItem3(id=4); Received MyItem3(id=5); Received MyItem3(id=6); Received
MyItem3(id=8); Received MyItem3(id=9); Received MyItem3(id=10);    Received MyItem3(id=11);    Received MyItem3(id=12);    Received MyItem3(id=13)
;  Received MyItem3(id=14);    Received MyItem3(id=15);    Received MyItem3(id=16);    Received MyItem3(id=17);    Received MyItem3(id=18);
Received MyItem3(id=19);    Received MyItem3(id=20);    Received MyItem3(id=21);    Received MyItem3(id=22);    Received MyItem3(id=23);    Received
MyItem3(id=24);    Received MyItem3(id=25);    Received MyItem3(id=26);    Received MyItem3(id=27);    Received MyItem3(id=28);    Received
MyItem3(id=29);    Received MyItem3(id=30);    Received MyItem3(id=31);    Received MyItem3(id=32);    Received MyItem3(id=33);    Received
MyItem3(id=34);    Received MyItem3(id=35);    Received MyItem3(id=36);    Received MyItem3(id=37);    Received MyItem3(id=38);    Received
MyItem3(id=39);    Received MyItem3(id=40);    Received MyItem3(id=41);    Received MyItem3(id=42);    Received MyItem3(id=43);    Received
MyItem3(id=44);    Received MyItem3(id=45);    Received MyItem3(id=46);    Received MyItem3(id=47);    Received MyItem3(id=48);    Received
MyItem3(id=49);    Received MyItem3(id=50);    Received MyItem3(id=51);    Received MyItem3(id=52);    Received MyItem3(id=53);    Received
MyItem3(id=54);    Received MyItem3(id=55);    Received MyItem3(id=56);    Received MyItem3(id=57);    Received MyItem3(id=58);    Received
MyItem3(id=59);    Received MyItem3(id=60);    Received MyItem3(id=61);    Received MyItem3(id=62);    Received MyItem3(id=63);    Received
MyItem3(id=64);    Received MyItem3(id=65);    Received MyItem3(id=66);    Received MyItem3(id=67);    Received MyItem3(id=68);    Received
MyItem3(id=69);    Received MyItem3(id=70);    Received MyItem3(id=71);    Received MyItem3(id=72);    Received MyItem3(id=73);    Received
MyItem3(id=74);    Received MyItem3(id=75);    Received MyItem3(id=76);    Received MyItem3(id=77);    Received MyItem3(id=78);    Received
MyItem3(id=79);    Received MyItem3(id=80);    Received MyItem3(id=81);    Received MyItem3(id=82);    Received MyItem3(id=83);

MyItem3(id=954);    Received MyItem3(id=955);    Received MyItem3(id=956);    Received MyItem3(id=957);    Received MyItem3(id=958);    Received
MyItem3(id=959);    Received MyItem3(id=960);    Received MyItem3(id=961);    Received MyItem3(id=962);    Received MyItem3(id=963);    Received
MyItem3(id=964);    Received MyItem3(id=965);    Received MyItem3(id=966);    Received MyItem3(id=967);    Received MyItem3(id=968);    Received
MyItem3(id=969);    Received MyItem3(id=970);    Received MyItem3(id=971);    Received MyItem3(id=972);    Received MyItem3(id=973);    Received
MyItem3(id=974);    Received MyItem3(id=975);    Received MyItem3(id=976);    Received MyItem3(id=977);    Received MyItem3(id=978);    Received
MyItem3(id=979);    Received MyItem3(id=980);    Received MyItem3(id=981);    Received MyItem3(id=982);    Received MyItem3(id=983);    Received
MyItem3(id=984);    Received MyItem3(id=985);    Received MyItem3(id=986);    Received MyItem3(id=987);    Received MyItem3(id=990);    Received
MyItem3(id=989);    Received MyItem3(id=990);    Received MyItem3(id=991);    Received MyItem3(id=992);    Received MyItem3(id=993);    Received
MyItem3(id=994);    Received MyItem3(id=995);    Received MyItem3(id=996);    Received MyItem3(id=997);    Received MyItem3(id=998);    Received
MyItem3(id=999);    Received MyItem3(id=1000);
Process finished with exit code 0
```

If you take a closer look at the output (screenshots), you will notice that the Observable (producer) continued to emit items, though the Observer (consumer) was not at all in pace with it. Until the time Observer (producer) finished emitting all the Items, the Observer (consumer) processed only the very first item (item 1). As mentioned earlier, this could lead to a lot of problems, including the OutOfMemory error. Now, let's replace Observable with Flowable in this code:

```
fun main(args: Array<String>) {
  Flowable.range(1,1000)//(1)
    .map { MyItem4(it) }//(2)
    .observeOn(Schedulers.io())
    .subscribe({//(3)
      println("Received $it")
      runBlocking { delay(50) }//(4)
    },{it.printStackTrace()})
    runBlocking { delay(60000) }//(5)
}
data class MyItem4 (val id:Int) {
  init {
    println("MyItem Created $id")
  }
}
```

The code is exactly the same as the previous one, just the single difference is that we wrote Flowable.range() instead of Observable. Now, let's see the output and note the difference:

```
"C:\Program Files\Java\jdk1.8.0_111\bin\java" ...
MyItem Created 1;   MyItem Created 2;   Received MyItem4(id=1); MyItem Created 3;   MyItem Created 4;   MyItem Created 5;   MyItem Created
6; MyItem Created 7;   MyItem Created 8;   MyItem Created 9;   MyItem Created 10;  MyItem Created 11;  MyItem Created 12;  MyItem Created
13;   MyItem Created 14;  MyItem Created 15;  MyItem Created 16;  MyItem Created 17;  MyItem Created 18;  MyItem Created 19;  MyItem Created
20;   MyItem Created 21;  MyItem Created 22;  MyItem Created 23;  MyItem Created 24;  MyItem Created 25;  MyItem Created 26;  MyItem Created
27;   MyItem Created 28;  MyItem Created 29;  MyItem Created 30;  MyItem Created 31;  MyItem Created 32;  MyItem Created 33;  MyItem Created
34;   MyItem Created 35;  MyItem Created 36;  MyItem Created 37;  MyItem Created 38;  MyItem Created 39;  MyItem Created 40;  MyItem Created
41;   MyItem Created 42;  MyItem Created 43;  MyItem Created 44;  MyItem Created 45;  MyItem Created 46;  MyItem Created 47;  MyItem Created
48;   MyItem Created 49;  MyItem Created 50;  MyItem Created 51;  MyItem Created 52;  MyItem Created 53;  MyItem Created 54;  MyItem Created
55;   MyItem Created 56;  MyItem Created 57;  MyItem Created 58;  MyItem Created 59;  MyItem Created 60;  MyItem Created 61;  MyItem Created
62;   MyItem Created 63;  MyItem Created 64;  MyItem Created 65;  MyItem Created 66;  MyItem Created 67;  MyItem Created 68;  MyItem Created
69;   MyItem Created 70;  MyItem Created 71;  MyItem Created 72;  MyItem Created 73;  MyItem Created 74;  MyItem Created 75;  MyItem Created
76;   MyItem Created 77;  MyItem Created 78;  MyItem Created 79;  MyItem Created 80;  MyItem Created 81;  MyItem Created 82;  MyItem Created
83;   MyItem Created 84;  MyItem Created 85;  MyItem Created 86;  MyItem Created 87;  MyItem Created 88;  MyItem Created 89;  MyItem Created
90;   MyItem Created 91;  MyItem Created 92;  MyItem Created 93;  MyItem Created 94;  MyItem Created 95;  MyItem Created 96;  MyItem Created
97;   MyItem Created 98;  MyItem Created 99;  MyItem Created 100; MyItem Created 101; MyItem Created 102; MyItem Created 103; MyItem Created
104;  MyItem Created 105; MyItem Created 106; MyItem Created 107; MyItem Created 108; MyItem Created 109; MyItem Created 110; MyItem Created
111;  MyItem Created 112; MyItem Created 113; MyItem Created 114; MyItem Created 115; MyItem Created 116; MyItem Created 117; MyItem Created
118;  MyItem Created 119; MyItem Created 120; MyItem Created 121; MyItem Created 122; MyItem Created 123; MyItem Created 124; MyItem Created
125;  MyItem Created 126; MyItem Created 127; MyItem Created 128; Received MyItem4(id=2); Received MyItem4(id=3); Received MyItem4(id=4); Received
MyItem4(id=5); Received MyItem4(id=6); Received MyItem4(id=7); Received MyItem4(id=8); Received MyItem4(id=9); Received MyItem4(id=10);  Received
MyItem4(id=11);   Received MyItem4(id=12);   Received MyItem4(id=13);   Received MyItem4(id=14);   Received MyItem4(id=15);   Received
MyItem4(id=16);   Received MyItem4(id=17);   Received MyItem4(id=18);   Received MyItem4(id=19);   Received MyItem4(id=20);   Received
MyItem4(id=21);   Received MyItem4(id=22);   Received MyItem4(id=23);   Received MyItem4(id=24);   Received MyItem4(id=25);   Received
MyItem4(id=26);   Received MyItem4(id=27);   Received MyItem4(id=28);   Received MyItem4(id=29);   Received MyItem4(id=30);   Received
MyItem4(id=31);   Received MyItem4(id=32);   Received MyItem4(id=33);   Received MyItem4(id=34);   Received MyItem4(id=35);   Received
MyItem4(id=36);   Received MyItem4(id=37);   Received MyItem4(id=38);   Received MyItem4(id=39);   Received MyItem4(id=40);   Received
MyItem4(id=41);   Received MyItem4(id=42);   Received MyItem4(id=43);   Received MyItem4(id=44);   Received MyItem4(id=45);   Received
MyItem4(id=46);   Received MyItem4(id=47);   Received MyItem4(id=48);   Received MyItem4(id=49);   Received MyItem4(id=50);   Received
MyItem4(id=51);   Received MyItem4(id=52);   Received MyItem4(id=53);   Received MyItem4(id=54);   Received MyItem4(id=55);   Received
MyItem4(id=56);   Received MyItem4(id=57);   Received MyItem4(id=58);   Received MyItem4(id=59);   Received MyItem4(id=60);   Received
MyItem4(id=61);   Received MyItem4(id=62);   Received MyItem4(id=63);   Received MyItem4(id=64);   Received MyItem4(id=65);   Received
MyItem4(id=66);   Received MyItem4(id=67);   Received MyItem4(id=68);   Received MyItem4(id=69);   Received MyItem4(id=70);   Received
MyItem4(id=71);   Received MyItem4(id=72);   Received MyItem4(id=73);   Received MyItem4(id=74);   Received MyItem4(id=75);   Received

Created 991;  MyItem Created 992; Received MyItem4(id=865); Received MyItem4(id=866);  Received MyItem4(id=867);  Received MyItem4(id=868);
Received MyItem4(id=869);  Received MyItem4(id=870);  Received MyItem4(id=871);  Received MyItem4(id=872);  Received MyItem4(id=873);  Received
MyItem4(id=874);  Received MyItem4(id=875);  Received MyItem4(id=876);  Received MyItem4(id=877);  Received MyItem4(id=878);  Received
MyItem4(id=879);  Received MyItem4(id=880);  Received MyItem4(id=881);  Received MyItem4(id=882);  Received MyItem4(id=883);  Received
MyItem4(id=884);  Received MyItem4(id=885);  Received MyItem4(id=886);  Received MyItem4(id=887);  Received MyItem4(id=888);  Received
MyItem4(id=889);  Received MyItem4(id=890);  Received MyItem4(id=891);  Received MyItem4(id=892);  Received MyItem4(id=893);  Received
MyItem4(id=894);  Received MyItem4(id=895);  Received MyItem4(id=896);  Received MyItem4(id=897);  Received MyItem4(id=898);  Received
MyItem4(id=899);  Received MyItem4(id=900);  Received MyItem4(id=901);  Received MyItem4(id=902);  Received MyItem4(id=903);  Received
MyItem4(id=904);  Received MyItem4(id=905);  Received MyItem4(id=906);  Received MyItem4(id=907);  Received MyItem4(id=908);  Received
MyItem4(id=909);  Received MyItem4(id=910);  Received MyItem4(id=911);  Received MyItem4(id=912);  Received MyItem4(id=913);  Received
MyItem4(id=914);  Received MyItem4(id=915);  Received MyItem4(id=916);  Received MyItem4(id=917);  Received MyItem4(id=918);  Received
MyItem4(id=919);  Received MyItem4(id=920);  Received MyItem4(id=921);  Received MyItem4(id=922);  Received MyItem4(id=923);  Received
MyItem4(id=924);  Received MyItem4(id=925);  Received MyItem4(id=926);  Received MyItem4(id=927);  Received MyItem4(id=928);  Received
MyItem4(id=929);  Received MyItem4(id=930);  Received MyItem4(id=931);  Received MyItem4(id=932);  Received MyItem4(id=933);  Received
MyItem4(id=934);  Received MyItem4(id=935);  Received MyItem4(id=936);  Received MyItem4(id=937);  Received MyItem4(id=938);  Received
MyItem4(id=939);  Received MyItem4(id=940);  Received MyItem4(id=941);  Received MyItem4(id=942);  Received MyItem4(id=943);  Received
MyItem4(id=944);  Received MyItem4(id=945);  Received MyItem4(id=946);  Received MyItem4(id=947);  Received MyItem4(id=948);  Received
MyItem4(id=949);  Received MyItem4(id=950);  Received MyItem4(id=951);  Received MyItem4(id=952);  Received MyItem4(id=953);  Received
MyItem4(id=954);  Received MyItem4(id=955);  Received MyItem4(id=956);  Received MyItem4(id=957);  Received MyItem4(id=958);  Received
MyItem4(id=959);  Received MyItem4(id=960);  MyItem Created 993; MyItem Created 994; MyItem Created 995; MyItem Created 996; MyItem Created
997;  MyItem Created 998; MyItem Created 999; MyItem Created 1000;  Received MyItem4(id=961);  Received MyItem4(id=962);  Received MyItem4
(id=963);  Received MyItem4(id=964);  Received MyItem4(id=965);  Received MyItem4(id=966);  Received MyItem4(id=967);  Received MyItem4(id=968)
;  Received MyItem4(id=969);  Received MyItem4(id=970);  Received MyItem4(id=971);  Received MyItem4(id=972);  Received MyItem4(id=973);
Received MyItem4(id=974);  Received MyItem4(id=975);  Received MyItem4(id=976);  Received MyItem4(id=977);  Received MyItem4(id=978);  Received
MyItem4(id=979);  Received MyItem4(id=980);  Received MyItem4(id=981);  Received MyItem4(id=982);  Received MyItem4(id=983);  Received
MyItem4(id=984);  Received MyItem4(id=985);  Received MyItem4(id=986);  Received MyItem4(id=987);  Received MyItem4(id=988);  Received
MyItem4(id=989);  Received MyItem4(id=990);  Received MyItem4(id=991);  Received MyItem4(id=992);  Received MyItem4(id=993);  Received
MyItem4(id=994);  Received MyItem4(id=995);  Received MyItem4(id=996);  Received MyItem4(id=997);  Received MyItem4(id=998);  Received
MyItem4(id=999);  Received MyItem4(id=1000);
Process finished with exit code 0
```

Have you noted the difference? Flowable, instead of emitting all the items, emitted few items in a chunk, waited for the consumer to coup up then again continued, and completed in an interleaved manner. This reduces a lot of problems itself.

When to use Flowables and Observables

By now, you may think Flowable is a handy tool to use, so you could replace Observable everywhere. However, this may not always be the case. Although Flowable provides us with backpressure strategies, Observables are here for a reason, and both of them have their own advantages and disadvantages. So, when to use which? Let's see.

When to use Flowables?

The following are the situations when you should consider using Flowables. Remember, Flowables are slower than Observables:

- Flowables and backpressure are meant to help deal with larger amounts of data. So, use flowable if your source may emit 10,000+ items. Especially when the source is asynchronous so that the consumer chain may ask the producer to limit/regulate emissions when required.
- If you are reading from/parsing a file or database.
- When you want to emit from network IO operations/Streaming APIs that support blocking while returning results, which is how many IO sources work.

When to use Observables?

Now you know when to use Flowables, take a look at the conditions where you should prefer Observables:

- When you are dealing with a smaller amount of data (less than 10,000 emissions)
- When you are performing strictly synchronous operations or operations with limited concurrency
- When you are emitting UI events (while working with Android, JavaFX, or Swing)

Also, keep in mind that Flowables are slower in comparison to Observables.

Flowable and Subscriber

Instead of Observer, Flowable uses Subscriber, which is backpressure compatible. However, if you use lambda expressions, then you will not notice any differences. So, why use Subscriber instead of Observer? Because Subscriber supports some extra operations and backpressure. For instance, it can convey how many items it wishes to receive as a message to upstream. Or rather, we can say while using Subscriber; you must specify how many items you want to receive (request) from upstream; if you don't specify it, you will not receive any emissions.

As we already mentioned, using lambda with Subscriber is similar to Observe; this implementation will automatically request an unbounded number of emissions from the upstream. As with our last code, we didn't specify how many emissions we want, but it internally requested unbounded number of emissions, and that's why we received all the items emitted.

So, let's try replacing the previous program with a Subscriber instance:

```kotlin
fun main(args: Array<String>) {
  Flowable.range(1, 1000)//(1)
    .map { MyItem5(it) }//(2)
    .observeOn(Schedulers.io())
    .subscribe(object : Subscriber<MyItem5> {//(3)
      override fun onSubscribe(subscription: Subscription) {
        subscription.request(Long.MAX_VALUE)//(4)
      }

      override fun onNext(s: MyItem5?) {
        runBlocking { delay(50) }
        println("Subscriber received " + s!!)
      }

      override fun onError(e: Throwable) {
        e.printStackTrace()
      }

      override fun onComplete() {
        println("Done!")
      }
    })
    runBlocking { delay(60000) }
}

data class MyItem5 (val id:Int) {
init {
  println("MyItem Created $id")
```

```
        }
    }
```

The output of the preceding program will be the same as for the previous one, so we are skipping the output here. Instead, let's understand the code. The program is almost identical to the previous one, until comment (3), where we created an instance of `Subscriber`. The methods of `Subscriber` are identical with `Observer`; however, as I mentioned earlier, on the `subscribe` method, you have to request for the number of emissions that you want initially. We did the same on comment (4); however, as we want to receive all emissions, we requested it with `Long.MAX_VALUE`.

So, how does the `request` method work? The `request()` method will request the number of emissions the `Subscriber` should listen on from the upstream, counting after the method is called. The `Subscriber` will ignore any further emissions after the requested emissions until you request for more.

So, let's modify this program to understand the `request` method better:

```
fun main(args: Array<String>) {
  Flowable.range(1, 15)
    .map { MyItem6(it) }
    .observeOn(Schedulers.io())
    .subscribe(object : Subscriber<MyItem6> {
      lateinit var subscription: Subscription// (1)
      override fun onSubscribe(subscription: Subscription) {
          this.subscription = subscription
          subscription.request(5)// (2)
      }

      override fun onNext(s: MyItem6?) {
        runBlocking { delay(50) }
        println("Subscriber received " + s!!)
          if(s.id == 5) {// (3)
            println("Requesting two more")
            subscription.request(2)// (4)
          }
      }

      override fun onError(e: Throwable) {
        e.printStackTrace()
      }

      override fun onComplete() {
        println("Done!")
      }
    })
```

```
        runBlocking { delay(10000) }
    }

data class MyItem6 (val id:Int) {
    init {
        println("MyItem Created $id")
    }
}
```

So, what are the tweaks we made in this program? Let's go through it. On comment (1), we declared a `lateinit` variable of type `Subscription`, we initialized that subscription inside the `onSubscribe` method, just before comment (2). On comment (2), we requested for 5 items with `subscription.request(5)`. Then, inside `onNext`, on comment (3), we checked if the received item is the 5th one (as we are using a range, the 5th item's value will be 5); if the item is the 5th one, then we are again requesting for 2 more. So, the program should print seven items instead of the 1-15 range. Let's check the following output:

```
"C:\Program Files\Java\jdk1.8.0_191\bin\java"...
MyItem Created 1
MyItem Created 2
MyItem Created 3
MyItem Created 4
MyItem Created 5
MyItem Created 6
MyItem Created 7
MyItem Created 8
MyItem Created 9
MyItem Created 10
MyItem Created 11
MyItem Created 12
MyItem Created 13
MyItem Created 14
MyItem Created 15
Subscriber received MyItem6(id=1)
Subscriber received MyItem6(id=2)
Subscriber received MyItem6(id=3)
Subscriber received MyItem6(id=4)
Subscriber received MyItem6(id=5)
Requesting two more
Subscriber received MyItem6(id=6)
Subscriber received MyItem6(id=7)

Process finished with exit code 0
```

So, although `Flowable` emitted all the items for the range, it was never passed to `Subscriber` after 7.

Note that the `request()` method just not goes all the way upstream, it just conveys to the latest preceding operator, which, in turn, decides on whether to/how to relay that information to further upstream.

So, we got some understanding on `Flowable` and `Subscriber`. Now, it's time to explore them in depth. We will start with creating a `Flowable` instance from scratch.

Creating Flowable from scratch

We learned about the `Observable.create` method in the previous chapter, but to make things less complicated, let's have a quick recap, and then we can continue with `Flowable.create`. Take a look at the following piece of code:

```kotlin
fun main(args: Array<String>) {
    val observer: Observer<Int> = object : Observer<Int> {
        override fun onComplete() {
            println("All Completed")
        }

        override fun onNext(item: Int) {
            println("Next $item")
        }

        override fun onError(e: Throwable) {
            println("Error Occured ${e.message}")
        }

        override fun onSubscribe(d: Disposable) {
            println("New Subscription ")
        }
    }//Create Observer

    val observable: Observable<Int> = Observable.create<Int> {//1
        for(i in 1..10) {
            it.onNext(i)
        }
        it.onComplete()
    }

    observable.subscribe(observer)

}
```

So, in this program, we created `Observable` with the `Observable.create` operator. This operator let's define our own custom `Observable`. We can write our own rules to emit items from `Observable`. It provides really great freedom, but the problem with `Observable` is here as well. It doesn't support backpressure. Wouldn't it be great if we could create a similar version with backpressure support? We will do it, but let's see the output first:

```
"C:\Program Files\Java\jdk1.8.0_131\bin\java" ...
New Subscription
Next 1
Next 2
Next 3
Next 4
Next 5
Next 6
Next 7
Next 8
Next 9
Next 10
All Completed

Process finished with exit code 0
```

So, as expected, it prints all the numbers from 1 through 10. Now, as discussed earlier, let's try with Flowable:

```kotlin
fun main(args: Array<String>) {
  val subscriber: Subscriber<Int> = object : Subscriber<Int> {
    override fun onComplete() {
      println("All Completed")
    }

    override fun onNext(item: Int) {
      println("Next $item")
    }

    override fun onError(e: Throwable) {
      println("Error Occured ${e.message}")
    }

    override fun onSubscribe(subscription: Subscription) {
      println("New Subscription ")
      subscription.request(10)
    }
  }// (1)

  val flowable: Flowable<Int> = Flowable.create<Int> ({
    for(i in 1..10) {
      it.onNext(i)
    }
```

```
    it.onComplete()
},BackpressureStrategy.BUFFER)//(2)

flowable
  .observeOn(Schedulers.io())
  .subscribe(subscriber)//(3)

runBlocking { delay(10000) }

}
```

So, on comment (1), we created an instance of `Subscriber`. Then, on comment (2), we created an instance of `Flowable` with the `Flowable.create()` method, and, on comment (3), we subscribed to it. However, focus on comment (2)—along with the `lambda`, we also passed another argument to the `Flowable.create` method, which is `BackpressureStrategy.BUFFER`. So, what is it? And what purpose does `BackpressureStrategy.BUFFER` serve? Let's inspect.

`Flowable.create()` takes two parameters to create an instance of `Flowable`. The following is the definition of the `Flowable.create()` method:

```
fun <T> create(source:FlowableOnSubscribe<T>,
mode:BackpressureStrategy):Flowable<T> {
  //...
}
```

First parameter is the source from where the emissions will generate, and the second one is `BackpressureStrategy`; it is an `enum` that helps supporting backpressure (it basically helps choosing which strategy to follow for backpressure) by caching/buffering or dropping some of the emissions if the downstream can't keep up. The `enum` `BackpressureStrategy` has five underlying options for different kinds of implementations of backpressure. In this example, `BackpressureStrategy.BUFFER` buffers all the emissions until they are consumed by the downstream. This, obviously, is not an optimal implementation of backpressure and can cause `OutOfMemoryError` while handling too many emissions, but, at least it prevents `MissingBackpressureException` and can make your custom `Flowable` workable to a small degree. We will learn about a more robust way to implement backpressure later in this chapter using `Flowable.generate()`; however, for now, let's know about the options we can choose from `BackpressureStrategyenum`:

- `BackpressureStrategy.MISSING`: This leads to no backpressure implementation at all; downstream has to deal with backpressure overflows. This option is helpful while using the `onBackpressureXXX()` operator. We will learn this example later in this chapter.

- `BackpressureStrategy.ERROR`: This, again, leads to no backpressure implementation and signals `MissingBackpressureException` the very moment the downstream cannot keep up with the source.
- `BackpressureStrategy.BUFFER`: This buffers all the emissions in an unbounded buffer until the downstream is able to consume them. This can lead to `OutOfMemoryError` if there are a lot of emissions to buffer.
- `BackpressureStrategy.DROP`: This strategy will let you drop all the emissions while the downstream is busy and can't keep up; when the downstream finishes the previous operation, it'll get the very first emission after its finishing time, and will miss any emissions in between. For example, say the source is emitting five values, 1, 2, 3, 4, and 5 respectively, the downstream got busy after receiving 1 and while the source emitted 2, 3, and 4, it got ready just before the source emitted 5; the downstream will receive 5 only and will miss all remaining.
- `BackpressureStrategy.LATEST`: This strategy will let you drop all the emissions, but keeps the latest one while the downstream is busy and can't keep up; when the downstream finishes the previous operation it'll get the last emission just before it finished, and will miss any emissions in between. For example, say the source is emitting five values 1, 2, 3, 4, and 5 respectively, the downstream got busy after receiving 1 and while the source emitted 2, 3, and 4, it got ready just before the source emitted 5; the downstream will receive both of them (if it didn't again get busy after receiving 4, that it can't receive 5).

Let's implement some of these backpressure strategies as operators while creating Flowables from Observables.

Creating Flowable from Observable

The `Observable.toFlowable()` operator provides you with another way to implement `BackpressureStrategy` into non-backpressured source. This operator turns any `Observable` into a `Flowable`, so let's get our hands dirty, and, first, let's try converting an `Observable` into `Flowable` with the buffering strategy, then we will try out a few other strategies in the same example to understand it better. Please refer to the following code:

```
fun main(args: Array<String>) {
  val source = Observable.range(1, 1000)//(1)
  source.toFlowable(BackpressureStrategy.BUFFER)//(2)
    .map { MyItem7(it) }
    .observeOn(Schedulers.io())
    .subscribe{//(3)
      print("Rec. $it;\t")
```

```
            runBlocking { delay(1000) }
        }
        runBlocking { delay(100000) }
    }

    data class MyItem7 (val id:Int) {
        init {
            print("MyItem init $id")
        }
    }
}
```

So, on comment (1), we created an `Observable` with the `Observable.range()` method. On comment (2), we converted it to `Flowable` with `BackpressureStrategy.BUFFER`. Then, we subscribed to it with a lambda as the `Subscriber`. Let's see some portions of the output as a screenshot (as the complete output will be too long to paste here):

So, as expected, the downstream here processes all the emissions, as the `BackpressureStrategy.BUFFER` buffers all the emissions until the downstream consumes.

So, now, let's try with `BackpressureStrategy.ERROR` and check what happens:

```kotlin
fun main(args: Array<String>) {
  val source = Observable.range(1, 1000)
  source.toFlowable(BackpressureStrategy.ERROR)
    .map { MyItem8(it) }
    .observeOn(Schedulers.io())
    .subscribe{
        println(it)
        runBlocking { delay(600) }
    }
    runBlocking { delay(700000) }
}

data class MyItem8 (val id:Int) {
init {
  println("MyItem Created $id")
}
}
}
```

The following is the output:

It showed an error as the downstream couldn't keep up with the upstream, as we described it earlier.

What would happen if we use the `BackpressureStrategy.DROP` option? Let's check:

```kotlin
fun main(args: Array<String>) {
  val source = Observable.range(1, 1000)
  source.toFlowable(BackpressureStrategy.DROP)
    .map { MyItem9(it) }
    .observeOn(Schedulers.computation())
    .subscribe{
      println(it)
      runBlocking { delay(1000) }
    }
    runBlocking { delay(700000) }
}

data class MyItem9 (val id:Int) {
init {
    println("MyItem Created $id")
  }
}
```

Everything is the same as in the previous example, except, here, we used the `BackpressureStrategy.DROP` option. Let's check the output:

So, as we can see in the preceding output, `BackpressureStrategy.DROP` stopped `Flowable` from emitting after `128`, as the downstream couldn't keep up with, just as we described earlier.

Now, as we have gained some grip on the options available in `BackpressureStrategy`, let's focus on the `BackpressureStrategy.MISSING` option and how to use them with the `onBackpressureXXX()` operators.

BackpressureStrategy.MISSING and onBackpressureXXX()

`BackpressureStrategy.MISSING` implies that it'll not implement any backpressure strategy, so you need to explicitly tell `Flowable` which backpressure strategy to follow. The `onBackpressureXXX()` operators help you achieve the same, while providing you with some additional configuration options.

There are mainly three types of `onBackpressureXXX()` operators available:

- `onBackpressureBuffer()`
- `onBackpressureDrop()`
- `onBackpressureLatest()`

Operator onBackpressureBuffer()

This operator serves the purpose of `BackpressureStrategy.BUFFER`; except that here, you'll get some extra configuration options, such as buffer size, bounded or unbounded, and more. You may omit the configurations as well to use the default behavior.

So, let's look at some examples:

```
fun main(args: Array<String>) {
  val source = Observable.range(1, 1000)
  source.toFlowable(BackpressureStrategy.MISSING)//(1)
    .onBackpressureBuffer()//(2)
    .map { MyItem11(it) }
    .observeOn(Schedulers.io())
    .subscribe{
      println(it)
      runBlocking { delay(1000) }
    }
    runBlocking { delay(600000) }
}

data class MyItem11 (val id:Int) {
```

```
init {
    println("MyItem Created $id")
}
}
```

Again, we are using the previous program with little tweaks. On comment (1), we created the `Flowable` instance with the `BackpressureStrategy.MISSING` option. On comment (2), to deal with backpressure, we used `onBackpressureBuffer`; the output is similar to the one in the `BackpressureStrategy.BUFFER` example, so we are omitting this.

You can specify the buffer size by using `onBackpressureBuffer()`. So let's modify the `onBackpressureBuffer()` method call with `onBackpressureBuffer(20)`. The following is the output:

Yes, that change resulted in an error—the buffer is full. We defined 20 to be the buffer size, but `Flowable` needed a lot more size. This could be avoided by implementing the `onError` method.

Operator onBackpressureDrop()

Like `onBackpressureBuffer` matches with `BackpressureStrategy.BUFFER`, `onBackpressureDrop` matches with `BackpressureStrategy.DROP` in terms of backpressure strategy, with some configuration options.

So, let's now try this:

```kotlin
fun main(args: Array<String>) {
    val source = Observable.range(1, 1000)
    source.toFlowable(BackpressureStrategy.MISSING)//(1)
        .onBackpressureDrop{ print("Dropped $it;\t") }//(2)
        .map { MyItem12(it) }
        .observeOn(Schedulers.io())
        .subscribe{
            print("Rec. $it;\t")
            runBlocking { delay(1000) }
        }
    runBlocking { delay(600000) }
}

data class MyItem12 (val id:Int) {
init {
    print("MyItem init $id;\t")
}
}
}
```

As shown in the previous program, we used `BackpressureStrategy.MISSING` on comment (1). On comment (2), we used the `onBackpressureDrop()` operator. This operator provides a configuration option to pass a consumer instance, which will, in turn, consume the dropped emissions so you can further process it. We used this configuration and passed a lambda, which will print the dropped emissions, as shown in this screenshot:

As we can see from the output, `Flowable` dropped emissions after `128` (as it has an internal buffer for `128` emissions). The consumer instance of `onBackpressureDrop` completed processing even before the `Subscriber` instance started.

Operator onBackpressureLatest()

This operator works exactly the same as the `BackpressureStrategy.LATEST`-it drops all the emissions keeping the latest one when the downstream is busy and can't keep up. When the downstream finishes the previous operation, it'll get the last emission just before it finished. Unfortunately, this doesn't provide any configurations; you will probably not need it.

Let's take a look at this code example:

```kotlin
fun main(args: Array<String>) {
  val source = Observable.range(1, 1000)
  source.toFlowable(BackpressureStrategy.MISSING)//(1)
    .onBackpressureLatest()//(2)
    .map { MyItem13(it) }
    .observeOn(Schedulers.io())
    .subscribe{
      print("-> $it;\t")
      runBlocking { delay(100) }
    }
    runBlocking { delay(600000) }
}
data class MyItem13 (val id:Int) {
init {
  print("init $id;\t")
}
}
}
```

Here is the output:

As we can see, the `Flowable` dropped all emissions after `128`, keeping only the last one (`1,000`).

Generating Flowable with backpressure at source

So far, we have learned to use standard libraries that handle backpressure at the downstream. However, is this optimal? Is it always desirable to cache and drop emissions whenever the downstream can't keep up? The answer to both questions is simply NO. Instead, the better policy would be to backpressure the source at the first place.

`Flowable.generate()` serves the exact same purpose. It's somewhat similar to `Flowable.create()`, but with a little difference. Let's take a look at an example, and then we will try to understand how it works and what are the differences between `Flowable.create()` and `Flowable.generate()`.

 Note that use `Flowable.fromIterable()` as it respects backpressure. So, consider using `Flowable.fromIterable()` whenever you can convert your source to an `Iterator`. Use `Flowable.generate()` only where you need something more specific, as it is way more complex.

Consider the following code:

```
fun main(args: Array<String>) {
  val flowable = Flowable.generate<Int> {
    it.onNext(GenerateFlowableItem.item)
  }// (1)

  flowable
    .map { MyItemFlowable(it) }
    .observeOn(Schedulers.io())
    .subscribe {
      runBlocking { delay(100) }
      println("Next $it")
    }// (2)

    runBlocking { delay(700000) }
}

data class MyItemFlowable(val id:Int) {
  init {
    println("MyItemFlowable Created $id")
  }
}

object GenerateFlowableItem {// (3)
  var item:Int = 0// (4)
```

```
get() {
    field+=1
    return field//(5)
    }
}
```

In that program, we created `Flowable` with the `Flowable.generate()` method. Unlike `Flowable.create()`, where `Flowable` emits items and `Subscriber` receives/waits for/buffers/drops them, `Flowable.generate()` generates items on request and emits them. `Flowable.generate()` accepts a lambda to use as the source, which may seem similar to `Flowable.create`, and calls it every time you request an item (unlike `Flowable.create`). So, for example, if you call the `onComplete` method inside the lambda, `Flowable` will emit only once. Also, you can't call `onNext` multiple times inside the lambda. If you called `onError`, then you will get an error on the very first call.

In this program, we created `object`, `GenerateFlowableItem`, with `var item`; the `var item` will automatically increment its value every time you access it (using a custom getter). So, the program should work like `Flowable.range(1, Int.MAX_VALUE)`, except that once the item reaches `Int.MAX_VALUE` instead of calling `onComplete`, it'll again repeat itself, starting from `Int.MIN_VALUE`.

In the output (omitted here as it is too large), `Flowable` emitted `128` items on the first go, then waited for the downstream to process `96` items, then `Flowable` again emitted `128` items, and the cycle continued. Until you unsubscribe from `Flowable` or the program execution stops, it will continue emitting items.

ConnectableFlowable

So far, in this chapter, we've dealt with `Cold Observables`. What if we want to deal with hot source? Every type of Observable has their counterpart in Flowable. In the previous chapter, we started hot source with `ConnectableObservable`, so let's start with `ConnectableFlowable`.

As with Observable, `ConnectableFlowable` resembles an ordinary Flowable, except that it does not begin emitting items when it is subscribed, but only when its `connect()` method is called. In this way, you can wait for all intended `Subscribers` to `Flowable.subscribe()`, before `Flowable` begins emitting items. Please refer to the following code:

```
fun main(args: Array<String>) {
    val connectableFlowable = listOf
```

```
("String 1","String 2","String   3","String 4",
"String  5").toFlowable()//(1)
.publish()//(2)
connectableFlowable.
 subscribe({
   println("Subscription 1: $it")
   runBlocking { delay(1000) }
   println("Subscription 1 delay")
 })
 connectableFlowable
 .subscribe({ println("Subscription 2 $it")})
 connectableFlowable.connect()
}
```

We tweaked the first example of `ConnectableObservable` from the previous chapter. As with `Observable`, you can use the `Iterable<T>.toFlowable()` extension function in the place of `Flowable.fromIterable()`. `Flowable.publish()` turns an ordinary `Flowable` into a `ConnectableFlowable`.

In this example, on comment `(1)`, we used the `Iterable<T>.toFlowable()` extension function to create `Flowable` from `List`, and on comment `(2)`, we used the `Flowable.publish()` operator to create `ConnectableFlowable` from `Flowable`.

The following is the output:

As we used `Flowable.fromIterable` (`Iterable<T>.toFlowable()` calls `Flowable.fromIterable` internally), which respects backpressure at the source, we can see `Flowable` waited for all the downstream to complete processing, then emitted the next item so that the downstreams can work in an interleaved manner.

By now, you may have been thinking of `Subjects`. It is a great tool, but, like `Observable`, `Subjects` also lack backpressure support. So, what is the counterpart for `Subjects` in Flowable?

Processor

Processors are the counterparts for `Subjects` in Flowable. Every type of `Subject` has its counterpart as processor with backpressure support.

In the previous chapter (Chapter 3, *Observables, Observers, and Subjects*), we started exploring `Subject`, with the `PublishSubject`; so, let's do the same here. Let's get started with `PublishProcessor`.

The following is an example of `PublishProcessor`:

```
fun main(args: Array<String>) {
  val flowable = listOf("String 1","String 2","String 3",
  "String 4","String 5").toFlowable()//(1)

  val processor = PublishProcessor.create<String>()//(2)

  processor.//(3)
    subscribe({
      println("Subscription 1: $it")
      runBlocking { delay(1000) }
      println("Subscription 1 delay")
    })
  processor//(4)
  .subscribe({ println("Subscription 2 $it")})

  flowable.subscribe(processor)//(5)

}
```

So, in this example, on comment `(1)`, we created a `Flowable` with the `Iterable<T>.toFlowable()` method. On comment `(2)`, we created a `processor` instance with the `PublishProcessor.create()` method. On comment `(3)` and `(4)`, we subscribed to the `processor` instance, and, on comment `(5)`. we subscribed to the `Flowable` with the `processor` instance.

The following is the output:

```
"C:\Program Files\Java\jdk1.6.0_131\bin\java" ...
Subscription 1: String 1
Subscription 1 delay
Subscription 2 String 1
Subscription 1: String 2
Subscription 1 delay
Subscription 2 String 2
Subscription 1: String 3
Subscription 1 delay
Subscription 2 String 3
Subscription 1: String 4
Subscription 1 delay
Subscription 2 String 4
Subscription 1: String 5
Subscription 1 delay
Subscription 2 String 5

Process finished with exit code 0
```

The `processor` is waiting for all its `Subscribers` to complete before pushing the next emission.

Learning Buffer, Throttle, and Window operators

So far, we have learned about backpressure. We slowed down the source, dropped items, or used buffer, which will hold items until the consumer consumes it; however, will all these suffice? While handling backpressure at the downstream is not a good solution always, we cannot always slow down the source as well.

While using `Observable.interval/Flowable.interval`, you cannot slow down the source. A stop gap could be some operators that would somehow allow us to process the emissions simultaneously.

There are the three operators that could help us in that way:

- `Buffer`
- `Throttle`
- `Window`

The buffer() operator

Unlike the `onBackPressureBuffer()` operator, which buffers emissions until the consumer consumes, the `buffer()` operator will gather emissions as a batch and will emit them as a list or any other collection type.

So, let's look at this example:

```
fun main(args: Array<String>) {
  val flowable = Flowable.range(1,111) // (1)
  flowable.buffer(10) // (2)
    .subscribe { println(it) }
}
```

On comment (1), we created a `Flowable` instance with the `Flowable.range()` method, which emits integers from 1 to 111. On comment (2), we used the `buffer` operator with 10 as the buffer size, so the `buffer` operator gathers 10 items from the `Flowable` and emits them as a list.

The following is the output, which satisfies the understanding:

```
"C:\Program Files\Java\jdk1.8.0_131\bin\java" ...
[1, 2, 3, 4, 5, 6, 7, 8, 9, 10]
[11, 12, 13, 14, 15, 16, 17, 18, 19, 20]
[21, 22, 23, 24, 25, 26, 27, 28, 29, 30]
[31, 32, 33, 34, 35, 36, 37, 38, 39, 40]
[41, 42, 43, 44, 45, 46, 47, 48, 49, 50]
[51, 52, 53, 54, 55, 56, 57, 58, 59, 60]
[61, 62, 63, 64, 65, 66, 67, 68, 69, 70]
[71, 72, 73, 74, 75, 76, 77, 78, 79, 80]
[81, 82, 83, 84, 85, 86, 87, 88, 89, 90]
[91, 92, 93, 94, 95, 96, 97, 98, 99, 100]
[101, 102, 103, 104, 105, 106, 107, 108, 109, 110]
[111]

Process finished with exit code 0
```

The `buffer` operator has quite good configuration options, such as the `skip` parameter.

It accepts a second integer parameter as the `skip` count. It works in a really interesting way. If the value of the `skip` parameter is exactly the same as the `count` parameter, then it will do nothing. Otherwise, it will first calculate the positive difference between the `count` and `skip` parameters as `actual_numbers_to_skip`, and, then, if the value of the `skip` parameter is greater than the value of the `count` parameter, it will skip the `actual_numbers_to_skip` items after the last item of each emission. Otherwise, if the value of the `count` parameter is greater than the value of the `skip` parameter, you'll get rolling buffers, that is, instead of skipping the items, it will skip the counts from the previous emissions.

Confused? Let's look at this example to clear things up:

```kotlin
fun main(args: Array<String>) {
    val flowable = Flowable.range(1,111)
    flowable.buffer(10,15)//(1)
        .subscribe { println("Subscription 1 $it") }

    flowable.buffer(15,7)//(2)
        .subscribe { println("Subscription 2 $it") }
}
```

On comment (1), we used buffer with count 10, skip 15, for the first subscription. On comment (2), we used it as count 15, skip 8, for the second subscription. The following is the output:

For the first subscription, it skipped 5 items after each subscription (15-10). However, for the second one, it repeated items from the 8th item in each emission (15-7).

If the preceding uses of the `buffer` operator were not enough for you, then let me tell you the `buffer` operator also lets you do time-based buffering. Put simply, it can gather emissions from a source and emit them at a time interval. Interesting right? Let's explore it:

```kotlin
fun main(args: Array<String>) {
    val flowable = Flowable.interval(100, TimeUnit:MILLISECONDS)//(1)
    flowable.buffer(1,TimeUnit.SECONDS)//(2)
     .subscribe { println(it) }

    runBlocking { delay(5, TimeUnit.SECONDS) }//(3)
}
```

To understand things better, we used `Flowable.interval` in this example to create a `Flowable` instance on comment `(1)`. On comment `(2)`, we used the `buffer(timespan:Long, unit:TimeUnit)` overload to instruct the operator to buffer all emissions for a second and emit them as a list.

This is the output:

```
"C:\Program Files\Java\jdk1.8.0_131\bin\java" ...
[0, 1, 2, 3, 4, 5, 6, 7, 8, 9]
[10, 11, 12, 13, 14, 15, 16, 17, 18, 19]
[20, 21, 22, 23, 24, 25, 26, 27, 28, 29]
[30, 31, 32, 33, 34, 35, 36, 37, 38, 39]
[40, 41, 42, 43, 44, 45, 46, 47, 48, 49]

Process finished with exit code 0
```

As you can see in the example, each of the emissions contains 10 items as `Flowable.interval()` is emitting one each 100 milliseconds and `buffer` is gathering emissions within a second timeframe (1 second = 1000 milliseconds, emission with a 100 milliseconds interval would result in 10 emissions in one second).

Another exciting feature of the buffer operator is that it can take another producer as the boundary, that is, the `buffer` operator will gather all the emissions of the source producer between two emissions of the boundary producer, and will emit the list on each boundary producer's emission.

Here is an example:

```
fun main(args: Array<String>) {
    val boundaryFlowable = Flowable.interval(350, TimeUnit.MILLISECONDS)

    val flowable = Flowable.interval(100, TimeUnit.MILLISECONDS)//(1)
    flowable.buffer(boundaryFlowable)//(2)
      .subscribe { println(it) }

    runBlocking { delay(5, TimeUnit.SECONDS) }//(3)
}
```

And the following is the output:

```
"C:\Program Files\Java\jdk1.8.0_131\bin\java" ...
[0, 1, 2]
[3, 4, 5]
[6, 7, 8, 9]
[10, 11, 12, 13]
[14, 15, 16]
[17, 18, 19]
[20, 21, 22, 23]
[24, 25, 26, 27]
[28, 29, 30]
[31, 32, 33, 34]
[35, 36, 37]
[38, 39, 40, 41]
[42, 43, 44]
[45, 46, 47, 48]

Process finished with exit code 0
```

The `buffer` operator emits a gathered list whenever `boundaryFlowable` emits.

The window() operator

The `window()` operator works almost the same, except that, instead of buffering items in a `Collection` object, it buffers items in another producer.

Here is an example:

```
fun main(args: Array<String>) {
    val flowable = Flowable.range(1,111)//(1)
    flowable.window(10)
      .subscribe {
        flo->flo.subscribe {//(2)
          print("$it, ")
        }
```

```
            println()
```

```
1, 2, 3, 4, 5, 6, 7, 8, 9, 10,
11, 12, 13, 14, 15, 16, 17, 18, 19, 20,
21, 22, 23, 24, 25, 26, 27, 28, 29, 30,
31, 32, 33, 34, 35, 36, 37, 38, 39, 40,
41, 42, 43, 44, 45, 46, 47, 48, 49, 50,
51, 52, 53, 54, 55, 56, 57, 58, 59, 60,
61, 62, 63, 64, 65, 66, 67, 68, 69, 70,
71, 72, 73, 74, 75, 76, 77, 78, 79, 80,
81, 82, 83, 84, 85, 86, 87, 88, 89, 90,
91, 92, 93, 94, 95, 96, 97, 98, 99, 100,
101, 102, 103, 104, 105, 106, 107, 108, 109, 110,
111,
Process finished with exit code 0
```

The `window` operator buffers `10` emissions in a new `Flowable` instance, which we will again subscribe to inside the `flowable.subscribe` lambda, and print them with a comma as a suffix.

The `window` operator also has same functionality as the other overloads of the `buffer` operator.

The throttle() operators

The `buffer()` and `window()` operators gather emissions. The `throttle` operators omit emissions. We will discuss it in greater detail in the later chapters, but we will take a look at it right now:

```kotlin
fun main(args: Array<String>) {
  val flowable = Flowable.interval(100, TimeUnit.MILLISECONDS)//(1)
  flowable.throttleFirst(200,TimeUnit.MILLISECONDS)//(2)
    .subscribe { println(it) }
  runBlocking { delay(1,TimeUnit.SECONDS) }
}
```

This is the output:

```
"C:\Program Files\Java\jdk1.8.0_131\bin\java" ...
0
3
5
7

Process finished with exit code 0
```

The `throttleFirst` skips the first emissions in every 200 milliseconds.

There are `throttleLast` and `throttleWithTimeout` operators as well.

Summary

In this chapter, we learned about backpressure. We learned how to support backpressure and Flowables as well as `processors`. We also learned how to support backpressure from consumers and producers.

Although we gained some grip on producers while working on real-time projects, we need to do asynchronous operations. In the next chapter, we will focus on the same. We will learn about asynchronous data operations, and we will learn more about the `map` operator, which we are already using.

Curious? Turn to `Chapter 5`, *Asynchronous Data Operators and Transformations* right now.

5

Asynchronous Data Operators and Transformations

Through the previous chapters, we got a strong grip on the producer (Observable and Flowable) and consumer (Observer and Subscriber). While learning them, we used the map method a lot. As already mentioned, the map method is actually an Rx-Operator. There are also a number of operators in RxKotlin. I can guess you have an itching question in your mind from the very first time we used the map operator. Why do we call it an operator when it looks like a method? Well, in this chapter, we will first try to answer this question by defining RxKotlin operators. We will then take a deeper look at the various operators available and their implementations. With the help of operators, we will transform, accumulate, map, group, and filter our data efficiently and with ease.

Operator

When we started with programming for the first time, we learned about operators. We learned that operators are those special characters/sequence of characters that perform some specific tasks on the operands and return the final results. In the reactive world, the definition remains merely the same; they take one or more Observable/Flowable as operands, transform them, and return the resultant Observable/Flowable.

Operators work such as a consumer to the preceding Observable/Flowable, listen to their emissions, transform them, and emit them to the downstream consumer. For instance, think of the map operator, it listens to the upstream producer, performs some operations on their emissions, and then emits those modified items to the downstream.

Operators help us leverage and express business logic and behaviors. There are a lot of operators available with RxKotlin. Throughout this book, we will be covering various types of operators comprehensively so that you know when to use which operator.

Remember, to implement business logic and behavior in your applications, you should use operators instead of writing blocking code or mixing imperative programming with reactive programming. By keeping algorithms and processes purely reactive, you can easily leverage lower memory usage, flexible concurrency, and disposability, which are reduced or not achieved if you mix reactive programming with imperative programming.

These are the five types of operators:

- `Filtering/suppressing` operators
- Transforming operators
- Reducing operators
- Collection operators
- Error handling operators
- Utility operators

So, now, let's take a closer look at them.

The filtering/suppressing operators

Think of a situation when you want to receive some emissions from the producer but want to discard the rest. There may be some logic to determine the qualifying emissions, or you may even wish to discard in bulk. The `filtering/suppressing` operators are there to help you in these situations.

Here is a brief list of `filtering/suppressing` operators:

- `debounce`
- `distinct` and `distinctUntilChanged`
- `elementAt`
- `Filter`
- `first` and `last`
- `ignoreElements`
- `skip`, `skipLast`, `skipUntil`, and `skipWhile`
- `take`, `takeLast`, `takeUntil`, and `takeWhile`

Let's now take a closer look at all of them.

The debounce operator

Think of a situation where you're receiving emissions rapidly, and are willing to take the last one after taking some time to be sure about it.

When developing an application UI/UX, we often come to such a situation. For example, you have created a text input and are willing to perform some operation when the user types something, but you don't want to perform this operation on each keystroke. You would like to wait a little bit for the user to stop typing (so you've got a good query matching what the user actually wants) and then send it to the downstream operator. The debounce operator serves that exact purpose.

For the sake of simplicity, we will not use any UI/UX code of any platform here (we will definitely try that in the later chapters while learning to implement RxKotlin in Android). Rather, we will try to simulate this using the Observable.create method (if you have any doubt about the Observable.create method, then rush to Chapter 3, *Observables, Observers, and Subjects* before this). Please refer to the following code:

```
fun main(args: Array<String>) {
  createObservable()//(1)
    .debounce(200, TimeUnit.MILLISECONDS)//(2)
    .subscribe {
      println(it)//(3)
    }
}

inline fun createObservable():Observable<String> =
Observable.create<String> {
  it.onNext("R")//(4)
  runBlocking { delay(100) }//(5)
  it.onNext("Re")
  it.onNext("Reac")
  runBlocking { delay(130) }
  it.onNext("Reactiv")
  runBlocking { delay(140) }
  it.onNext("Reactive")
  runBlocking { delay(250) }//(6)
  it.onNext("Reactive P")
  runBlocking { delay(130) }
  it.onNext("Reactive Pro")
  runBlocking { delay(100) }
  it.onNext("Reactive Progra")
```

```
        runBlocking { delay(100) }
        it.onNext("Reactive Programming")
        runBlocking { delay(300) }
        it.onNext("Reactive Programming in")
        runBlocking { delay(100) }
        it.onNext("Reactive Programming in Ko")
        runBlocking { delay(150) }
        it.onNext("Reactive Programming in Kotlin")
        runBlocking { delay(250) }
        it.onComplete()
    }
```

In this program, we tried to keep the `main` function clean by exporting the Observable creation to another function (`createObservable()`) to help you understand better. On comment (1), we called the `createObservable()` function to create an `Observable` instance.

Inside the `createObservable()` function, we tried to simulate user typing behavior by emitting a series of incremental `Strings` with intervals, until it reached the final version (`Reactive Programming in Kotlin`). We provided bigger intervals after completing each word depicting an ideal user behavior.

On comment (2), we used the `debounce()` operator with 200 and `TimeUnit.MILLISECONDS` as parameters that'll make the downstream wait for 200 milliseconds after each emission and take the emissions only if no other emissions occurred in between.

The output is as follows:

Observer receives only three emits, after which the Observable took at least 200 milliseconds before emitting the next one.

The distinct operators – distinct, distinctUntilChanged

This operator is quite simple; it helps you filter duplicate emissions from the upstream. Take a look at the following example for better understanding:

```
fun main(args: Array<String>) {
    listOf(1,2,2,3,4,5,5,5,6,7,8,9,3,10)//(1)
        .toObservable()//(2)
        .distinct()//(3)
        .subscribe { println("Received $it") }//(4)
}
```

On comment (1), we created a list of Int containing many duplicate values. On comment (2), we created an Observable instance from that list with the help of the toObservable() method. On comment (3), we used the distinct operator to filter out all duplicate emissions.

Here is the output:

```
"C:\Program Files\Java\jdk1.8.0_131\bin\java" ...
Received 1
Received 2
Received 3
Received 4
Received 5
Received 6
Received 7
Received 8
Received 9
Received 10

Process finished with exit code 0
```

What the distinct operator does is remember all the emissions that took place and filters any such emissions in future.

The `distinctUntilChange` operator is slightly different. Instead of discarding all duplicate emissions, it discards only consecutive duplicate emissions, keeping the rest at its place. Please, refer to the following code:

```
fun main(args: Array<String>) {
    listOf(1,2,2,3,4,5,5,5,6,7,8,9,3,10)// (1)
        .toObservable()// (2)
        .distinctUntilChanged()// (3)
        .subscribe { println("Received $it") }// (4)
}
```

Here is the output:

```
"C:\Program Files\Java\jdk1.8.0_131\bin\java" ...
Received 1
Received 2
Received 3
Received 4
Received 5
Received 6
Received 7
Received 8
Received 9
Received 3
Received 10

Process finished with exit code 0
```

Take a cautious look at the output; item 3 is printed twice, second time after 9. The `distinct` operator remembers each item until it receives `onComplete`, but the `distinctUntilChanged` operator remembers them only until it receives a new item.

The elementAt operator

With imperative programming, we have the ability to access the nth element of any array/list, which is quite a common requirement. The `elementAt` operator is really helpful in this regard; it pulls the nth element from the producer and emits it as its own sole emission.

Take a look at the following piece of code:

```
fun main(args: Array<String>) {
  val observable = listOf(10,1,2,5,8,6,9)
    .toObservable()

  observable.elementAt(5)//(1)
    .subscribe { println("Received $it") }

  observable.elementAt(50)//(2)
    .subscribe { println("Received $it") }
}
```

Take a look at the following output before we continue to inspect the code:

```
"C:\Program Files\Java\jdk1.8.0_131\bin\java" ...
Received 6

Process finished with exit code 0
```

On comment (1), we requested the 5th element from Observable, and it emitted the same (count starts with zero). However, on comment (2), we requested the 50th element, which doesn't even exist in Observable, so it didn't emit anything.

This operator achieves this behavior with the help of the Maybe monad, which will be covered later.

Filtering emissions - filter operator

The filter operator is arguably the most used filtering/suppressing operator. It lets you implement custom logic to filter emissions.

The following code snippet is the simplest implementation of the filter operator:

```
fun main(args: Array<String>) {
  Observable.range(1,20)//(1)
    .filter{//(2)
      it%2==0
  }
    .subscribe {
      println("Received $it")
    }
}
```

On comment `(1)`, we created an `Observable` instance with the help of the `Observable.range()` operator. We filtered out odd numbers from the emissions with the help of the `filter` operator on comment `(2)`.

The following is the output:

```
"C:\Program Files\Java\jdk1.8.0_131\bin\java" ...
Received 2
Received 4
Received 6
Received 8
Received 10
Received 12
Received 14
Received 16
Received 18
Received 20

Process finished with exit code 0
```

The first and last operator

These operators help you listen only for the first or last emission and discard the remaining ones.

Check out the following example:

```
fun main(args: Array<String>) {
  val observable = Observable.range(1,10)
  observable.first(2)//(1)
    .subscribeBy { item -> println("Received $item") }

  observable.last(2)//(2)
    .subscribeBy { item -> println("Received $item") }

  Observable.empty<Int>().first(2)//(3)
    .subscribeBy { item -> println("Received $item") }
}
```

The output is as follows:

```
"C:\Program Files\Java\jdk1.8.0_131\bin\java" ...
Received 1
Received 10
Received 2

Process finished with exit code 0
```

On comment (1), we used the `first` operator, with the `defaultValue` parameter set to 2 so that it will emit the `defaultValue` parameter if it can't access the first element. On comment (2), we used the `last` operator. On comment (3), we used the `first` operator again, this time, with an empty `Observable`; so, instead of emitting the first element, it emits `defaultValue`.

The ignoreElements operator

Sometimes, you may require to listen only on the `onComplete` of a producer. The `ignoreElements` operator helps you to do that. Please refer to the following code:

```kotlin
fun main(args: Array<String>) {
  val observable = Observable.range(1,10)
  observable
    .ignoreElements()
    .subscribe { println("Completed") }// (1)
}
```

```
"C:\Program Files\Java\jdk1.8.0_131\bin\java" ...
Completed

Process finished with exit code 0
```

The `ignoreElements` operator returns a Completable monad, which only has the `onComplete` event.

We will look into the `skip` and `take` operators in `Chapter 6`, *More on Operators and Error Handling* while discussing conditional operators.

The transforming operators

As the name suggests, the `transforming` operators help you transform items emitted by a producer.

Here is a brief list of `transforming` operators:

- `map`
- `flatMap`, `concatMap`, and `flatMapIterable`
- `switchMap`
- `switchIfEmpty`
- `scan`
- `groupBy`
- `startWith`
- `defaultIfEmpty`
- `sorted`
- `buffer`
- `window`
- `cast`
- `delay`
- `repeat`

The map operator

The `map` operator performs a given task (lambda) on each of the emitted items and emits them to the downstream. We have already seen a little use of the `map` operator. For a given `Observable<T>` or `Flowable<T>`, the `map` operator will transform an emitted item of type `T` into an emission of type `R` by applying the provided lambda of `Function<T, R>` to it.

So, now, let's take a look at another example with the `map` operator:

```
fun main(args: Array<String>) {
  val observable = listOf(10,9,8,7,6,5,4,3,2,1).toObservable()
  observable.map {//(1)
    number-> "Transforming Int to String $number"
  }.subscribe {
    item-> println("Received $item")
  }
}
```

On comment `(1)`, we used the `map` operator, which will transform the emitted item of type `Int` to an emission of type `String`. Although we have a clear idea of what the output will be, let's validate that by taking a look at the following screenshot:

```
"C:\Program Files\Java\jdk1.8.0_131\bin\java" ...
Received Transforming Int to String 10
Received Transforming Int to String 9
Received Transforming Int to String 8
Received Transforming Int to String 7
Received Transforming Int to String 6
Received Transforming Int to String 5
Received Transforming Int to String 4
Received Transforming Int to String 3
Received Transforming Int to String 2
Received Transforming Int to String 1

Process finished with exit code 0
```

Casting emissions (cast operator)

Think of a situation where you want to cast emissions from the Observable to another data type. Passing a lambda just to cast the emissions doesn't seem like a good idea. The `cast` operator is here to help in this scenario. Let's take a look:

```kotlin
fun main(args: Array<String>) {
  val list = listOf<MyItemInherit>(
      MyItemInherit(1),
      MyItemInherit(2),
      MyItemInherit(3),
      MyItemInherit(4),
      MyItemInherit(5),
      MyItemInherit(6),
      MyItemInherit(7),
      MyItemInherit(8),
      MyItemInherit(9),
      MyItemInherit(10)
  )// (1)

  list.toObservable()// (2)
     .map { it as MyItem }// (3)
     .subscribe {
        println(it)
     }
```

```
        println("cast")

        list.toObservable()
            .cast(MyItem::class.java)//(4)
            .subscribe {
                println(it)
            }
    }

    open class MyItem(val id:Int) {//(5)
    override fun toString(): String {
      return "[MyItem $id]"
    }
  }

  class MyItemInherit(id:Int):MyItem(id) {//(6)
    override fun toString(): String {
      return "[MyItemInherit $id]"
    }
  }
```

In this program, we have defined two classes: MyItem and MyItemInherit on comment
(5) and (6) respectively. We will be using these two classes to demonstrate the uses of the
cast operator. So, on comment (1), we created a list of MyItemInherit; for this program,
our approach is to try the same thing, first with the map operator, and then we will do the
same with the cast operator. On comment (2), we created an observable with a list, and
then, on comment (3), we used the map operator and passed a lambda, where we type-
casted the emission to MyItemInherit.

We did the same on comment (4), but, this time with the cast operator. Just look at the
simplicity of the code now, it looks a lot cleaner and simpler.

The flatMap operator

Where the map operator takes each emission and transforms them, the flatMap operator
creates a new producer, applying the function you passed to each emission of the source
producer.

So, let's look at this example:

```kotlin
fun main(args: Array<String>) {
    val observable = listOf(10,9,8,7,6,5,4,3,2,1).toObservable()
    observable.flatMap {
        number-> Observable.just("Transforming Int to String $number")
    }.subscribe {
        item-> println("Received $item")
    }
}
```

Here is the output:

```
"C:\Program Files\Java\jdk1.8.0_131\bin\java" ...
Received Transforming Int to String 10
Received Transforming Int to String 9
Received Transforming Int to String 8
Received Transforming Int to String 7
Received Transforming Int to String 6
Received Transforming Int to String 5
Received Transforming Int to String 4
Received Transforming Int to String 3
Received Transforming Int to String 2
Received Transforming Int to String 1

Process finished with exit code 0
```

The output is similar to the previous one, but the logic is different. Instead of just returning the `String`, we are returning `Observable` with the desired `String`. Although, for this example, you seem to have no benefit using it, think of a situation when you need to derive multiple items from a single emission. Consider the following example where we will create multiple items from each emission:

```kotlin
fun main(args: Array<String>) {
    val observable = listOf(10,9,8,7,6,5,4,3,2,1).toObservable()
    observable.flatMap {
        number->
        Observable.create<String> {//(1)
            it.onNext("The Number $number")
            it.onNext("number/2 ${number/2}")
            it.onNext("number%2 ${number%2}")
            it.onComplete()//(2)
        }
    }.subscribeBy (
        onNext = {
            item-> println("Received $item")
```

```
        },
        onComplete = {
            println("Complete")
        }
    )
}
```

Let's take a look at the output, and then we will try to understand the program:

```
"C:\Program Files\Java\jdk1.8.0_131\bin\java" ...
Received The Number 10
Received number/2 5
Received number%2 0
Received The Number 9
Received number/2 4
Received number%2 1
Received The Number 8
Received number/2 4
Received number%2 0
Received The Number 7
Received number/2 3
Received number%2 1
Received The Number 6
Received number/2 3
Received number%2 0
Received The Number 5
Received number/2 2
Received number%2 1
Received The Number 4
Received number/2 2
Received number%2 0
Received The Number 3
Received number/2 1
Received number%2 1
Received The Number 2
Received number/2 1
Received number%2 0
Received The Number 1
Received number/2 0
Received number%2 1
Complete

Process finished with exit code 0
```

In this program, we've created a new instance of `Observable` inside the `flatMap` operator, which will emit three strings. On comment `(1)`, we created the `Observable` instance with the `Observable.create` operator. We will emit three strings from the `Observable.create` operator, and, on comment `(2)`, we will send an `onComplete` notification after emitting three items from `Observable`.

However, take a look at the output; it emitted all the items before sending the `onComplete` notification. The reason is that all `Obervables` are combined together and then subscribed to the downstream. The `flatMap` operator internally uses the `merge` operator to combine multiple `Observables`.

The `concatMap` performs the same operation using the `concat` operator instead of the `merge` operator to combine two `Observable/Flowables`.

We will learn more about these operators (`merge`, `concat`, and other combining operators) in the next chapter.

We will again take a look at `flatMap`, along with `concatMap`, `switchMap`, and `flatMapIterable` in `Chapter 6`, *More on Operators and Error Handling* after gaining some knowledge on merging and concatenating producers.

The defaultIfEmpty operator

While working with filtering operators and/or working on complex requirements, it may occur that we encounter an empty producer (see the following code block):

```
fun main(args: Array<String>) {
  Observable.range(0,10)//(1)
    .filter{it>15}//(2)
    .subscribe({
      println("Received $it")
  })
}
```

Here, on comment `(1)`, we will create `Observable` of range 0 to 10; however, on comment `(2)`, we will filter it for emission value >15. So, basically, we will end up with an empty `Observable`.

The `defaultIfEmpty` operator helps us deal with such situations. The preceding example, with `defaultIfEmpty` looks like this:

```
fun main(args: Array<String>) {
  Observable.range(0,10)//(1)
    .filter{it>15}//(2)
    .defaultIfEmpty(15)//(3)
    .subscribe({
        println("Received $it")
    })
}
```

This is the same program, but, just on comment `(3)`, we added the `defaultIfEmpty` operator.

The output looks like the following screenshot:

```
"C:\Program Files\Java\jdk1.8.0_131\bin\java" ...
Received 15

Process finished with exit code 0
```

The output shows that, although `Observable` doesn't contain any number above `10`, `defaultIfEmpty` adds `15` to the `Observable` as it's empty after filtering.

The switchIfEmpty operator

This operator is similar to the `defaultIfEmpty` operator; the only difference is that, for the `defaultIfEmpty` operator, it adds an emission to empty producers, but for the `switchIfEmpty` operator, it starts emitting from the specified alternative producer if the source producer is empty.

Unlike the `defaultIfEmpty` operator, where you needed to pass an item, here, you have to pass an alternate producer to the `switchIfEmpty` operator. If the source producer is empty, it will start taking emissions from the alternate producer.

Here is an example:

```
fun main(args: Array<String>) {
  Observable.range(0,10)//(1)
    .filter{it>15}//(2)
    .switchIfEmpty(Observable.range(11,10))//(3)
    .subscribe({
```

```
        println("Received $it")
    })
}
```

This is the same example as the previous one; just on comment (3), we used
`switchIfEmpty` **instead of** `defaultIfEmpty` with an alternate Observable. The following
output shows that the emissions were taken from the alternate Observable passed with the
`switchIfEmpty` operator:

```
"C:\Program Files\Java\jdk1.8.0_131\bin\java" ...
Received 11
Received 12
Received 13
Received 14
Received 15
Received 16
Received 17
Received 18
Received 19
Received 20

Process finished with exit code 0
```

The startWith operator

The `startWith` operator is simple; it enables you to add an item to the producer at the top
of all preexisting items.

Let's take a look at how it works:

```
fun main(args: Array<String>) {
  Observable.range(0,10)//(1)
    .startWith(-1)//(2)
    .subscribe({
      println("Received $it")
    })
  listOf("C","C++","Java","Kotlin","Scala","Groovy")//(3)
    .toObservable()
    .startWith("Programming Languages")//(4)
    .subscribe({
      println("Received $it")
    })
}
```

The output is as follows:

```
"C:\Program Files\Java\jdk1.8.0_131\bin\java" ...
Received -1
Received 0
Received 1
Received 2
Received 3
Received 4
Received 5
Received 6
Received 7
Received 8
Received 9
Received Programming Languages
Received C
Received C++
Received Java
Received Kotlin
Received Scala
Received Groovy

Process finished with exit code 0
```

As we can see, the startWith operator on comment (2) and (4) worked just like a prefix on the existing list of emissions.

Sorting emissions (sorted operator)

There are some scenarios where you would like to sort the emissions. The sorted operator helps you do that. It will internally collect and reemit all the emissions from the source producer after sorting.

Let's take a look at this example and try to understand this operator better:

```
fun main(args: Array<String>) {
  println("default with integer")
  listOf(2,6,7,1,3,4,5,8,10,9)
    .toObservable()
    .sorted()//(1)
    .subscribe { println("Received $it") }

  println("default with String")
  listOf("alpha","gamma","beta","theta")
    .toObservable()
    .sorted()//(2)
    .subscribe { println("Received $it") }

  println("custom sortFunction with integer")
  listOf(2,6,7,1,3,4,5,8,10,9)
    .toObservable()
    .sorted { item1, item2 -> if(item1>item2) -1 else 1 }//(3)
    .subscribe { println("Received $it") }

  println("custom sortFunction with custom class-object")
  listOf(MyItem1(2),MyItem1(6),
    MyItem1(7),MyItem1(1),MyItem1(3),
    MyItem1(4),MyItem1(5),MyItem1(8),
    MyItem1(10),MyItem1(9))
    .toObservable()
    .sorted { item1, item2 ->
    if(item1.item<item2.item) -1 else 1 }//(4)
    .subscribe { println("Received $it") }
}

data class MyItem1(val item:Int)
```

Take a look at the output first, and then we will explore the program:

```
"C:\Program Files\Java\jdk1.8.0_131\bin\java" ...
default with integer
Received 1
Received 2
Received 3
Received 4
Received 5
Received 6
Received 7
Received 8
Received 9
Received 10
default with String
Received alpha
Received beta
Received gamma
Received theta
custom sortFunction with integer
Received 10
Received 9
Received 8
Received 7
Received 6
Received 5
Received 4
Received 3
Received 2
Received 1
custom sortFunction with custom class-object
Received MyItem1(item=1)
Received MyItem1(item=2)
Received MyItem1(item=3)
Received MyItem1(item=4)
Received MyItem1(item=5)
Received MyItem1(item=6)
Received MyItem1(item=7)
Received MyItem1(item=8)
Received MyItem1(item=9)
Received MyItem1(item=10)

Process finished with exit code 0
```

Now, let's explore the program. As we already know, the `sorted` operator helps sorting emissions; to sort, we need to compare, thus, the `sorted` operator requires a `Comparable` instance to compare emitted items and sort them respectively. This operator has two overloads, one with no parameter—it assumes that the producer (here `Observable`) type will implement `Comparable` and calls `compareTo` function, failing which will generate error; the other overload is with a method (lambda) for comparing. On comment (1) and (2), we implemented the `sorted` operator with a default `sort` function, that is, it will call the `compareTo` function from the item instance and will throw error if the datatype doesn't implement `Comparable`.

On comment (3), we used our own custom `sortFunction` to sort the integers in descending order.

On comment (4), we used an Observable of type `MyItem1`, which obviously is a custom class and doesn't implement `Comparable`, so we passed the `sortFunction` lambda here as well.

Caution: As we already mentioned, the `sorted` operator collects all emissions and then sorts them before reemitting them in a sorted order; thus, using this operator can cause significant performance implications. Moreover, while using with large producers, it can cause `OutOfMemory Error` as well. So, use the sorted operator cautiously, or try to avoid it unless extensively required.

Accumulating data – scan operator

The `scan` operator is a rolling aggregator; it emits incremental accumulation by adding previous emissions to it.

Let's take a look at the following example before delving deeper:

```
fun main(args: Array<String>) {
  Observable.range(1,10)
  .scan { previousAccumulation, newEmission ->
  previousAccumulation+newEmission }//(1)
  .subscribe { println("Received $it") }

  listOf("String 1","String 2", "String 3", "String 4")
   .toObservable()
   .scan{ previousAccumulation, newEmission ->
   previousAccumulation+" "+newEmission }//(2)
   .subscribe { println("Received $it") }
```

```
    Observable.range(1,5)
    .scan { previousAccumulation, newEmission ->
    previousAccumulation*10+newEmission }//(3)
    .subscribe { println("Received $it") }
}
```

The output is as follows:

```
"C:\Program Files\Java\jdk1.8.0_131\bin\java" ...
Received 1
Received 3
Received 6
Received 10
Received 15
Received 21
Received 28
Received 36
Received 45
Received 55
Received String 1
Received String 1 String 2
Received String 1 String 2 String 3
Received String 1 String 2 String 3 String 4
Received 1
Received 12
Received 123
Received 1234
Received 12345

Process finished with exit code 0
```

So, in this program, we used the scan operator to implement three types of operations, which we will discuss in detail, but, first, let's try to understand the scan operator itself. It takes a lambda with two arguments. The first parameter is the result of a rolling aggregation of all previous emissions; the second one is the current emission.

The following graph will allow you to understand it better:

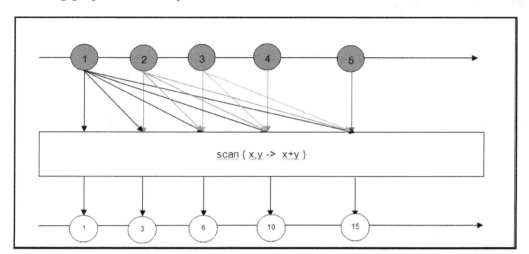

As we can see in the graph, the scan operator will accumulate all the previous emissions with the current emission based on the provided accumulation function.

So, in the preceding program, on comment (1), we did the same thing with the scan operator as it is described in the graph. We used it to get the sum of all integers emitted up until then. On comment (2), we used it with Observable of type String and got concatenated strings.

On comment (3), we used the scan operator to concatenate the integers by multiplying the previous accumulation by 10 and adding the present emission to it.

One thing to note is that we can use the scan operator for almost any operation, not just for summing, as long as it returns items of the same datatype.

 Note that the scan operator has similarities with the reduce operator, which we will cover soon in this chapter; however, be cautious not to get confused. The scan operator is a rolling aggregator, which transforms all the emissions it receives into accumulation; whereas, the reduce operator reduces emissions to just one by accumulating all the emissions once it receives the onComplete notification.

Reducing operators

While developing applications, you may face such a situation where you may need to accumulate and consolidate emissions. Note that nearly all the operators under this criteria will only work on a finite producer (Observable/Flowable) that calls `onComplete()` because typically, we can consolidate only finite datasets. We will explore this behavior as we cover these operators.

Here is a short list of reducing operators, which we will cover in this chapter:

- `count`
- `reduce`
- `all`
- `any`
- `contains`

Counting emissions (count operator)

The `count` operator subscribes to a producer, counts the emissions, and emits a `Single`, containing the count of emissions by the producer.

Here is an example:

```
fun main(args: Array<String>) {
    listOf(1,5,9,7,6,4,3,2,4,6,9).toObservable()
    .count()
    .subscribeBy { println("count $it") }
}
```

The following is the output:

```
"C:\Program Files\Java\jdk1.8.0_131\bin\java" ...
count 11

Process finished with exit code 0
```

As we can see from the output, this operator counts the emissions from the producer, and emits the count once it receives the `onComplete` notification.

Accumulating emissions – reduce operator

Reduce is a perfect accumulation operator. It accumulates all the emissions by the producer and emits them once it receives the `onComplete` notification from the producer.

Here is an example:

```
fun main(args: Array<String>) {
  Observable.range(1,10)
  .reduce { previousAccumulation, newEmission ->
  previousAccumulation+newEmission   }
  .subscribeBy { println("accumulation $it") }

  Observable.range(1,5)
  .reduce { previousAccumulation, newEmission ->
  previousAccumulation*10+newEmission   }
  .subscribeBy { println("accumulation $it") }
}
```

The output is shown as follows:

```
"C:\Program Files\Java\jdk1.8.0_131\bin\java" ...
accumulation 55
accumulation 12345

Process finished with exit code 0
```

The `reduce` operator works similar to the `scan` operator, the only difference is that instead of accumulating and emitting them on each emission, it accumulates all the emissions and emits them on receiving the `onComplete` notification.

The `all` and `any` operators help validate emissions by the producer; we will look into them in the next chapter.

The collection operators

Though it is not good practice, keeping some rare situations in mind, RxKotlin provides you with operators that can listen to all the emissions and accumulate them to a collection object.

The `collection` operators are basically a subset of the reducing operators.

The following list consists of the most important `collection` operators:

- `toList` and `toSortedList`
- `toMap`
- `toMultiMap`
- `collect`

We will be covering `collection` operators in detail later in this book.

The error handling operators

We already learned about the `onError` event in the Subscriber/Observer. However, the problem with the `onError` event is that the error is emitted to the downstream consumer chain, and the subscription is terminated instantly. For example, take a look at the following program:

```
fun main(args: Array<String>) {
  Observable.just(1,2,3,5,6,7,"Errr",8,9,10)
    .map { it.toIntOrError() }
    .subscribeBy (
        onNext = {
            println("Next $it")
        },
        onError = {
            println("Error $it")
        }
    )
}
```

The output of the program is shown in the following screenshot:

```
"C:\Program Files\Java\jdk1.8.0_131\bin\java" ...
Next 1
Next 2
Next 3
Next 5
Next 6
Next 7
Error java.lang.NumberFormatException: For input string: "Errr"

Process finished with exit code 0
```

The program throws an exception in the `map` operator when the string **Errr** is emitted from the Observable. The exception was caught by the `onError` handler, but the Subscription doesn't get any further emissions.

This may not be the desired behavior every time. Although we cannot pretend the error never happened and continue (we should not do this either), there should be a way to at least resubscribe or switch to an alternate source producer.

Error handling operators help you achieve the same.

The following are the error handling operators.

- `onErrorResumeNext()`
- `onErrorReturn()`
- `onExceptionResumeNext()`
- `retry()`
- `retryWhen()`

We will cover error handling operators in detail in `Chapter 6`, *More on Operators and Error Handling*.

The utility operators

These operators help us to perform various utility operations, such as performing some action on emissions, remembering timestamps of each items emitted, caching, and much more.

The following is the list of utility operators:

- `doOnNext`, `doOnComplete`, and `doOnError`
- `doOnSubscribe`, `doOnDispose`, and `doOnSuccess`
- `serialize`
- `cache`

We will cover utility operators in detail in the next chapter.

Summary

In this chapter, we learned about operators and the types of operators available, and we learned in detail about operators, especially the ones useful for transforming, filtering, and accumulating emissions by the source producer. We also learned about the necessity of the error handling operators, which we will cover in the next chapter.

This chapter and the next chapter, that is, Chapter 6, *More on Operators and Error Handling* are highly related; while discussing topics in this chapter, we got a glance about the contents of the next chapter. In the next chapter as well, we will refer to and use the contents learned in this chapter.

While in this chapter we focused on the basics of operators, operator types, and operators specifically useful for filtering, transforming, and accumulating emissions (aka data), in the next chapter, we will cover the operators useful to combine Observable/Flowables and error handling and for conditional purposes.

Turn the page right now to get started.

6
More on Operators and Error Handling

In the previous chapter, we learned about operators and how to use them. We learned how operators can help us in solving complex problems with ease. We got a grip on operators and their types, and we learned basic filtering operators and transforming operators in detail. It's time to move on to some interesting and advanced things you can do with operators.

We will cover the following topics in this chapter:

- Combining producers (Observable/Flowable)
- Grouping emissions
- Filtering/suppressing operators
- Error handling operators
- Real-world HTTP client example

So, what are we waiting for? Let's get started with combining producer (Observable/Flowable) instances.

Combining producers (Observable/Flowable)

While developing applications, it's a common situation to combine data from multiple sources before using them. One such situation is when you are building some offline application following an offline-first approach, and you want to combine the resultant data you got from the HTTP call with the data from the local database.

Now, without wasting much time, let's take a look at the operators that can help us combine producers:

- `startWith()`
- `merge()`, `mergeDelayError()`
- `concat()`
- `zip()`
- `combineLatest()`

Basically, there are a few mechanisms to combine producers (Observables/Flowables). They are as follows:

- Merging producers
- Concatenating producers
- Ambiguous combination of producers
- Zipping
- Combine latest

We will discuss all the previously mentioned techniques to combine producers in this chapter. However, let's start with an operator that we are already aware of.

The startWith operator

We got introduced to the `startWith` operator in the previous chapter, but there's still a lot to cover. This operator also lets you combine multiple producers. Take a look at the following example:

```
fun main(args: Array<String>) {
  println("startWith Iterator")
  Observable.range(5,10)
    .startWith(listOf(1,2,3,4))//(1)
    .subscribe {
      println("Received $it")
    }
  println("startWith another source Producer")
  Observable.range(5,10)
    .startWith(Observable.just(1,2,3,4))//(2)
    .subscribe {
      println("Received $it")
    }
}
```

We can pass another source `Observable` or an `Iterator` instance to be prepended before the source `Observable` that the operator has subscribed to starts emitting.

In the preceding program, on comment `(1)`, we used the `startWith` operator and passed an `Interator` instance to it. The `startWith` operator internally converts the passed `Iterator` instance to an `Observable` instance (it'll convert it to a `Flowable` instance in case you're using `Flowable`). Here is the signature of the `startWith` operator:

```
fun startWith(items: Iterable<T>): Observable<T> {
  return concatArray<T>(fromIterable<out T>(items), this)
}
```

From the preceding signature of the `startWith` operator, we can also see that it uses `concatArray` internally, which we will be covering very soon in this chapter.

On comment `(2)`, we used the `startWith` operator with another source `Observable`.

Here is the output of the program:

```
"C:\Program Files\Java\jdk1.8.0_131\bin\java" ...
startWith Iterator
Received 1
Received 2
Received 3
Received 4
Received 5
Received 6
Received 7
Received 8
Received 9
Received 10
Received 11
Received 12
Received 13
Received 14
startWith another source Producer
Received 1
Received 2
Received 3
Received 4
Received 5
Received 6
Received 7
Received 8
Received 9
Received 10
Received 11
Received 12
Received 13
Received 14

Process finished with exit code 0
```

As we have got some grip on the `startWith` operator, now let's move forward with the `zip` operator. The `zip` operator implements a zipping mechanism to combine producers.

Zipping emissions – zip operator

The `zip` operator is quite interesting. Think of a situation where you're working with multiple `Observable/Flowables` and want to perform some kind of operation on each subsequent emission of each producer. The `zip` operator enables you to perform exactly that. It accumulates emissions of multiple producers to create a new emission via the specified function. So, let's look at a pictorial representation to delve deeper:

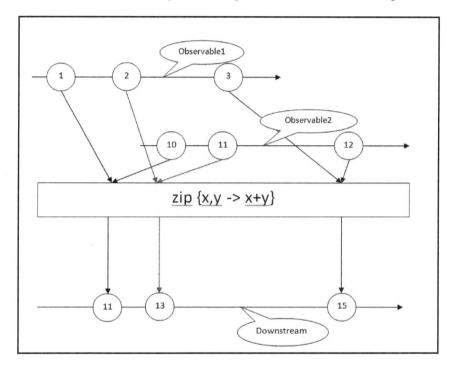

As the picture depicts, the `zip` operator accumulates emissions from multiple producers into a single emission. It also takes a function to apply on the emissions as the `scan` or `reduce` operator, but applies them to emissions from different producers.

For the sake of simplicity, we used two `Observable` in the preceding picture and the following example, but the `zip` operator works with up to nine `Observables/Flowables`.

Consider the following code:

```
fun main(args: Array<String>) {
  val observable1 = Observable.range(1,10)
  val observable2 = Observable.range(11,10)
  Observable.zip(observable1,observable2,
  io.reactivex.functions.BiFunction
  <Int, Int, Int> { emission01, emission02 ->
  emission01+emission02
  }).subscribe {
      println("Received $it")
  }
}
```

The `zip` operator is defined in `companion object` (`static` method in Java) of the `Observable` class, thus can be directly accessed by writing `Observable.zip` itself. No need to access it through another instance. So, let's take a look at the output before we proceed:

```
"C:\Program Files\Java\jdk1.8.0_131\bin\java" ...
Received 12
Received 14
Received 16
Received 18
Received 20
Received 22
Received 24
Received 26
Received 28
Received 30

Process finished with exit code 0
```

In order to understand and use the zip operator better, you need to keep the following points about it in mind:

- The zip operator works on each emission of the supplied producers. For example, if you pass three producers *x*, *y*, and *z* to the zip operator, it will accumulate the nth emission of *x* with the nth emission of *y* and *z*.
- The zip operator waits for each of its producers to emit, before applying the function to them. For example, if you use Observable.interval as one of the producers in the zip operator, the zip operator will wait for each emission and will emit the accumulated values at the specified intervals as well.
- If any of the producers notify onComplete or onError without emitting the item it was waiting for, then it'll discard all emissions afterwards, including that particular one from other producers as well. For example, if producer *x* emits 10 items, producer *y* emits 11 items, and producer *z* emits 8 items, the zip operator will accumulate the first 8 emissions from all the producers and will discard all remaining emissions from producer *x* and *y*.

The zipWith operator

The instance version (that is, the copy of the function, which should be called with an instance rather than static) of the zip operator is zipWith, which can be called from the Observable instance itself. The only problem with this version is that you can pass only another source Observable. If you need to work with three or more Observable instances, you should rather consider using the zip operator instead of zipWith.

Here's an example:

```
fun main(args: Array<String>) {
  val observable1 = Observable.range(1,10)
  val observable2 = listOf("String 1","String 2","String 3",
  "String 4","String 5","String 6","String 7","String 8",
  "String 9","String 10").toObservable()

  observable1.zipWith(observable2,{e1:Int,e2:String ->
  "$e2 $e1"})//(1)
    .subscribe {
        println("Received $it")
    }
}
```

The output is as follows:

```
"C:\Program Files\Java\jdk1.8.0_131\bin\java" ...
Received String 1 1
Received String 2 2
Received String 3 3
Received String 4 4
Received String 5 5
Received String 6 6
Received String 7 7
Received String 8 8
Received String 9 9
Received String 10 10


Process finished with exit code 0
```

On comment (1), we used the zipWith operator on the Observable instance, observable1, and passed another Observable instance, observable2, to it with a lambda to apply to the emissions. From the output, we can tell that the zipWith operator accumulates the producer it's subscribed to, with the producer it is provided with.

The combineLatest operator

The combineLatest operator works in a similar way like the zip operator. It accumulates the emissions of the provided producers. The only difference between combineLatest and zip is that the zip operator waits for each of its source producers to emit, before it starts processing all the emissions to create its new one, but the combineLatest operator starts as soon as it receives any emit from any of its source producers.

To understand this operator better, we will see an example with both, the zip and the combineLatest operator. Let's first try the example with the zip operator, as we gained some grip on it already:

```
fun main(args: Array<String>) {
  val observable1 =
  Observable.interval(100,TimeUnit.MILLISECONDS)//(1)
  val observable2 =
  Observable.interval(250,TimeUnit.MILLISECONDS)//(2)

  Observable.zip(observable1,observable2,
    BiFunction { t1:Long, t2:Long -> "t1: $t1, t2: $t2" })//(3)
```

```
      .subscribe{
         println("Received $it")
      }

   runBlocking { delay(1100) }
}
```

The output is as follows. As expected, it accumulates each and every emission and prints them:

```
"C:\Program Files\Java\jdk1.8.0_131\bin\java" ...
Received t1: 0, t2: 0
Received t1: 1, t2: 1
Received t1: 2, t2: 2
Received t1: 3, t2: 3

Process finished with exit code 0
```

In this program, we created `Observable` with a 100 milliseconds interval on comment `(1)`. On comment `(2)`, we created another `Observable` with a 250 milliseconds interval. In the output, we can see 3 emits, as, after zipping them, the total interval becomes 350 milliseconds, and within 1,100 milliseconds of delay, there is room for only 3 emits with 350 milliseconds interval in between them.

Now, let's test the same code with `combineLatest`:

```
fun main(args: Array<String>) {
   val observable1 = Observable.interval(100, TimeUnit.MILLISECONDS)
   val observable2 = Observable.interval(250, TimeUnit.MILLISECONDS)

   Observable.combineLatest(observable1,observable2,
      BiFunction { t1:Long, t2:Long -> "t1: $t1, t2: $t2" })
      .subscribe{
         println("Received $it")
      }

   runBlocking { delay(1100) }
}
```

Here is the output:

```
"C:\Program Files\Java\jdk1.8.0_131\bin\java" ...
Received t1: 1, t2: 0
Received t1: 2, t2: 0
Received t1: 3, t2: 0
Received t1: 3, t2: 1
Received t1: 4, t2: 1
Received t1: 5, t2: 1
Received t1: 6, t2: 1
Received t1: 6, t2: 2
Received t1: 7, t2: 2
Received t1: 8, t2: 2
Received t1: 9, t2: 2
Received t1: 9, t2: 3
Received t1: 10, t2: 3
Received t1: 11, t2: 3

Process finished with exit code 0
```

As the output suggests, the `combineLatest` operator processes and emits the value as soon as it gets an emit from any of its source producers by using the last emitted value for all other source producers.

Now, let's move forward with merging producers, with the help of the `merge` operator.

Merging Observables/Flowables – merge operator

The zipping operation will let you accumulate emissions, but what if you want to subscribe to each emission by all the source producers? Say you have two different producers and have the same set of actions to be applied when subscribing to them; there's no way to mix imperative programming and reactive programming and repeatedly subscribe to both of the producers separately with the same code. It'll also result in redundant code. So, what is the solution here? You got it right; merging all the emissions of all the source producers together and subscribing to them as a whole is the solution.

So, let's get an example here:

```kotlin
fun main(args: Array<String>) {
    val observable1 = listOf("Kotlin", "Scala",
    "Groovy").toObservable()
    val observable2 = listOf("Python", "Java", "C++",
    "C").toObservable()

    Observable
```

```
    .merge(observable1,observable2)//(1)
    .subscribe {
        println("Received $it")
    }
}
```

In this program, on comment (1), we will merge two `observable` and subscribe to them as a whole. The output is as follows:

As the output shows, the `merge` operator merged two `Observables` and put the emissions of both the `Observables` in their order of emission.

The merging operation, however, doesn't maintain the order specified; rather, it'll start listening to all the provided producers instantly and will fire emissions as soon as they are emitted from the source. Let's look at an example that illustrates this:

```
fun main(args: Array<String>) {
    val observable1 = Observable.interval(500,
    TimeUnit.MILLISECONDS).map { "Observable 1 $it" }//(1)
    val observable2 = Observable.interval(100,
    TimeUnit.MILLISECONDS).map { "Observable 2 $it" }//(2)

    Observable
        .merge(observable1,observable2)
        .subscribe {
            println("Received $it")
        }
        runBlocking { delay(1500) }
}
```

In the preceding example, on comment (1) and (2), we created two Observable<Long> instances with the Observable.interval operator, then mapped it with Observable numbering and got instances of Observable<String>. The objective of the map operator here is to inject an Observable identification in the output so we can easily identify the Observable source from the merged output.

So, here is the much discussed output:

```
"C:\Program Files\Java\jdk1.8.0_131\bin\java" ...
Received Observable 2 0
Received Observable 2 1
Received Observable 2 2
Received Observable 2 3
Received Observable 1 0
Received Observable 2 4
Received Observable 2 5
Received Observable 2 6
Received Observable 2 7
Received Observable 2 8
Received Observable 2 9
Received Observable 1 1
Received Observable 2 10
Received Observable 2 11
Received Observable 2 12
Received Observable 2 13
Received Observable 2 14
Received Observable 1 2

Process finished with exit code 0
```

The output clearly shows that the merge operator took emissions from observable2 first, as they came first, even though we put observable1 first in the merge operator.

The merge operator, however, supports up to four parameters. As a fallback, we have the mergeArray operator, which accepts vararg of Observable; the following is an example:

```kotlin
fun main(args: Array<String>) {
    val observable1 = listOf("A", "B", "C").toObservable()
    val observable2 = listOf("D", "E", "F", "G").toObservable()
    val observable3 = listOf("I", "J", "K", "L").toObservable()
    val observable4 = listOf("M", "N", "O", "P").toObservable()
    val observable5 = listOf("Q", "R", "S", "T").toObservable()
    val observable6 = listOf("U", "V", "W", "X").toObservable()
    val observable7 = listOf("Y", "Z").toObservable()
```

```
Observable.mergeArray(observable1, observable2, observable3,
    observable4, observable5, observable6, observable7)
    .subscribe {
        println("Received $it")
    }
}
```

The output is as follows:

```
"C:\Program Files\Java\jdk1.8.0_131\bin\java" ...
Received A
Received B
Received C
Received D
Received E
Received F
Received G
Received I
Received J
Received K
Received L
Received M
Received N
Received O
Received P
Received Q
Received R
Received S
Received T
Received U
Received V
Received W
Received X
Received Y
Received Z

Process finished with exit code 0
```

As with the `zip` operator, the `merge` operator also has a version for calling on instances of `Observable`'s rather than, statically, `mergeWith`; we can call this operator on `Observable` instances. So, let's look at an example:

```
fun main(args: Array<String>) {
    val observable1 = listOf("Kotlin", "Scala",
    "Groovy").toObservable()
    val observable2 = listOf("Python", "Java", "C++",
    "C").toObservable()

    observable1
        .mergeWith(observable2)
        .subscribe {
            println("Received $it")
        }
}
```

The program is simple enough. We are creating two `Observable` instances, and then merging `observable1` with `observable2` with the `mergeWith` operator called on the `observable1` instance.

The output is as follows:

```
"C:\Program Files\Java\jdk1.8.0_131\bin\java" ...
Received Kotlin
Received Scala
Received Groovy
Received Python
Received Java
Received C++
Received C

Process finished with exit code 0
```

The literal meaning of merging is combining two things together to create a new one, irrespective of any order; all the merging operators do the same thing. If you want to maintain the order, you have to concatenate one after another.

Concatenating producers (Observable/Flowable)

Concatenating operators are almost the same with `merge` operators, except that the concatenating operators respect the prescribed ordering. Instead of subscribing to all provided producers in one go, it subscribes to the producers one after another; only once, it received `onComplete` from the previous subscription.

So, let's modify our last program with the `concatenate` operator and see the changes:

```
fun main(args: Array<String>) {
  val observable1 = Observable.interval(500, TimeUnit.MILLISECONDS)
    .take(2)//(1)
    .map { "Observable 1 $it" }//(2)
  val observable2 = Observable.interval(100,
  TimeUnit.MILLISECONDS).map { "Observable 2 $it" }//(3)

 Observable
   .concat(observable1,observable2)
   .subscribe {
      println("Received $it")
   }

   runBlocking { delay(1500) }
}
```

As we already mentioned, the `concat` operator subscribes to the next source `Observable` in the queue only after it got `onComplete` from its current source `Observable`; we also know that the `Observable` instances created with `Observable.interval` never emit `onComplete`. Rather, they keep emitting numbers until `Long.MAX_VALUE` is reached. So, as a quick fix, we used the `take` operator on comment (1), which will take the first two emissions from `Observable.interval` and then will append an `onComplete` notification to it so that the `concat` operator can start listening to the next source Observable as well.

> We are discussing the `take` operators in this chapter in the *Skipping and taking emissions* section. Don't forget to take a look.

So, here is the output:

```
"C:\Program Files\Java\jdk1.8.0_131\bin\java" ...
Received Observable 1 0
Received Observable 1 1
Received Observable 2 0
Received Observable 2 1
Received Observable 2 2
Received Observable 2 3
Received Observable 2 4

Process finished with exit code 0
```

From the output, we can clearly see that the `concat` operator is subscribed to the next supplied source `Observable` only after it got the `onComplete` notification from its first one.

Just like the `merge` operator, the `concat` operator also has `concatArray` and `concatWith` variants, and they work in almost the same way, just concatenating instead of merging.

Ambiguously combining producers

The ambiguous combination of producers is probably the easiest among all combination types. Think of a situation where you're fetching data from two data sources (may be two separate APIs or database tables), and want to proceed with the first one you got and discard the other one. In the imperative programming technique, you would probably be required to write checks for that; however, with RxKotlin, the `amb` operator is there to hold your back.

The `amb` operator takes a list of `Observable` (`Iterable<Observable>` instance) as parameter, subscribes to all `Observables` present in the `Iterable` instance, emits the items that it got from the first `Observable` it got an emit from, and discards the rest of `Observables` present on the `Iterable` instance.

The following example will help us understand better:

```kotlin
fun main(args: Array<String>) {
  val observable1 = Observable.interval(500,
  TimeUnit.MILLISECONDS).map { "Observable 1 $it" }// (1)
  val observable2 = Observable.interval(100,
  TimeUnit.MILLISECONDS).map { "Observable 2 $it" }// (2)
```

```
Observable
  .amb(listOf(observable1,observable2))// (3)
  .subscribe {
      println("Received $it")
  }

  runBlocking { delay(1500) }
}
```

So, in this program, we created two `Observable`'s with a `500` and a `100` milliseconds interval on comment `(1)` and `(2)` respectively. On comment `(3)`, we used the `listOf` function to create a `List<Observable>` from those two `Observable` and passed it to the `amb` operator. Here's the output:

```
"C:\Program Files\Java\jdk1.8.0_131\bin\java" ...
Received Observable 2 0
Received Observable 2 1
Received Observable 2 2
Received Observable 2 3
Received Observable 2 4
Received Observable 2 5
Received Observable 2 6
Received Observable 2 7
Received Observable 2 8
Received Observable 2 9
Received Observable 2 10
Received Observable 2 11
Received Observable 2 12
Received Observable 2 13
Received Observable 2 14
Received Observable 2 15

Process finished with exit code 0
```

We can see from the output that the `amb` operator took the emissions from `observable2` and didn't care about `observable1`, as the `observable2` instance emitted first.

Just like other combination operators, `amb` also has `ambArray` and `ambWith` operator variants.

Grouping

Grouping is a powerful operation that can be achieved using RxKotlin. This operation allows you to group emissions based on their property. Say, for example, you have an `Observable`/`Flowable` emitting integer numbers (`Int`), and, as per your business logic, you have some separate code for even and odd numbers and want to handle them separately. Grouping is the best solution in that scenario.

Let's take an example:

```
fun main(args: Array<String>) {
  val observable = Observable.range(1,30)

  observable.groupBy {//(1)
    it%5
  }.blockingSubscribe {//(2)
    println("Key ${it.key} ")
    it.subscribe {//(3)
        println("Received $it")
    }
  }
}
```

In this example, I've grouped emissions based on their remainder when divided by 5, so, basically, there should be 5 groups (0 through 4). On comment (1) of this example, we used the `groupBy` operator and passed a predicate to it, upon which the grouping should be performed. The `groupBy` operator takes the result of the predicate to group emissions.

On comment (2) of this example, we used the `blockingSubscribe` operator to subscribe to the newly created `Observable<GroupedObservable<K, T>>` instance. We could also use the simple `subscribe` operator; however, as we are printing the output to the console, by using `subscribe`, everything will look like a mess. Mainly because the `subscribe` operator doesn't wait for the given task on emission to complete before taking the next emission. On the other hand, `blockingSubscribe` will make the program wait until it completes processing an emission, before proceeding to a new one.

The `groupBy` operator returns `Observable` that emits `GroupedObservable`, containing our groups; so, inside `blockingSubscribe`, we need to subscribe to the emitted `GroupedObservable` instance. On comment (3), we did the same, after printing the `key` of the emitted `GroupedObservable` instance.

The output is as follows:

```
"C:\Program Files\Java\jdk1.8.0_131\bin\java" ...
Key 1
Received 1
Received 6
Received 11
Received 16
Received 21
Received 26
Key 2
Received 2
Received 7
Received 12
Received 17
Received 22
Received 27
Key 3
Received 3
Received 8
Received 13
Received 18
Received 23
Received 28
Key 4
Received 4
Received 9
Received 14
Received 19
Received 24
Received 29
Key 0
Received 5
Received 10
Received 15
Received 20
Received 25
Received 30

Process finished with exit code 0
```

flatMap, concatMap – In details

As promised in the previous chapter, now we will take a deeper dive into the `flatMap` and `concatMap` operators, as, by now, we have already gained some sort of expertise on the `merge` and `concat` operators and know the differences between them.

Let's start with the differences between `flatMap` and `concatMap`, after which, we will also discuss their ideal implementation scenarios. We will also discuss some of their variants to know them better.

In the previous chapter, we mentioned that `flatMap` internally uses the `merge` operator and `concatMap` internally uses the `concat` operator. However, what difference does that make? You just learned the differences between the `merge` and the `concat` operator, but what is the point of having two separate mapping operators based on them? So, let's start with an example. We will see an example with `flatMap`, and then we will try to implement the same with `concatMap`:

```
fun main(args: Array<String>) {
  Observable.range(1,10)
    .flatMap {
        val randDelay = Random().nextInt(10)
        return@flatMap Observable.just(it)
        .delay(randDelay.toLong(),TimeUnit.MILLISECONDS)//(1)
    }
    .blockingSubscribe {
        println("Received $it")
    }
}
```

In the preceding program, we created an `Observable` instance. We then used the `flatMap` operator with the `delay` operator on it to add a random delay to the emissions.

The output is as follows:

From the output, we can see that the downstream didn't get the emissions in their prescribed order; I think you got the reason behind it, didn't you? That's right; the cause behind it is simply the `merge` operator, as the `merge` operator subscribes and reemits the emissions asynchronously all at one go, thus the order is not maintained.

Now, let's implement the code with the `concatMap` operator:

```
fun main(args: Array<String>) {
   Observable.range(1,10)
      .concatMap {
          val randDelay = Random().nextInt(10)
          return@concatMap Observable.just(it)
          .delay(randDelay.toLong(), TimeUnit.MILLISECONDS)//(1)
      }
      .blockingSubscribe {
          println("Received $it")
      }
}
```

The output is as follows:

```
"C:\Program Files\Java\jdk1.8.0_131\bin\java" ...
Received 1
Received 2
Received 3
Received 4
Received 5
Received 6
Received 7
Received 8
Received 9
Received 10

Process finished with exit code 0
```

As the `concatMap` operator uses `concat` internally, it maintains the prescribed order of emissions.

So, when to use which operator? Let's take a look at the following real-time scenarios; all of them are applicable, especially when you are building an app.

When to use flatMap operator

Take a look at the following list—it contains the contexts and situations where flatMap will fit best:

- When you're working with a list of data within a page, activity, or fragment and want to send some data to a server or a database per item of the list. The concatMap operator will also do here; however, as the flatMap operator works asynchronously, it'll be faster, and, as you're sending data, the order doesn't really matter.
- Whenever you want to perform any operation on list items asynchronously and in a comparatively short time period.

When to use concatMap operator

So, when to use concatMap?

The following list contains the contexts and situations where concatMap will fit best:

- When you are downloading the list of data to display to the user. The order really matters here, you will surely not want to load and display the second item of the list after the third and fourth one are already displayed, would you?
- Performing some operation on a sorted list, making sure the list stays the same.

Understanding switchMap operator

The switchMap operator is really interesting. It listens to all the emissions of the source producer (Observable/Flowable) asynchronously, but emits only the latest one within the timeframe. Let's explain it a bit more.

When the source Observable emits more than one item consecutively before the switchMap has emitted any of them, switchMap will take the last one and discard any emission that came in between. Let's take an example to understand it better:

```
fun main(args: Array<String>) {
  println("Without delay")
  Observable.range(1,10)
  .switchMap {
    val randDelay = Random().nextInt(10)
    return@switchMap Observable.just(it)//(1)
```

```
      }
      .blockingSubscribe {
         println("Received $it")
      }
   println("With delay")
   Observable.range(1,10)
      .switchMap {
         val randDelay = Random().nextInt(10)
         return@switchMap Observable.just(it)
            .delay(randDelay.toLong(), TimeUnit.MILLISECONDS)// (2)
      }
      .blockingSubscribe {
         println("Received $it")
      }
}
```

The output is as follows:

In the program, we took two approaches at first, we used the `delay` operator, and then we reused the same with the `delay` operator. From the output, we can see that, for the second one, `switchMap` only emitted the last item, as it got consecutive emission for each one before it reemitted them. However, for the first one, it reemitted all the items before receiving any further emit.

Still confused? Let's modify the program a bit more:

```kotlin
fun main(args: Array<String>) {
    Observable.range(1,10)
        .switchMap {
            val randDelay = Random().nextInt(10)
            if(it%3 == 0)
                Observable.just(it)
            else
                Observable.just(it)
                    .delay(randDelay.toLong(), TimeUnit.MILLISECONDS)
        }
        .blockingSubscribe {
            println("Received $it")
        }
}
```

In this program, instead of adding delay to all the emissions, we emitted all the numbers divisible by 3 without delay, and added a delay to the rest.

The output is as follows:

```
"C:\Program Files\Java\jdk1.8.0_131\bin\java" ...
Received 3
Received 6
Received 9
Received 10

Process finished with exit code 0
```

As expected, the `switchMap` operator emits the only those items which were emitted by the source without delay, and the last emitted item by the source. The reason is quite simple; the `switchMap` operator was able to emit them before it received the following item.

Skipping and taking emissions

Just like the preceding situation in this chapter, where we used the `take` operator, there are often some scenarios where you would like to take some of the emissions and skip the remaining ones. The `skip` and `take` operators are of huge help in those scenarios. They are actually a part of the filtering operators we discussed in the previous chapter; however, honestly, they do deserve a dedicated discussion. So, here it is.

Skipping emissions (skip, skipLast, skipUntil, and skipWhile)

There may be a requirement where you would like to skip some emissions at the beginning or skip emissions until a particular condition is met. You may even have to wait for another producer before taking emissions and skip all remaining ones.

These operators are designed keeping the exact scenario in mind. They help you skip emissions in various ways.

RxKotlin provides us with many variations and overloads of the `skip` operator; we will discuss the most important ones among them:

- `skip`
- `skipLast`
- `skipWhile`
- `skipUntil`

We will take a look at all of the preceding listed operators one by one.

Let's start with `skip`:

```kotlin
fun main(args: Array<String>) {
  val observable1 = Observable.range(1,20)
  observable1
  .skip(5)//(1)
  .subscribe(object:Observer<Int> {
    override fun onError(e: Throwable) {
      println("Error $e")
    }

    override fun onComplete() {
      println("Complete")
    }

    override fun onNext(t: Int) {
      println("Received $t")
    }

    override fun onSubscribe(d: Disposable) {
      println("starting skip(count)")
    }

  })
```

```
val observable2 = Observable.interval(100,TimeUnit.MILLISECONDS)
observable2
    .skip(400,TimeUnit.MILLISECONDS)//(2)
    .subscribe(
        object:Observer<Long> {
            override fun onError(e: Throwable) {
              println("Error $e")
            }

            override fun onComplete() {
              println("Complete")
            }

            override fun onNext(t: Long) {
                println("Received $t")
            }

            override fun onSubscribe(d: Disposable) {
                println("starting skip(time)")
            }

        }
    )

    runBlocking {
      delay(1000)
    }

}
```

The `skip` operator has two important overloads: `skip(count:Long)` and `skip(time:Long, unit:TimeUnit)`; the first overload works on count, discarding the first *n* number of emissions, while the second overload works on time, discarding all the emissions that came in the specified time duration.

In this program, on comment (1), we used the `skip(count)` operator to skip the first 5 emissions. On comment (2), we used the `skip(time,unit)` operator to skip all emissions in the first 400 milliseconds (4 seconds) of the subscription.

Here is the output:

Now, let's take a look at how the `skipLast` operator works:

```kotlin
fun main(args: Array<String>) {
  val observable = Observable.range(1,20)
  observable
    .skipLast(5) // (1)
    .subscribe(object: Observer<Int> {
      override fun onError(e: Throwable) {
        println("Error $e")
      }

      override fun onComplete() {
        println("Complete")
      }

      override fun onNext(t: Int) {
        println("Received $t")
      }
```

```
override fun onSubscribe(d: Disposable) {
    println("starting skipLast(count)")
}

})
}
```

The `skipLast` operator has many overloads like the `skip` operator. The only difference is that this operator discards emissions from last. In this program, we used the `skipLast(count)` operator to skip the last 5 emissions on comment (1).

Here is the output:

```
"C:\Program Files\Java\jdk1.8.0_131\bin\java" ...
starting skipLast(count)
Received 1
Received 2
Received 3
Received 4
Received 5
Received 6
Received 7
Received 8
Received 9
Received 10
Received 11
Received 12
Received 13
Received 14
Received 15
Complete

Process finished with exit code 0
```

Unlike `skip` and `skipLast`, both of which skip emissions on the basis of count or time, `skipWhile` skips them on the base of a predicate (logical expression). You've to pass a predicate to the `skipWhile` operator, just like the `filter` operator. It will keep skipping emissions while the predicate evaluates to true. It will start passing all emissions downstream as soon as the predicate returns false. Let's take a look at the following piece of code:

```kotlin
fun main(args: Array<String>) {
  val observable = Observable.range(1,20)
  observable
    .skipWhile {item->item<10}//(1)
    .subscribe(object: Observer<Int> {
      override fun onError(e: Throwable) {
        println("Error $e")
      }

      override fun onComplete() {
        println("Complete")
      }

      override fun onNext(t: Int) {
        println("Received $t")
      }

      override fun onSubscribe(d: Disposable) {
        println("starting skipWhile")
      }

    })
}
```

The output is as follows:

Note that, unlike filter, the `skipWhile` operator will execute the predicate until it returns false and pass all the emissions thereafter. If you want the predicate, check on all the emissions; you should rather consider the `filter` operator.

Think of a situation where you're working with two producers, producer1 and producer2, and want to start processing emissions from producer1 as soon as producer2 starts emitting. In this scenario, `skipUntil` can help you out. Let's look at this example:

```kotlin
fun main(args: Array<String>) {
    val observable1 = Observable.interval(100, TimeUnit.MILLISECONDS)
    val observable2 =
    Observable.timer(500,TimeUnit.MILLISECONDS)//(1)

    observable1
        .skipUntil(observable2)//(2)
        .subscribe(
            object: Observer<Long> {
                override fun onError(e: Throwable) {
                    println("Error $e")
                }

                override fun onComplete() {
                    println("Complete")
                }

                override fun onNext(t: Long) {
                    println("Received $t")
                }

                override fun onSubscribe(d: Disposable) {
                    println("starting skip(time)")
                }

            }
        )

        runBlocking { delay(1500) }
}
```

We will explain the code, but take a look at the output first:

```
"C:\Program Files\Java\jdk1.8.0_131\bin\java" ...
starting skipUntil
Received 5
Received 6
Received 7
Received 8
Received 9
Received 10
Received 11
Received 12
Received 13
Received 14

Process finished with exit code 0
```

On comment (1), we created an `Observable` instance (`observable2`) with `Observable.timer`, which should trigger emission after `500` milliseconds. On comment (2), we used that `Observable` instance (`observable2`) as the parameter to the `skipUntil` operator, which will make it discard all the emissions of `observable1` until `observable2` emits.

Take operators (take, takeLast, takeWhile, and takeUntil)

The `take` operators work in exactly the opposite way than the `skip` operators. Let's take an example of them one by one and understand how they work:

```
fun main(args: Array<String>) {
  val observable1 = Observable.range(1,20)
  observable1
    .take(5)//(1)
    .subscribe(object:Observer<Int> {
      override fun onError(e: Throwable) {
        println("Error $e")
      }

      override fun onComplete() {
        println("Complete")
```

```
        }

    override fun onNext(t: Int) {
        println("Received $t")
    }

    override fun onSubscribe(d: Disposable) {
        println("starting skip(count)")
    }

  })

val observable2 = Observable.interval(100,TimeUnit.MILLISECONDS)
observable2
    .take(400,TimeUnit.MILLISECONDS)//(2)
    .subscribe(
       object:Observer<Long> {
          override fun onError(e: Throwable) {
             println("Error $e")
          }

          override fun onComplete() {
             println("Complete")
          }

          override fun onNext(t: Long) {
             println("Received $t")
          }

          override fun onSubscribe(d: Disposable) {
             println("starting skip(time)")
          }

       }
    )

    runBlocking {
      delay(1000)
    }

}
```

This program is almost like the program with `skip`. The difference is that here, we used `take` instead of `skip`. Let's check the difference to understand better:

The output shows it clearly. In the exact opposite way than the `skip` operator, the `take` operator passes the specified emissions to downstream, discarding the remaining ones. Most importantly, it also sends `onComplete` notifications to downstream on its own, as soon as it completes passing all the specified emissions.

Let's test it with `takeLast` operator:

```
fun main(args: Array<String>) {
  val observable = Observable.range(1,20)
  observable
    .takeLast(5)//(1)
    .subscribe(object: Observer<Int> {
      override fun onError(e: Throwable) {
        println("Error $e")
      }

      override fun onComplete() {
        println("Complete")
      }

      override fun onNext(t: Int) {
        println("Received $t")
      }

      override fun onSubscribe(d: Disposable) {
        println("starting skipLast(count)")
```

```
        }

    })
}
```

And, here is the output; it prints the last 5 numbers in the emission:

```
"C:\Program Files\Java\jdk1.8.0_131\bin\java" ...
starting skipLast(count)
Received 16
Received 17
Received 18
Received 19
Received 20
Complete

Process finished with exit code 0
```

Now take a look at the `takeWhile`:

```kotlin
fun main(args: Array<String>) {
    val observable = Observable.range(1,20)
    observable
        .takeWhile{item->item<10}//(1)
        .subscribe(object: Observer<Int> {
            override fun onError(e: Throwable) {
                println("Error $e")
            }

            override fun onComplete() {
                println("Complete")
            }

            override fun onNext(t: Int) {
                println("Received $t")
            }

            override fun onSubscribe(d: Disposable) {
                println("starting skipWhile")
            }

        })
}
```

The output is the exact opposite of `skipWhile`; instead of skipping the first `10` numbers, it prints them and discards the remaining ones:

```
"C:\Program Files\Java\jdk1.8.0_131\bin\java" ...
starting skipWhile
Received 1
Received 2
Received 3
Received 4
Received 5
Received 6
Received 7
Received 8
Received 9
Complete

Process finished with exit code 0
```

The error handling operators

While developing applications, errors may occur. We have to handle those errors properly to make sure our applications perform seamlessly on the user's end. Take the following program as an example:

```kotlin
fun main(args: Array<String>) {
    Observable.just(1,2,3,4,5)
        .map { it/(3-it) }
        .subscribe {
            println("Received $it")
        }
}
```

Here is the output:

```
"C:\Program Files\Java\jdk1.8.0_131\bin\java" ...
Received 0
io.reactivex.exceptions.OnErrorNotImplementedException: / by zero
Received 2
    at io.reactivex.internal.functions.Functions$OnErrorMissingConsumer.accept(Functions.java:704)
    at io.reactivex.internal.functions.Functions$OnErrorMissingConsumer.accept(Functions.java:701)
    at io.reactivex.internal.observers.LambdaObserver.onError(LambdaObserver.java:74)
    at io.reactivex.internal.observers.BasicFuseableObserver.onError(BasicFuseableObserver.java:100)
    at io.reactivex.internal.observers.BasicFuseableObserver.fail(BasicFuseableObserver.java:110)
    at io.reactivex.internal.operators.observable.ObservableMap$MapObserver.onNext(ObservableMap.java:61)
    at io.reactivex.internal.operators.observable.ObservableFromArray$FromArrayDisposable.run(ObservableFromArray.java:107)
    at io.reactivex.internal.operators.observable.ObservableFromArray.subscribeActual(ObservableFromArray.java:36)
    at io.reactivex.Observable.subscribe(Observable.java:10842)
    at io.reactivex.internal.operators.observable.ObservableMap.subscribeActual(ObservableMap.java:33)
    at io.reactivex.Observable.subscribe(Observable.java:10842)
    at io.reactivex.Observable.subscribe(Observable.java:10828)
    at io.reactivex.Observable.subscribe(Observable.java:10731)
    at com.rivuchk.packtpub.reactivekotlin.chapter6.Chapter6_17Kt.main(chapter6_17.kt:8)
Caused by: java.lang.ArithmeticException: / by zero
    at com.rivuchk.packtpub.reactivekotlin.chapter6.Chapter6_17Kt$main$1.apply(chapter6_17.kt:7)
    at com.rivuchk.packtpub.reactivekotlin.chapter6.Chapter6_17Kt$main$1.apply(chapter6_17.kt)
    at io.reactivex.internal.operators.observable.ObservableMap$MapObserver.onNext(ObservableMap.java:59)
    ... 8 more
Exception in thread "main" io.reactivex.exceptions.OnErrorNotImplementedException: / by zero
```

As expected, the program threw an error and that is a bad thing if that occurs on the user end. So, let's take a look at how we can handle errors in a reactive way. RxKotlin provides us with a few operators for error handling, which we'll take a look at. We will use the previous program and apply various error handling operators to them to understand them better.

onErrorReturn – return a default value on error

The `onErrorReturn` provides you with a technique to specify a default value to return to the downstream in case an error occurred in the upstream. Take a look at the following code snippet:

```kotlin
fun main(args: Array<String>) {
  Observable.just(1,2,3,4,5)
    .map { it/(3-it) }
    .onErrorReturn { -1 }//(1)
    .subscribe {
        println("Received $it")
    }
}
```

We used the `onErrorReturn` operator to return −1 whenever an error occurs. The output is as follows:

```
"C:\Program Files\Java\jdk1.8.0_131\bin\java" ...
Received 0
Received 2
Received -1

Process finished with exit code 0
```

As we can see in the output, the `onErrorReturn` operator returns the specified default value. The downstream didn't receive any item further as the upstream stopped emitting items as soon as the error occurred.

As we mentioned earlier, both `onError` and `onComplete` are terminal operators, so the downstream stops listening to that upstream as soon as it receives any of them.

The onErrorResumeNext operator

The `onErrorResumeNext` operator helps you subscribe to a different producer in case any error occurs.

Here is an example:

```
fun main(args: Array<String>) {
  Observable.just(1,2,3,4,5)
    .map { it/(3-it) }
    .onErrorResumeNext(Observable.range(10,5))//(1)
    .subscribe {
      println("Received $it")
    }
}
```

The output is as follows:

```
"C:\Program Files\Java\jdk1.8.0_131\bin\java" ...
Received 0
Received 2
Received 10
Received 11
Received 12
Received 13
Received 14

Process finished with exit code 0
```

This operator is especially useful when you want to subscribe to another source producer in case any error occurs.

Retrying on error

The `retry` operator is another error handling operator that enables you to retry/re-subscribe to the same producer when an error occurs. You just need to provide a predicate or retry-limit when it should stop retrying. So, let's look at an example:

```
fun main(args: Array<String>) {
  Observable.just(1,2,3,4,5)
    .map { it/(3-it) }
    .retry(3)//(1)
    .subscribeBy (
        onNext  = {println("Received $it")},
        onError = {println("Error")}
    )
    println("\n With Predicate \n")
    var retryCount = 0
    Observable.just(1,2,3,4,5)
    .map { it/(3-it) }
    .retry {//(2)
        _, _->
        (++retryCount)<3
    }
    .subscribeBy (
        onNext  = {println("Received $it")},
        onError = {println("Error")}
    )
}
```

On comment (1), we used the `retry` operator with a retry limit, and on comment (2), we used the `retry` operator with a predicate. The `retry` operator will keep retrying until the predicate returns true and will pass the error to downstream whenever the predicate returns false.

Here is the output:

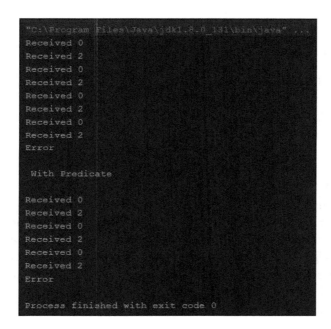

An HTTP example

Any learning is not complete until and unless we apply it to a real-time scenario. So far, you have learned many concepts of reactive programming. Now, it's time to apply them to a real-world scenario, where we will use an API to get some data through an HTTP request and print the response data to the console.

We used one additional plugin for this example—RxJava-Apache-HTTP. If you're using Gradle as your build tool, add the following dependency:

```
//RxJava - Apache - HTTP
compile "com.netflix.rxjava:rxjava-apache-http:0.20.7"
```

Here is the code:

```
fun main(args: Array<String>) {
  val httpClient = HttpAsyncClients.createDefault()//(1)
  httpClient.start()//(2)
  ObservableHttp.createGet("http://rivuchk.com/feed/json",
  httpClient).toObservable()//(3)
    .flatMap{ response ->
      response.content.map{ bytes ->
      String(bytes)
    }//(4)
  }
  .onErrorReturn {//(5)
    "Error Parsing data "
  }
  .subscribe {
    println(it)//(6)
    httpClient.close()//(7)
  }
}
```

In this program, we used `HttpAsyncClients.createDefault()` to get an instance of `CloseableHttpAsyncClient`. Before starting an HTTP request, we first need to start the client. We did this in the code on comment `(2)`, with `httpClient.start()`. On comment `(3)`, we created a GET request and converted it to an observable of type `ObservableHttpResponse`, so we used the `flatMap` operator to get access to the content of the response. Inside the `flatMap` operator, we used the `map` operator to convert the byte response into a `String` on comment `(4)`.

On comment `(5)`, we used the `onErrorReturn` operator to return a default `String` in case there's an error.

Finally, after the `onErrorReturn` operator, we subscribed to the chain and printed the response on comment `(6)`. We closed the `httpClient` as soon as we were done with the response.

The following is partly a screenshot of the output:

```
"items": [
    {
        "id": "http://rivuchk.com/community-gdg-kolkata-kotlinkolkata/gdg-kolkata/gdg-kolkata-august-kotlin-meetup-slide/",
        "url": "http://rivuchk.com/community-gdg-kolkata-kotlinkolkata/gdg-kolkata/gdg-kolkata-august-kotlin-meetup-slide/",
        "title": "GDG-Kolkata August &#8211; Kotlin Meetup Slide",
        "date_published": "2017-08-19T00:00:06+00:00",
        "date_modified": "2017-08-19T05:18:13+00:00",
        "author": {
            "name": "Rivu Chakraborty"
        }
    },
    {
        "id": "http://rivuchk.com/community-gdg-kolkata-kotlinkolkata/google-solve-india-kolkata-notes/",
        "url": "http://rivuchk.com/community-gdg-kolkata-kotlinkolkata/google-solve-india-kolkata-notes/",
        "title": "Google Solve For India &#8211; Kolkata Notes",
        "date_published": "2017-06-04T07:20:14+00:00",
        "date_modified": "2017-06-04T11:38:42+00:00",
        "author": {
            "name": "Rivu Chakraborty"
        }
    },
    {
        "id": "https://rivuchk.com/development/android-runtime-permission-manager/",
        "url": "http://rivuchk.com/development/android-runtime-permission-manager/",
        "title": "Android Runtime Permission Manager",
        "date_published": "2017-04-23T06:19:25+00:00",
        "date_modified": "2017-06-04T11:32:59+00:00",
        "author": {
            "name": "Rivu Chakraborty"
        }
    },
    {
        "id": "http://rivuchk.com/rivu-chakraborty/articles-and-tutorials/",
        "url": "http://rivuchk.com/rivu-chakraborty/articles-and-tutorials/",
        "title": "Articles and Tutorials",
        "date_published": "2016-12-18T18:49:46+00:00",
        "date_modified": "2017-05-20T15:41:06+00:00",
        "author": {
            "name": "Rivu Chakraborty"
        }
    }
]

Process finished with exit code 0
```

Summary

This was a rather a long chapter. You learned about combining producers, and learned, in depth, about the `flatMap`, `concatMap`, and `switchMap` operators. You got introduced to the `take` and `skip` operators and their variants. You learned about the error handling approaches in reactive programming. We also tried our skills with an HTTP client example, where we requested an API to fetch JSON data and print it to the console. We didn't try to parse the JSON data, as it could increase complexity at this level. Later in this book, we will definitely parse data and display that properly.

While this and Chapter 5, *Asynchronous Data Operators and Transformations* were more about operators, the next chapter, Chapter 7, *Concurrency and Parallel Processing in RxKotlin with Schedulers*, is mainly about schedulers, handling concurrency, and multi-threading, and we will get a deeper dive in asynchronous programming with RxKotlin. As we are gradually moving to more advanced topics and chapters through this book, you need to pay more attention to each chapter to get a proper grasp on each aspect of reactive programming in Kotlin.

So, what are you waiting for? Turn the page, Chapter 7, *Concurrency and Parallel Processing in RxKotlin with Schedulers* is waiting for you.

7
Concurrency and Parallel Processing in RxKotlin with Schedulers

So, up until now, you have learned the basics of reactive programming. You learned about Observable, Observers, and Subjects, as well as backpressure, Flowable, processors, and operators. Now, it's time for us to learn some other new topics in reactive programming, probably the most important ones—concurrency and parallel processing.

A popular misconception regarding reactive programming is that reactive programming is multi-threaded by default. The truth is actually that RxKotlin works on a single thread by default, although it provides us with loads of operators to implement multi-threading as per our business logic and requirements with ease.

In this chapter, we will cover the following topics:

- Introduction to concurrency
- The `subscribeOn()` and `observeOn()` operator
- Parallelization

Introduction to concurrency

The definition of concurrency can be described as follows:

> *As a programming paradigm, concurrent computing is a form of modular programming, namely factoring an overall computation into subcomputations that may be executed concurrently.*
>
> *– Wikipedia*

As the definition says, concurrency is all about breaking the entire task into small parts and then executing them concurrently (there's a small difference between concurrent execution and parallel execution, which we will discuss shortly).

So, what does it mean to execute subcomputations concurrently? Let's look at a real-life example. Think of a situation where you're cooking a new dish at your home and you have three chores—bring the spices, cut the vegetables, and also marinate something. Now, if you're doing it all alone, you have to do them one by one, but if you have a family member at your disposal, then you can distribute the tasks between the two of you. You can cut the vegetables while the other person is bringing the spices, and whoever between you two completes early can continue on the third task—marinating the food.

You can think of you and the family member (who helped you) as two threads, or, to be more specific, you're the main thread of the program (here, cooking) as you're the responsible person for the entire job, and you'll be distributing tasks between you and the family member, who is a worker thread. Together, you and your family member form a thread pool.

The entire program will execute faster if there are more threads and the complete task is divided properly among them.

Parallel execution versus concurrency

The concepts of concurrency and parallelization are not only related, but they are deeply connected to each other; you may think of them as identical twin brothers. They look almost the same, but there are differences. Let's try to discover.

In the previous example, we discussed concurrency, but it seemed to execute in parallel. Now, let's take a better example, which will not only help us understand parallelization, but will allow us to understand the differences between concurrency and parallelization as well.

Think of a hotel with 5 customers who ordered 15 dishes. These 15 dishes represent identical tasks, and each of them require to be cooked by a chef. Now, as with the previous example, think of the cooks as threads (in the previous example, you and your family member were playing the role of a cook in your home), but rather than sharing sub-parts of a dish, they will cook each dish at a time (because, obviously, there are 15 orders!).

Now, if you get 15 cooks at your disposal (along with 15 ovens and other resources), then you can get all the dishes to be cooked in one go, but that's not quite economical. You cannot infinitely increase your cooks and resources with the number of orders. The more economical solution would be to hire 5 cooks and make a pool (or you may say a queue) of orders and execute orders one after another. So, each cook has to make three dishes (or iterations of tasks). If there are more orders, then the pool would grow bigger.

Parallelization says to wisely divide tasks in a pool; instead of creating threads for each task, create a pool of tasks, and assign them to an existing thread, and reuse them.

The conclusion is, parallelization is achieved with concurrency, but it is not the same thing; rather, it is about how to use concurrency.

Now, why is it so important? Or rather, why is it required at all? I think you already got the answer, but let's inspect.

Think of a situation where you're working with a large dataset, and also have a long chain of operations to be performed on them before being displayed to the user. If you're an application developer, you'd probably want to perform all the operations in the background and pass the resultant data to the foreground for displaying it to the user. Concurrency is useful for this same scenario.

As I mentioned earlier, RxKotlin doesn't perform actions concurrently, but provides you with loads of options to perform the selected operations concurrently, leaving the choice to you.

You're probably wondering if RxKotlin really is single threaded by default, then how is the subscription handled by it? Should the subscription be concurrent? Let's find the answers before we proceed further with concurrent computing with RxKotlin.

So, whenever you subscribe to an Observable and/or Flowable, the current thread is blocked until all the items are emitted and received by the Observer chain (except for the cases with interval and timer factory methods). Surprising, right? However, it's actually good, because, for an Observable chain, if a separate thread is assigned to each operator (any operator generally subscribes to the source Observable and performs operations on the emissions, the next operator subscribes to the emissions by the current one), then it would be totally messy.

To resolve this scenario, ReactiveX provided us with scheduler and scheduling operators. By using them, thread management becomes easy, as the synchronization is almost automatic and there's no shared data between threads (as a basic property of functional programming, thus functional reactive programming).

Now that we have got some hands on the ideas behind concurrency, we can move forward with implementing concurrency using RxKotlin.

What is a scheduler?

In ReactiveX, the heart of concurrency lies in schedulers. As I have already mentioned, by default, the Observable and the chain of operators applied to it will do the work on the same thread where subscribe is called, and the thread will be blocked until Observer receives the `onComplete` or `onError` notification. We can use schedulers to change this behavior.

A scheduler can be thought of as a thread pool, from which ReactiveX can pool a thread and execute its task on it. It's basically an abstraction over multithreading and concurrency, making the implementation of concurrency a lot easier in ReactiveX.

Types of scheduler

As an abstraction layer for thread pool management, the scheduler API provides you with some pre-composed scheduler. It also allows you to create a new user-defined scheduler. Let's take a look at the available scheduler types:

- `Schedulers.io()`
- `Schedulers.computation()`
- `Schedulers.newThread()`
- `Schedulers.single()`
- `Schedulers.trampoline()`
- `Schedulers.from()`

We will look into their definitions and their prescribed use-cases, but first, let's get started with some code.

We will start with a usual example without a scheduler, and then we will implement a scheduler in the same example to observe the difference, as follows:

```kotlin
fun main(args: Array<String>) {
  Observable.range(1,10)
    .subscribe {
       runBlocking { delay(200) }
       println("Observable1 Item Received $it")
     }

  Observable.range(21,10)
    .subscribe {
       runBlocking { delay(100) }
       println("Observable2 Item Received $it")
     }
}
```

In this program, we used two `Observable`; we used delay inside their subscription to simulate long running tasks.

The following output displays the expected result. The Observers run one after another:

The total execution time of this program would be around 3,100 milliseconds (as the delay is performed before printing), while the thread pool was sitting idle in between. Using scheduler, this time can be significantly reduced. Let's get it done:

```kotlin
fun main(args: Array<String>) {
  Observable.range(1, 10)
    .subscribeOn(Schedulers.computation())//(1)
    .subscribe {
      runBlocking { delay(200) }
      println("Observable1 Item Received $it")
    }

  Observable.range(21, 10)
    .subscribeOn(Schedulers.computation())//(2)
    .subscribe {
      runBlocking { delay(100) }
      println("Observable2 Item Received $it")
    }
  runBlocking { delay(2100) }//(3)
}
```

This program contains three new lines as compared to the previous one. On comment (1) and (2), subscribeOn(Schedulers.computation()), and runBlocking { delay(2100) } on comment (3). We will inspect the significance of those lines after taking a look at the output:

```
"C:\Program Files\Java\jdk1.8.0_131\bin\java" ...
Observable2 Item Received 21
Observable1 Item Received 1
Observable2 Item Received 22
Observable2 Item Received 23
Observable1 Item Received 2
Observable2 Item Received 24
Observable2 Item Received 25
Observable1 Item Received 3
Observable2 Item Received 26
Observable2 Item Received 27
Observable1 Item Received 4
Observable2 Item Received 28
Observable2 Item Received 29
Observable1 Item Received 5
Observable2 Item Received 30
Observable1 Item Received 6
Observable1 Item Received 7
Observable1 Item Received 8
Observable1 Item Received 9
Observable1 Item Received 10

Process finished with exit code 0
```

As the output shows, Observable in this example is emitted concurrently. The line of the subscribeOn(Schedulers.computation()) code enabled both downstreams to subscribe to the Observable in a different (background) thread, which influenced concurrency. You should already be used to it with using it runBlocking { delay(2100) } on comment (3); we use it to keep the program alive. As all the operations are being performed in different threads, we need to block the main thread to keep the program alive. However, notice the time duration of the delay we passed; it's only 2,100 milliseconds, and the output confirms both the subscriptions processed all the emissions. So, it's clear, we saved 1,000 milliseconds right away.

Let's now continue discussions on different types of schedulers available—we will then dive into different ways to use them.

Schedulers.io() - I/O bound scheduler

`Schedulers.io()` provides us with I/O bound threads. To be more accurate, `Schedulers.io()` provides you with `ThreadPool`, which can create an unbounded number of worker threads that are meant to be performing I/O bounded tasks.

Now, what exactly does the I/O bounded thread mean? And why are we calling it I/O bounded? Let's inspect.

All the threads in this pool are blocking and are meant to perform more I/O operations than computationally intense tasks, giving less load to CPUs, but may take longer due to waiting for I/O. By I/O operations, we mean interactions with file systems, databases, services, or I/O devices.

We should be cautious about using this scheduler as it can create an infinite number of threads (until the memory lasts) and can cause `OutOfMemory` errors.

Schedulers.computation() - CPU bound schedulers

The `Schedulers.computation()` is probably the most useful scheduler for programmers. It provides us with a bounded thread-pool, which can contain a number of threads equal to the number of available CPU cores. As the name suggests, this scheduler is meant for CPU intense works.

We should use this scheduler only for CPU—intense tasks and not for any other cause. The reason is that the threads in this scheduler keeps the CPU cores busy, and may slow down the entire application if it is used for I/O bound or any other tasks that involves non-computational tasks.

The main reason why we should consider `Schedulers.io()` for I/O bound tasks and `Schedulers.computation()` for computational purposes is that `computation()` threads utilize the processors better and create no more threads than the available CPU cores, and reuses them. While `Schedulers.io()` is unbounded, and if you schedule 10,000 computational tasks on `io()` in parallel, then each of those 10,000 tasks each have their own thread and be competing for CPU incurring context switching costs.

Schedulers.newThread()

The `Schedulers.newThread()` provides us with a scheduler that creates a new thread for each task provided. While at first glance it may seem similar to `Schedulers.io()`, there's actually a huge difference.

The `Schedulers.io()` uses a thread pool, and whenever it gets a new unit of work, it first looks into the thread pool to see if any idle thread is available to take up the task; it proceeds to create a new thread if no pre-existing thread is available to take up the work.

However, `Schedulers.newThread()` doesn't even use a thread pool; instead, it creates a new thread for every request and forgets them forever.

In most of the cases, when you're not using `Schedulers.computation()`, you should consider `Schedulers.io()` and should predominantly avoid using `Schedulers.newThread()`; threads are very expensive resources, you should try to avoid the creation of new threads as much as possible.

Schedulers.single()

The `Schedulers.single()` provides us with a scheduler that contains only one thread and returns the single instance for every call. Confused? Let's make it clear. Think of a situation where you need to execute tasks that are strongly sequential—`Schedulers.single()` is the best available option for you here. As it provides you with only one thread, every task that you enqueue here is bound to be executed sequentially.

Schedulers.trampoline()

`Schedulers.single()` and `Schedulers.trampoline()` sound somewhat similar, both the schedulers are for sequential execution. While `Schedulers.single()` guarantees that all its task will run sequentially, it may run parallel to the thread it was called upon (if not, that thread is from `Schedulers.single()` as well); the `Schedulers.trampoline()` is different in that sector.

Unlike maintaining a thread to its disposal like `Schedulers.single()`, `Schedulers.trampoline()` queues up the task on the thread it was called on.

So, it'll be sequential with the thread it was called upon.

Let's look at some examples of `Schedulers.single()` and `Schedulers.trampoline()` to understand them better:

```
fun main(args: Array<String>) {

  async(CommonPool) {
    Observable.range(1, 10)
      .subscribeOn(Schedulers.single())//(1)
      .subscribe {
        runBlocking { delay(200) }
        println("Observable1 Item Received $it")
      }

    Observable.range(21, 10)
      .subscribeOn(Schedulers.single())//(2)
      .subscribe {
        runBlocking { delay(100) }
        println("Observable2 Item Received $it")
      }

    for (i in 1..10) {
      delay(100)
      println("Blocking Thread $i")
    }
  }

  runBlocking { delay(6000) }
}
```

The output is as follows:

```
"C:\Program Files\Java\jdk1.8.0_131\bin\java" ...
Blocking Thread 1
Observable1 Item Received 1
Blocking Thread 2
Blocking Thread 3
Observable1 Item Received 2
Blocking Thread 4
Blocking Thread 5
Observable1 Item Received 3
Blocking Thread 6
Blocking Thread 7
Observable1 Item Received 4
Blocking Thread 8
Observable1 Item Received 5
Blocking Thread 9
Blocking Thread 10
Observable1 Item Received 6
Observable1 Item Received 7
Observable1 Item Received 8
Observable1 Item Received 9
Observable1 Item Received 10
Observable2 Item Received 21
Observable2 Item Received 22
Observable2 Item Received 23
Observable2 Item Received 24
Observable2 Item Received 25
Observable2 Item Received 26
Observable2 Item Received 27
Observable2 Item Received 28
Observable2 Item Received 29
Observable2 Item Received 30

Process finished with exit code 0
```

The output clearly shows that despite the fact that both the subscriptions run sequentially, they run in parallel to the calling thread.

Now, let's implement the same code with `Schedulers.trampoline()` and observe the difference:

```
fun main(args: Array<String>) {

    async(CommonPool) {
        Observable.range(1, 10)
            .subscribeOn(Schedulers.trampoline())//(1)
            .subscribe {
                runBlocking { delay(200) }
                println("Observable1 Item Received $it")
            }

        Observable.range(21, 10)
            .subscribeOn(Schedulers.trampoline())//(2)
            .subscribe {
                runBlocking { delay(100) }
                println("Observable2 Item Received $it")
            }

        for (i in 1..10) {
            delay(100)
            println("Blocking Thread $i")
        }
    }

    runBlocking { delay(6000) }
}
```

The following output shows that the scheduler ran sequentially to the calling thread:

```
"C:\Program Files\Java\jdk1.8.0_131\bin\java" ...
Observable1 Item Received 1
Observable1 Item Received 2
Observable1 Item Received 3
Observable1 Item Received 4
Observable1 Item Received 5
Observable1 Item Received 6
Observable1 Item Received 7
Observable1 Item Received 8
Observable1 Item Received 9
Observable1 Item Received 10
Observable2 Item Received 21
Observable2 Item Received 22
Observable2 Item Received 23
Observable2 Item Received 24
Observable2 Item Received 25
Observable2 Item Received 26
Observable2 Item Received 27
Observable2 Item Received 28
Observable2 Item Received 29
Observable2 Item Received 30
Blocking Thread 1
Blocking Thread 2
Blocking Thread 3
Blocking Thread 4
Blocking Thread 5
Blocking Thread 6
Blocking Thread 7
Blocking Thread 8
Blocking Thread 9
Blocking Thread 10

Process finished with exit code 0
```

Schedulers.from

So far, we've seen the default/predefined schedulers available within RxKotlin. However, while developing applications, you may need to define your custom scheduler. Keeping that scenario in mind, ReactiveX has provided you with `Schedulers.from(executor:Executor)`, which lets you convert any executor into a scheduler.

Let's look at the following example:

```
fun main(args: Array<String>) {

    val executor:Executor = Executors.newFixedThreadPool(2)//(1)
    val scheduler:Scheduler = Schedulers.from(executor)//(2)

    Observable.range(1, 10)
      .subscribeOn(scheduler)//(3)
      .subscribe {
        runBlocking { delay(200) }
        println("Observable1 Item Received $it -
        ${Thread.currentThread().name}")
      }

    Observable.range(21, 10)
      .subscribeOn(scheduler)//(4)
      .subscribe {
          runBlocking { delay(100) }
          println("Observable2 Item Received $it -
          ${Thread.currentThread().name}")
      }

    Observable.range(51, 10)
       .subscribeOn(scheduler)//(5)
       .subscribe {
           runBlocking { delay(100) }
           println("Observable3 Item Received $it -
           ${Thread.currentThread().name}")
       }
       runBlocking { delay(10000) }//(6)
}
```

In this example, we've created a custom Scheduler from an Executor (for the sake of simplicity, we've used a standard Thread Pool Executor; you're free to use your own custom executor).

On comment (1), we created the executor with the Executors.newFixedThreadPool() method, on comment (2), we created the scheduler instance with the help of Schedulers.from(executor:Executor). We used the scheduler instance on comment (3), comment (4), and comment (5).

Here is the output:

```
"c:\Program Files\Java\jdk1.8.0_131\bin\java" ...
Observable2 Item Received 21 - pool-1-thread-2
Observable1 Item Received 1 - pool-1-thread-1
Observable2 Item Received 22 - pool-1-thread-2
Observable2 Item Received 23 - pool-1-thread-2
Observable1 Item Received 2 - pool-1-thread-1
Observable2 Item Received 24 - pool-1-thread-2
Observable2 Item Received 25 - pool-1-thread-2
Observable1 Item Received 3 - pool-1-thread-1
Observable2 Item Received 26 - pool-1-thread-2
Observable2 Item Received 27 - pool-1-thread-2
Observable1 Item Received 4 - pool-1-thread-1
Observable2 Item Received 28 - pool-1-thread-2
Observable2 Item Received 29 - pool-1-thread-2
Observable1 Item Received 5 - pool-1-thread-1
Observable2 Item Received 30 - pool-1-thread-2
Observable3 Item Received 51 - pool-1-thread-2
Observable1 Item Received 6 - pool-1-thread-1
Observable3 Item Received 52 - pool-1-thread-2
Observable3 Item Received 53 - pool-1-thread-2
Observable1 Item Received 7 - pool-1-thread-1
Observable3 Item Received 54 - pool-1-thread-2
Observable3 Item Received 55 - pool-1-thread-2
Observable1 Item Received 8 - pool-1-thread-1
Observable3 Item Received 56 - pool-1-thread-2
Observable1 Item Received 9 - pool-1-thread-1
Observable3 Item Received 57 - pool-1-thread-2
Observable3 Item Received 58 - pool-1-thread-2
Observable1 Item Received 10 - pool-1-thread-1
Observable3 Item Received 59 - pool-1-thread-2
Observable3 Item Received 60 - pool-1-thread-2

Process finished with exit code 1
```

How to use schedulers – subscribeOn and observeOn operators

Now that we have gained some grip on what schedulers are, how many types of schedulers are available, and how to create a `scheduler` instance, we will focus on how to use schedulers.

There are basically two operators that help us implement schedulers. Up until now, in this chapter, we've used the subscribeOn operator in all the examples with a scheduler; however, there's another operator—observeOn. We will now focus on these two operators, learning how they work, and how they differ.

Let's start with the subscribeOn operator.

Changing thread on subscription – subscribeOn operator

We need to understand how the Observable works before delving any further in how to use scheduler. Let's take a look at the following graphics:

```
"C:\Program Files\Java\jdk1.8.0_131\bin\java" ...
Mapping 1 - main
Received 1 - main
Mapping 2 - main
Received 2 - main
Mapping 3 - main
Received 3 - main
Mapping 4 - main
Received 4 - main
Mapping 5 - main
Received 5 - main
Mapping 6 - main
Received 6 - main
Mapping 7 - main
Received 7 - main
Mapping 8 - main
Received 8 - main
Mapping 9 - main
Received 9 - main
Mapping 10 - main
Received 10 - main

Process finished with exit code 0
```

As the preceding image depicts, it's the threads that are responsible for carrying items from the source all the way to the Subscriber through operators. It may be a single thread throughout the subscription, or it may even be different threads at different levels.

By default, the thread in which we perform the subscription is the responsible of bringing all the emissions down to the Subscriber, unless we instruct it otherwise.

Let's take a look at the code example first:

```
fun main(args: Array<String>) {
    listOf("1","2","3","4","5","6","7","8","9","10")
        .toObservable()
        .map {
            item->
            println("Mapping $item ${Thread.currentThread().name}")
            return@map item.toInt()
        }
        .subscribe {
            item -> println("Received $item
            ${Thread.currentThread().name}")
        }

}
```

It's a simple RxKotlin code example; we are creating `Observable`, mapping it, and then subscribing to it. The only difference here is that I've printed the `Thread` name inside both the `map` and the `subscribe` lambdas.

Let's take a look at the output:

```
"C:\Program Files\Java\jdk1.8.0_131\bin\java" ...
Mapping 1 - RxComputationThreadPool-1
Received 1 - RxComputationThreadPool-1
Mapping 2 - RxComputationThreadPool-1
Received 2 - RxComputationThreadPool-1
Mapping 3 - RxComputationThreadPool-1
Received 3 - RxComputationThreadPool-1
Mapping 4 - RxComputationThreadPool-1
Received 4 - RxComputationThreadPool-1
Mapping 5 - RxComputationThreadPool-1
Received 5 - RxComputationThreadPool-1
Mapping 6 - RxComputationThreadPool-1
Received 6 - RxComputationThreadPool-1
Mapping 7 - RxComputationThreadPool-1
Received 7 - RxComputationThreadPool-1
Mapping 8 - RxComputationThreadPool-1
Received 8 - RxComputationThreadPool-1
Mapping 9 - RxComputationThreadPool-1
Received 9 - RxComputationThreadPool-1
Mapping 10 - RxComputationThreadPool-1
Received 10 - RxComputationThreadPool-1

Process finished with exit code 0
```

From the output, we can determine that the main thread executes the entire subscription.

The `subscribeOn` operator, as the name suggests, helps us change the thread of a subscription. Let's modify the program once and take a look:

```kotlin
fun main(args: Array<String>) {
  listOf("1","2","3","4","5","6","7","8","9","10")
    .toObservable()
    .map {
      item->
      println("Mapping $item - ${Thread.currentThread().name}")
      return@map item.toInt()
    }
```

```
.subscribeOn(Schedulers.computation())//(1)
.subscribe {
    item -> println("Received $item -
    ${Thread.currentThread().name}")
}

runBlocking { delay(1000) }
}
```

The entire program remains the same, except that, in between `map` and `subscribe`, we used the `subscribeOn` operator at comment `(1)`. Let's check the output:

```
"C:\Program Files\Java\jdk1.8.0_131\bin\java" ...
Mapping 1 - RxComputationThreadPool-1
Mapping 2 - RxComputationThreadPool-1
Mapping 3 - RxComputationThreadPool-1
Mapping 4 - RxComputationThreadPool-1
Mapping 5 - RxComputationThreadPool-1
Mapping 6 - RxComputationThreadPool-1
Mapping 7 - RxComputationThreadPool-1
Mapping 8 - RxComputationThreadPool-1
Mapping 9 - RxComputationThreadPool-1
Mapping 10 - RxComputationThreadPool-1
Received 1 - RxCachedThreadScheduler-1
Received 2 - RxCachedThreadScheduler-1
Received 3 - RxCachedThreadScheduler-1
Received 4 - RxCachedThreadScheduler-1
Received 5 - RxCachedThreadScheduler-1
Received 6 - RxCachedThreadScheduler-1
Received 7 - RxCachedThreadScheduler-1
Received 8 - RxCachedThreadScheduler-1
Received 9 - RxCachedThreadScheduler-1
Received 10 - RxCachedThreadScheduler-1

Process finished with exit code 0
```

The `subscribeOn` operator changes the thread for the entire subscription; you can use it wherever you want in the subscription flow. It will change the thread once and for all.

Observing on a different thread – observeOn operator

While `subscribeOn` looks like an awesome gift from heaven, it may not be suited in some cases. For example, you may want to do computations on the `computation` threads and display the results from the `io` threads, which actually you should do. The `subscribeOn` operator requires a companion for all these things; while it'll specify the thread for the entire subscription, it requires its companion to specify threads for specific operators.

The perfect companion to the `subscribeOn` operator is the `observeOn` operator. The `observéOn` operator specifies the scheduler for all the operators called after it.

Let's modify our program with `observeOn` to perform the `map` operation in the `Schedulers.computation()` and receive the result of the subscription (`onNext`) in the `Schedulers.io()`:

```kotlin
fun main(args: Array<String>) {
    listOf("1","2","3","4","5","6","7","8","9","10")
        .toObservable()
        .observeOn(Schedulers.computation())//(1)
        .map {
            item->
            println("Mapping $item - ${Thread.currentThread().name}")
            return@map item.toInt()
        }
        .observeOn(Schedulers.io())//(2)
        .subscribe {
            item -> println("Received $item -
            ${Thread.currentThread().name}")
        }

    runBlocking { delay(1000) }
}
```

Chapter 7

The following output clearly shows we're successful in achieving our objective:

```
"C:\Program Files\Java\jdk1.8.0_131\bin\java" ...
Mapping 1 - RxComputationThreadPool-1
Mapping 2 - RxComputationThreadPool-1
Mapping 3 - RxComputationThreadPool-1
Mapping 4 - RxComputationThreadPool-1
Mapping 5 - RxComputationThreadPool-1
Mapping 6 - RxComputationThreadPool-1
Mapping 7 - RxComputationThreadPool-1
Mapping 8 - RxComputationThreadPool-1
Mapping 9 - RxComputationThreadPool-1
Mapping 10 - RxComputationThreadPool-1
Received 1 - RxCachedThreadScheduler-1
Received 2 - RxCachedThreadScheduler-1
Received 3 - RxCachedThreadScheduler-1
Received 4 - RxCachedThreadScheduler-1
Received 5 - RxCachedThreadScheduler-1
Received 6 - RxCachedThreadScheduler-1
Received 7 - RxCachedThreadScheduler-1
Received 8 - RxCachedThreadScheduler-1
Received 9 - RxCachedThreadScheduler-1
Received 10 - RxCachedThreadScheduler-1

Process finished with exit code 0
```

So, what did we do? We specified the computation threads for the map operator by calling observeOn(Schedulers.computation()) just before it, and called observeOn(Schedulers.io()) before subscribe to switch to io threads to receive the results.

In this program, we did a context switch; we exchanged data with threads and implemented communication in between threads with such an ease, with merely 7-8 lines of code—that's the abstraction schedulers provides us with.

Summary

In this chapter, you learned about concurrent execution and parallelism and how to achieve multithreading in RxKotlin. Multithreading is a necessity in today's app driven era, as modern users don't like to wait, or, to be blocked, you need to constantly switch threads to perform computations and UX operations.

In this chapter, you learned how schedulers in RxKotlin can help you, or, rather, how schedulers abstract the complexities of multithreading.

While concurrent execution and parallelism is an essential part of modern application development, testing is probably the most crucial part. We cannot deliver any app without testing it. Agile methodology (though we are not discussing agile here) says we should perform testing repeatedly and with every iteration of our product (application) development.

In the Chapter 8, *Testing RxKotlin Applications*, we will discuss testing. Don't dare miss it out, turn the page right now!

8
Testing RxKotlin Applications

We have covered more than 60% of the book and have learned a lot of concepts. From the first chapter, starting with concepts of reactive programming till the previous chapter about concurrent execution and parallelism. But we cannot complete the application development without introducing a few tests. It is probably the most crucial point in the process of application development.

This chapter is dedicated to testing. As Kotlin itself is relatively new, our first objective would be to learn testing in Kotlin. We will then proceed with testing in RxKotlin. The following are the topics we are going to cover in this chapter:

- Introduction to unit testing and its importance
- Kotlin and JUnit, Kotlin-test
- Testing tools in RxKotlin
- Blocking subscribers
- Blocking operators
- `TestObserver` and `TestSubscriber`

So let's get started.

Introduction to unit testing and its importance

While testing is absolute necessary in application development, many novice developers get away with a few basic questions regarding testing. They are:

- What is unit testing? and why is it a developer's job?
- Why is unit testing so important?
- And, do we need to write unit tests for each section of our programs?

We will start this chapter by answering these basic questions. If you would like to rather start with testing using RxKotlin directly, you can skip the first few sections in this chapter and start from *Testing tools in RxKotlin*. Though I would encourage you to read the chapter throughout, even if you have previous experience in testing with Kotlin.

Let's start by defining unit testing. Unit testing is a level of software testing where the individual smallest testable components of a software (aka application), called **units** are tested. The purpose is to validate that each unit of the software performs as it was supposed to.

Unit tests can be done manually, but they are often automated. The sole purpose of automated unit testing is to reduce human error and eliminate any extra bugs/errors caused by them. To explain let's first remember the proverb:

To err is human

So, if we do the unit tests manually, the chances of additional errors or bugs will rise. Automated unit tests can eliminate this risk as they include minimal human effort.

Also, we need to document the tests we've performed, and we need to perform the same tests again with new ones with each incremental build of our product. Automated unit tests eliminate that extra effort, as you would be required to write the test once and then you can run them any time in the future. Also, automated unit tests also reduce documentation efforts.

Why is it a developer's job? Who would write the code for automated testing other than the developers?

Also, it is not possible for developers to give understanding to tester after completing each small units of an application. Even you may have completed some module, which is not yet on the GUI, so the tester or anyone else than you may not even be able to reach that unit to test. Also, it may not have any direct impact or relation with the UI/UX, it may be a small internal code part.

To summarize, a developer better understands his code and he knows well what exactly he wants from that bunch of code. So the developer is the best person to write unit tests on that module.

Why is unit testing so important?

Let's have a real-life example. Think of an engineer, creating a new motor or device. The engineer will test the functionality after completing each unit of that motor, rather than testing the whole motor at the end (though he / she will test the whole motor at the end, but will also test it repeatedly and incrementally while building it). The main reason behind this behavior is that if he / she doesn't do that, at the end it would take a lot effort to identify the exact problems (if any). While testing incrementally will allow you to fix any problem right away as soon as it arises. The same applies for software (applications) as well.

You should perform unit tests periodically and repeatedly as you develop each module of your application the more you test the better is the out product. And yes, **we should write unit tests for each and every functional section of our applications**.

 By **functional section** we mean each section that performs any small operation and/or function. We can skip testing a POJO class with just getters and setters, but we must test the code which uses that POJO class to accomplish something.

So, as we've understood the importance of testing, let's start by writing JUnit tests in Kotlin.

Writing JUnit tests in Kotlin

If you've any experience with Java development, you've heard of or most probably worked with JUnit. It is a testing framework, for Java (as well as Kotlin).

Typically unit tests are created in a separate source folder than real source codes, to keep it separated. The standard Maven/Gradle convention uses `src/main` for real codes (Java/Kotlin files or classes) and `src/test` for test classes. The following screenshot shows the structure for the project we're using in this book:

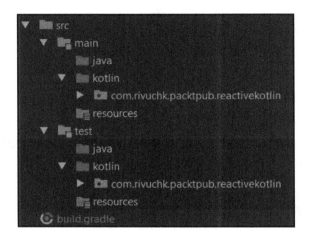

Before beginning to write test cases we've to add the following Gradle dependencies:

```
testCompile 'junit:junit:4.12'
testCompile "org.mockito:mockito-core:1.9.5"
testCompile "org.jetbrains.kotlin:kotlin-test-
   junit:$kotlin_version"
```

We've added a dependency to Mockito as well, which we are going to cover soon.

So, we have got everything ready, let's write our first test case. Please refer to the following code:

```
package com.rivuchk.packtpub.reactivekotlin

import org.junit.Test
import kotlin.test.assertEquals

class TestClass {
  @Test//(1)
  fun `my first test`() {//(2)
    assertEquals(3,1+2)//(3)
  }
}
```

Have a close look at the preceding program. Each JUnit test case should be defined as a function inside a class. The class that contains the JUnit test functions should only be used for testing purposes and should not serve any other purpose. The `test` function should be annotated with the `@Test` annotation, as we did in comment (1). This annotation helps JUnit to detect and execute the tests.

Now, give a cautious look at the line containing comment (2). The function name is `` `my first test` `` (). Yes, it contains space within the function name. That is probably the best thing you can get while writing test cases in Kotlin. Kotlin allows you to have functions that have names without spaces, while they aren't good practice while writing codes, they are quite a life saver while writing tests; as you don't need to call the `test` functions elsewhere, they actually serve as readable test names.

In comment (3), we wrote the actual test. The `assertEquals` test checks for equality between `expected` and `actual` values. The first parameter in this test is the expected value, and the second one is the actual one, which should be equal to the expected one.

If you run the test, you'll get the following output:

If we modify the program and pass 2+3 instead of 1+2 as the actual parameter, then the test would fail and give the following output:

You can also pass a failure message, that would be shown in case of failure, as follows:

```
class TestClass {
  @Test//(1)
  fun `my first test`() {//(2)
    assertEquals(3,2+3, "Actual value is not equal to the expected
    one.")//(3)
  }
}
```

The message would be shown in the error report if the test fails. Have a look at the following output:

Testing your code

In the earlier section, we learned how to write test cases, but did we test our code? No. We did the tests with some oblivious values. And we know that is not the purpose of tests. Tests are there to make sure that our functions, classes, and code blocks are working as expected.

We should write the tests on top of our existing code (unless we are following **Test-driven development (TDD)**).

Test-driven development is a development methodology where tests are written first, and then the actual source code is written that would pass the test cases. Test-driven development is hugely popular among developers and architects and many companies follow TDD as their development process.

The following is a small Kotlin file that contains a few methods for calculations, we would perform tests on top of this file:

```
package com.rivuchk.packtpub.reactivekotlin.chapter8

fun add(a:Int, b:Int):Int = a+b
fun substract(a:Int, b:Int):Int = a-b
fun mult(a:Int, b:Int):Int = a*b
fun divide(a:Int, b:Int):Int = a/b
```

And, following class is with the test cases, go through the code carefully, and then we will describe it:

```
package com.rivuchk.packtpub.reactivekotlin.chapter8//(1)

import org.junit.Test
import kotlin.test.*

class TestCalculator {
  @Test
  fun `addition test`() {//(2)
    assertEquals(1 + 2, add(1,2))
  }
  @Test
  fun `substraction test`() {//(3)
    assertEquals(8-5, substract(8,5))
  }
  @Test
  fun `multiplication test`() {//(4)
    assertEquals(4 * 2, mult(4,2))
   }
  @Test
  fun `division test`() {//(5)
    assertEquals(8 / 2, divide(8,2))
  }
}
```

Have a look at the package declarations. Both files share the same package name, we deliberately did this, so that we would not have to import the functions.

We used the simplest functions in the source code so that you can understand the code easily. Also notice that we wrote each test case separately, just like a function, we can obviously call multiple test functions within a test case, though. Confused? Let's elaborate, when you're testing multiple aspects of a single function or property you can (and should) group them all inside a test function (a function with an `@Test` annotation). Generally, compilers display test results as they encounter test functions, irrespective of how many tests each test function performs. So rest assured that your tests will be performed if you group them inside a single test function, they will however be shown as a single test. However when you're writing tests for separate functions or properties you would obviously want a separate report for all of them, in that case you should write them separately just like the earlier example.

Have a look at the output now:

But in each of the earlier examples, we used only `assertEquals`; seeing this, you may have a question, is `assertEquals` the only test function available? The answer is a big no. We've plenty of test functions available with Kotlin. The following are a few test cases with oblivious values, just to have an idea about the most useful test functions in Kotlin. Please refer to the following code:

```
package com.rivuchk.packtpub.reactivekotlin.chapter8

import org.junit.Test
import java.util.*
import kotlin.test.*

class TestFunctions {

  @Test
  fun `expected block evaluation`() {
    expect(10,{
      val x=5
      val y=2
      x*y
    })
  }

  @Test
  fun `assert illegal value`() {
```

```
      assertNotEquals(-1,Random().nextInt(1))
    }

    @Test
    fun `assert true boolean value`() {
        assertTrue(true)
    }

    @Test
    fun `assert false boolean value`() {
        assertFalse(false)
    }

    @Test
    fun `assert that passed value is null`() {
        assertNull(null)
    }

    @Test
    fun `assert that passed value is not null`() {
        assertNotNull(null)
    }
}
```

Before inspecting the test cases here, let's have a look at the following test output screenshot:

Now, let's try to understand the code. We will start with the `expected block evaluation`() test. The `expect` test function takes the expected value as the first parameter and a block (lambda) as the second parameter, executes the lambda, and checks the return value against the expected value for equality.

The second test case was `assert illegal value` (), in that test case we are using the `assertNotEquals()` test method. This test method does the exact opposite than the `assertEquals()`. It fails the test if both parameters are equal. The `assertNotEquals()` is especially useful when you've a function that should return any value except a particular one.

In the `assert true boolean value` () and `assert true boolean value` () test cases we used `assertTrue()` and `assertFalse()` respectively. Both test methods takes a `Boolean` value as parameter. As the name suggests, `assertTrue()` expects the value to be `true`, while `assertFalse()` expects to be `false`.

The next two test cases are for nulls. The first one `assert that passed value is null` () uses `assertNull()`, which expects the passed value to contain `null`. The second one uses `assertNotNull()` in complete opposite way, expects the value would not be `null`.

So, as we got some hands-on idea on writing test cases, let's get started with testing in **RxKotlin**.

Testing in RxKotlin

Now, as you've some hands-on testing in Kotlin and have some idea about RxKotlin as well, you may be wondering how to implement test cases in RxKotlin? It is true that testing in RxKotlin may not seem straightforward; the reason is that ReactiveX defines behavior rather than states, and most testing frameworks, including JUnit and kotlin—test are good for testing states.

To the aid of developers, RxKotlin comes with a set of tools for testing, which you can use with your favorite testing frameworks. In this book, we will cover testing in RxKotlin with JUnit and Kotlin-test.

So, what are we waiting for? Let's get started.

Blocking subscribers

Try to remember the code blocks from previous chapters, where we used `delay` to make the main thread wait whenever we used an `Observable` or `Flowable` that operates on a different thread. A perfect example of this scenario is when we used `Observable.interval` as a factory method or when we used the `subscribeOn` operator. To get you refreshed, following is such a code example:

```
fun main(args: Array<String>) {
  Observable.range(1,10)
      .subscribeOn(Schedulers.computation())
      .subscribe {
          item -> println("Received $item")
      }
  runBlocking { delay(10) }
}
```

In this example, we switched to `Schedulers.computation` for the subscription. Now let's see, how we can test this Observable and check that we received exactly `10` emissions:

```
@Test
fun `check emissions count` () {
  val emissionsCount = AtomicInteger()//(1)
  Observable.range(1,10)
      .subscribeOn(Schedulers.computation())
      .blockingSubscribe {//(2)
        _ -> emissionsCount.incrementAndGet()
      }

      assertEquals(10,emissionsCount.get())//(3)
}
```

Let's have a look at the testing result first before digging into the code:

There are a few things that need explanations in this code. The first one is `AtomicInteger`. `AtomicInteger` is a wrapper around integer in Java, that allows an `Int` value to be updated atomically. Though `AtomicInteger` extends `Number` to allow uniform access by tools and utilities that deal with numerically-based classes, it cannot be used as a replacement of `Integer`. We used `AtomicInteger` in this code to ensure atomicity, as the subscription was running in the `computationScheduler` (thus in multiple threads).

The line, that demands our attention is where we put comment `(2)`. We used `blockingSubscribe` instead of just `subscribe`. When we subscribe to a producer with the `subscribe` operator and the subscription is not in the current thread, the current thread doesn't wait for the subscription to complete and moves to the next line instantly. That's why we used delay to make the current thread wait. Using `delay` inside `tests` is troublesome. While `blockingSubscribe` blocks the current running thread until the subscription finishes up (even if the subscription occurs in a separate thread), that is useful while writing tests.

Blocking operators

While `blockingSubscribe` is useful in testing, it cannot always serve your purpose. You might need to test the first, last or all the values of the producer. For that purpose you would need the data in its pure imperative nature.

The set of yet uncovered operators in RxKotlin is at your helm in that scenario. The blocking operators serve as an immediate accessible bridge between the reactive world and the imperative world. They block the current thread and make it wait for the results to be emitted, but returns them in a non-reactive way.

The only similarity between `blockingSubscribe` and blocking operators are that both block the declaring thread even if the reactive operations are performed in a different thread.

Other than this one, there are no more similarities. The `blockingSubscribe` treats the data as reactive and doesn't return anything. It rather pushes them to the subscriber (or lambda) specified. Whereas blocking operators will return the data in a non-reactive nature.

The following list contains the blocking operators we are going to cover:

- `blockingFirst()`
- `blockingGet()`
- `blockingLast()`

- blockingIterable()
- blockingForEach()

Though we should avoid using them in production as they encourage anti-patterns and reduce the benefits of reactive programming, however we can surely use them for testing purposes.

Getting the first emitted item – blockingFirst()

The first blocking operator we are going discuss is the blockingFirst operator. This operator blocks the calling thread until the first item is emitted and returns it. The following is an ideal test case for blockingFirst(), where we are performing a sorting operation on Observable and we are testing it by checking if the first emitted item is the smallest. Please refer to the following code:

```
@Test
fun `test with blockingFirst`() {
    val observable = listOf(2,10,5,6,9,8,7,1,4,3).toObservable()
            .sorted()
    val firstItem = observable.blockingFirst()
    assertEquals(1,firstItem)
}
```

The test result is as follows:

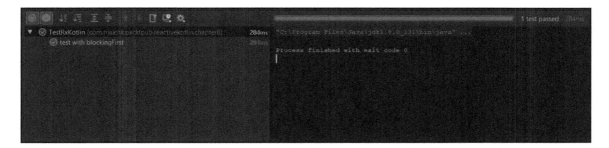

In the program, we created an unsorted list of integers from 1 to 10 and created an Observable with the list, so the smallest item from that Observable should be 1. We obtained the first item and made the thread to wait till we get it with the help of the blockingFirst() operator.

Then used the assertEquals testing function to assert that the first emitted item is 1.

Getting the only item from single or maybe - blockingGet

When you're working with single or maybe, you just can't use any other blocking operator other than blockingGet(). The reason is quite simple, both monads can contain only one item.

So, let's create two new test cases by modifying the last test case as follows:

```
@Test
fun `test Single with blockingGet`() {
  val observable = listOf(2,10,5,6,9,8,7,1,4,3).toObservable()
          .sorted()

  val firstElement:Single<Int> = observable.first(0)

  val firstItem = firstElement.blockingGet()
  assertEquals(1,firstItem)
}

@Test
fun `test Maybe with blockingGet`() {
  val observable = listOf(2,10,5,6,9,8,7,1,4,3).toObservable()
          .sorted()

  val firstElement:Maybe<Int> = observable.firstElement()

  val firstItem = firstElement.blockingGet()
  assertEquals(1,firstItem)
}
```

In the first test case, we used observable.first() with a default value, this operator returns a Single; on the second operator, we used observable.firstElement() this operator returns a Maybe. Then we used blockingGet in both test cases to get the first element as an Int and execute the test function.

So, following screenshot is the test result:

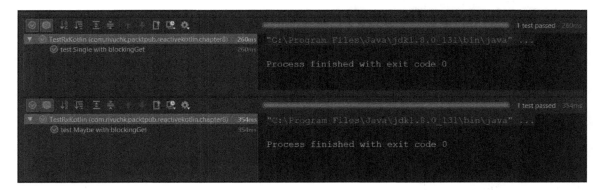

Getting the last Item - blockingLast

We have `blockingFirst`, so it's quite obvious that we would have `blockingLast`. As expected, it gets you the last emitted item while blocking the thread until the source emits it. The following is the code example:

```
@Test
fun `test with blockingLast`() {
  val observable = listOf(2,10,5,6,9,8,7,1,4,3).toObservable()
          .sorted()

  val firstItem = observable.blockingLast()
  assertEquals(10,firstItem)
}
```

As we are expecting the last emitted item, we are checking equality with 10.

Following is the screenshot of the testing result:

Getting all emissions as iterable - blockingIterable operator

So, we fetched the first emitted item, we fetched the last emitted item, but what if we want all the items emitted for testing? The `blockingIterable` operator gets you with the same. The `blockingIterable` operator works in an interesting way, it passes an emission to the `Iterable`, then the `Iterable` will keep blocking the iterating thread until the next emission is available. This operator queues up unconsumed values until the `Iterator` can consume them, and this can cause `OutOfMemory` exceptions.

So following is an example, where we are obtaining the complete list and then we are checking if the emissions were sorted by converting the returned `Iterable` to `List` and checking equality with the source `list` after sorting. Please refer to the following code:

```
@Test
fun `test with blockingIterable`() {
  val list = listOf(2,10,5,6,9,8,7,1,4,3)

  val observable = list.toObservable()
          .sorted()

  val iterable = observable.blockingIterable()
  assertEquals(list.sorted(),iterable.toList())
}
```

If the emissions were sorted, the `iterable`, when converted to `list`, should be equal to `list.sorted()`.

Following is the screenshot of the test result:

Looping through all emissions - blockingForEach

If you want to loop through all the emissions then `blockingForEach` is probably a better solution. It's better than `blockingIterable` as it will not queue up the emissions. Rather will it block the calling thread and wait for each emission to be processed before allowing the thread to continue.

In the following example, we created an `Observable` from a list of `Int`. Then applied a filter for even numbers only and then within the `blockingForEach` we are testing whether all the received numbers are even:

```
@Test
fun `test with blockingForEach`() {
  val list =
  listOf(2,10,5,6,9,8,7,1,4,3,12,20,15,16,19,18,17,11,14,13)

  val observable = list.toObservable()
    .filter { item -> item%2==0 }

  observable.forEach {
      item->
      assertTrue { item%2==0 }
  }
}
```

The result of the test is as follows:

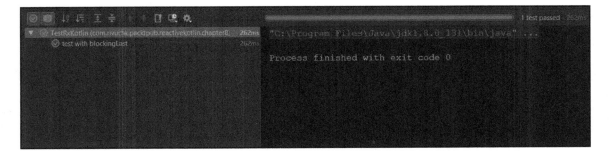

We covered the most useful blocking operators up until now. They are useful for simple assertions and can effectively block the code so that we can perform our testing operations.

However, using blocking code does no good in production. While it seems that using blocking code for testing is ok, but it is actually not. It can do significant harm to keep you from the benefits of testing. How? Just think of multiple Observables/Flowables are emitting concurrently for your application, if you put them on the blocking code their complete behavior may change and as a result you'll be deprived from the benefits of unit testing.

So, what is the way out? Let's see.

Introducing TestObserver and TestSubscriber

As you read through this chapter, you may have developed an idea that the only way we can perform tests are through blocking the code, either by using `blockingSubscribe` or by using blocking operators. *But this is not the case.* In fact, there are more comprehensive ways to reactive code, or rather we can say that we can test reactive code reactively.

To say it more precisely, in a Subscriber we have `onError` and `onComplete` that demands testing along with `onNext`, which is not always possible with just blocking. Yes some sort of blocking is necessary, but it cannot alone do all the things and it also needs to be managed reactively.

So, here are your two superheroes to make the developers life easy—`TestObserver` and `TestSubscriber`. As with `Subscriber` and `Observer`, you can use `TestSubscriber` with `Flowables` and `TestObserver` with `Observables`, everything except that is similar between these two.

So, let's get started with an example:

```
@Test
fun `test with TestObserver`() {
 val list =
 listOf(2,10,5,6,9,8,7,1,4,3,12,20,15,16,19,18,17,11,14,13)

 val observable = list.toObservable().sorted()

 val testObserver = TestObserver<Int>()
 observable.subscribe(testObserver)//(1)

 testObserver.assertSubscribed()//(2)

 testObserver.awaitTerminalEvent()//(3)
```

```
testObserver.assertNoErrors()//(4)
testObserver.assertComplete()//(5)
testObserver.assertValueCount(20)//(6)
testObserver.assertValues
(1,2,3,4,5,6,7,8,9,10,11,12,13,14,15,16,17,18,19,20)//(7)
}

@Test
fun `test with TestSubscriber`() {
val list =
listOf(2,10,5,6,9,8,7,1,4,3,12,20,15,16,19,18,17,11,14,13)

val flowable = list.toFlowable().sorted()

val testSubscriber = TestSubscriber<Int>()

flowable.subscribe(testSubscriber)//(1)

testSubscriber.assertSubscribed()//(2)

testSubscriber.awaitTerminalEvent()//(3)

testSubscriber.assertNoErrors()//(4)
testSubscriber.assertComplete()//(5)
testSubscriber.assertValueCount(20)//(6)
testSubscriber.assertValues
(1,2,3,4,5,6,7,8,9,10,11,12,13,14,15,16,17,18,19,20)//(7)
}
```

So we did perform the same set of tests with `TestObserver` and `TestSubscriber`. The test result is obviously passed:

Let's now understand the test cases. On comment (1), we are subscribing to the Observable/Flowable. On comment (2), we are checking if the Subscription was successful and was only one with the help of the `assertSubscribed()` test. On comment (3), we are blocking the thread until the Observable/Flowable completes its execution with the `awaitTerminalEvent()` method. This terminal event can be `onComplete` or `onError` as well. On comments (4) and (5), we are checking whether the `Observable` and/or `Flowable` has completed successfully without any errors, `assertNoErrors()` will test whether the Subscription hasn't received any errors and `assertComplete()` will test whether the producer has completed successfully . On comment (6), we are testing that the total received emission count was 20 (there were 20 items in the list), `assertValuesCount()` helps us with this objective. On comment (6), with the help of `assertValues()` we are testing the expected and actual values of each of the emissions in its order.

So it was cool, right? The next thing I'm going to show is probably cooler.

Understanding TestScheduler

Think of an Observable/Flowable created with the `Observable.interval()` / `Flowable.interval()` factory method. If you have given a long interval (say five minutes) in them and have tested at least say 100 emissions then it would take a long time for testing to complete (500 minutes = 8.3 hours, that is, a complete man-hour just to test a single producer). Now if you have more producers like that with a larger interval and more emissions to test then it would probably take the whole lifetime to test, when would you ship the product then?

`TestScheduler` is here to save your life. They can effectively simulate time with time-driven producers so that we can do assertions by fast-forwarding it by a specific amount.

So, the following is the respective implementation:

```
@Test
fun `test by fast forwarding time`() {
  val testScheduler = TestScheduler()

  val observable =
  Observable.interval(5,TimeUnit.MINUTES,testScheduler)
  val testObserver = TestObserver<Long>()

  observable.subscribe(testObserver)
  testObserver.assertSubscribed()
  testObserver.assertValueCount(0)//(1)
```

```
    testScheduler.advanceTimeBy(100,TimeUnit.MINUTES)//(2)
    testObserver.assertValueCount(20)//(3)

    testScheduler.advanceTimeBy(400,TimeUnit.MINUTES)//(4)
    testObserver.assertValueCount(100)//(5)
}
```

So, here we created an `Observable` with `Observable.interval` with a 5 minute interval and `TestScheduler` as its `Scheduler`.

On comment `(1)`, it should not receive any emissions (as there are still 5 minutes before it should receive its first emission) and we are testing it with `assertValuesCount(0)`.

We then fast-forwarded the time by `100` minutes on comment `(2)`, and tested whether we received `20` emissions on comment `(3)`. `TestScheduler` provides us with the `advanceTimeBy` method, which takes a timespan and unit as parameters and simulates that for us.

We then fast-forwarded time by another `400` minutes and tested if we received a total of 100 emissions on comment `(4)` and comment `(5)`.

As you would expect, the test passes.

Summary

So, in this chapter, we learned about testing in Kotlin. We started with the benefits of testing and then moved on to testing in Kotlin, using JUnit and Kotlin-test.

As we got some hands-on testing experience in Kotlin, we gradually moved to testing in RxKotlin, we learned a few technique to test RxKotlin and learnt about the super-convenient testing tools that RxKotlin provides for us.

As we have built a strong base of knowledge in RxKotlin, in the next chapter—`Chapter 9`, *Resource Management and Extending RxKotlin* we are going to discuss some advanced topics. We will discuss managing resources—how to free allocated memory and prevent memory leaks. We will also learn to create our own custom operators, which can be chained in the RxKotlin logic just like those predefined operators.

So, what are you waiting for? Get started on `Chapter 9`, *Resource Management and Extending RxKotlin*, right now, and from now on don't forget to test every code you write.

9
Resource Management and Extending RxKotlin

So far, you've learned about Observables, Flowables, Subjects, processors, operators, combining producers, testing, and many more things. We have gained most of the necessary knowledge to start coding our applications. The only remaining topic to look at is resource management—the technique of creating, accessing, and cleaning up resources. Also if you're one of the developers who is hungry for a challenge, then you'll always look for ways to customize everything. So far in this book, we've seen how to use operators in their prescribed way. We did nothing innovative and didn't try to customize the operators. So, this chapter is dedicated to resource management and extending RxKotlin through custom operators.

The following list contains the topics we will cover in this chapter:

- Resource management with the `using` method
- Creating custom operators with the `lift` operator
- Creating custom transformers (transforming operators) with the `compose` operator

So, first things first, let's get started with resource management.

Resource management

Resource management, what does it mean? Why should we care about it? If you've a little experience in application development with Java,Kotlin,JavaScript, or any other language, then you're probably familiar with the fact that while developing applications, we often need to access resources, and we must close them when we are done.

If you're not experienced with that phrase, resource management, then let's break things down. We will be starting from the ground by exploring the definition of a resource.

So, what is resource? When developing applications, you may often need to access an API (through an HTTP connection), access a database, read from/write to a file, or you may even need to access any I/O ports/sockets/devices. All these things are considered **resources** in general.

Why do we need to manage/close them? Whenever we are accessing a resource, especially to write, the system often locks it for us, and blocks its access to any other program. If you don't release or close a resource when you're done, system performance may degrade and there may even be a deadlock. Even if the system doesn't lock the resource for us, it will keep it open for us until we release or close it, resulting in poor performance.

So, we must close or release a resource whenever we are done working with it.

Generally, on the JVM, we access resources through a class. Often, that class implements the `Closable` interface, making releasing a resource easy for us by calling its `close` method. It's quite easy in imperative programming, but you're probably wondering how to do it in reactive programming.

You're probably thinking of mixing imperative programming with reactive programming and making the resources global properties, and then, inside the `subscribe` method, you'll dispose them after using. This is basically what we did in `Chapter 5`, *Asynchronous Data Operators and Transformations* HTTP Request.

Sorry to break your heart, but that is the wrong procedure; in `Chapter 5`, *Asynchronous Data Operators and Transformations*, we did it to avoid further complexities in order to make you understand the code better, but we should learn the correct approach now.

To make things less complex, we will create a dummy resource with a custom implementation of the `Closable` interface. So, no more suspense; take a look at the following code snippet:

```
class Resource():Closeable {
  init {
```

```
    println("Resource Created")
  }

  val data:String = "Hello World"

  override fun close() {
    println("Resource Closed")
  }
}
```

In the preceding code, we created a `Resource` class and implemented `Closeable` in this class (just to mock a typical Java resource class). We also created a `val` property named `data` inside that class, which will be used to mock data fetching from `Resource`.

Now, how do we use it in a reactive chain? RxKotlin provides a very convenient way to deal with disposable resources. To save your life with disposable resources, RxKotlin has a gift for you—the `using` operator.

The `using` operator lets you create a resource that'll exist only during the life span of the `Observable`, and it will be closed as soon as the `Observable` completes.

The following diagram describes the relation of lifespans of `Observable` created with the `using` operator and the resource attached to it, which has been taken from ReactiveX documentation (`http://reactivex.io/documentation/operators/using.html`):

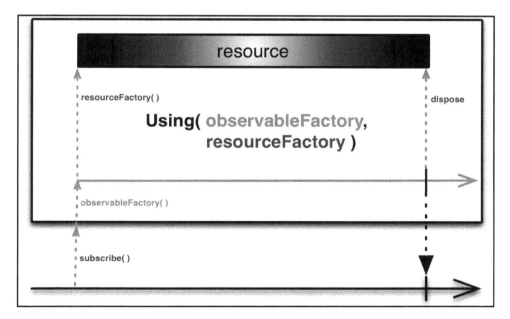

The preceding image clearly displays that the resource will live during the lifespan of the Observable only—a perfect life partner, wouldn't you say?

Here is the definition of the using operator:

```
fun <T, D> using(resourceSupplier: Callable<out D>, sourceSupplier:
Function<in D, out ObservableSource<out T>>,
  disposer: Consumer<in D>): Observable<T> {
    return using(resourceSupplier, sourceSupplier, disposer, true)
}
```

It looks confusing, but it's easy when we break it down. The using method accepts a Callable instance, which will create a resource and return it (out D is for that purpose). And, the last one is to release/close the resource. The using operator will call the first lambda before creating the Resource instance. Then, it'll pass the Resource instance to the second lambda for you to create Observable and return it so that you can subscribe. Finally, when the Observable calls its onComplete event, it will call the third lambda to close the resource.

You're now dying to see the example, right? The following is the example:

```
fun main(args: Array<String>) {
  Observable.using({// (1)
    Resource()
  },{// (2)
    resource:Resource->
    Observable.just(resource)
  },{// (3)
    resource:Resource->
    resource.close()
  }).subscribe {
    println("Resource Data ${it.data}")
  }
}
```

In the preceding program, we passed three lambdas to the using operator. In the first lambda (comment one), we created an instance of Resource and returned it (in a lambda, the last statement works as return, you don't have to write it).

The second lambda will take resource as parameter and will create the Observable from it to return.

The third lambda will again take `resource` as a parameter and close it.

The `using` operator will return the `Observable` you created in the second lambda for you to apply the RxKotlin chain to it.

So, here is a screenshot of the output, if you're curious:

```
"C:\Program Files\Java\jdk1.8.0_131\bin\java" ...
Resource Created
Resource Data Hello World
Resource Closed

Process finished with exit code 0
```

So, that is resource management made easy. Also note that you can create and pass as many resources as you want to the `using` operator. We implemented the `Closable` interface for ease of understanding, but it's not mandatory; you can easily create and pass an array of resources.

Creating your own operators

So far, we have used lots of operators, but are we sure they will meet all our needs? Or, can we always find a fitting operator for each requirement we face? No, that's not possible. Sometimes, we may have to create our own operators for our own needs, but how?

RxKotlin is always there to make your life easier. It has an operator just for this purpose—the `lift` operator. The `lift` operator receives an instance of `ObservableOperator`; so, to create your own operator, you have to implement that interface.

In my opinion, the best way to learn something is by doing it. What about creating a custom operator that would add a sequential number to every emission? Let's create it as per the following list of requirements:

- The operator should emit a pair, with an added sequential number as the first element. The second element of the pair should be the actual emission.
- The operator should be generic and should work with any type of Observable.
- As with other operators, the operator should work concurrently with other operators.

The preceding points are our basic requirements; and, as per the preceding requirement, we must use `AtomicInteger` for the counter (which will count the emissions, and we will pass that count as a sequential number) so that the operator will work seamlessly with any `Scheduler`.

Every custom operator should implement the `ObservableOperator` interface, which looks like this:

```
interface ObservableOperator<Downstream, Upstream> {
  /**
   * Applies a function to the child Observer and returns a new
   parent Observer.
   * @param observer the child Observer instance
   * @return the parent Observer instance
   * @throws Exception on failure
   */
  @NonNull
  @Throws(Exception::class)
  fun apply(@NonNull observer: Observer<in Downstream>):
  Observer<in Upstream>;
}
```

`Downstream` and `Upstream` are two generic types here. `Downstream` specifies the type that will be passed to the Downstream of the operator, and `Upstream` specifies the type that the operator will receive from `upstream`.

The `apply` function has a parameter called the `Observer` that should be used to pass the emission to the `Downstream`, and the function should return another `Observer` that will be used to listen to the `upstream` emissions.

Enough theory. The following is the definition of our `AddSerialNumber` operator. Take a careful look at it here:

```
class AddSerialNumber<T> : ObservableOperator<Pair<Int,T>,T> {
  val counter:AtomicInteger = AtomicInteger()

  override fun apply(observer: Observer<in Pair<Int, T>>):
  Observer<in T> {
    return object : Observer<T> {
      override fun onComplete() {
        observer.onComplete()
      }

      override fun onSubscribe(d: Disposable) {
        observer.onSubscribe(d)
      }
```

```
        override fun onError(e: Throwable) {
            observer.onError(e)
        }

        override fun onNext(t: T) {
            observer.onNext(Pair(counter.incrementAndGet(),t))
        }

    }
  }
}
```

Let's start describing this from the very first feature—the definition of the `AddSerialNumber` class. This implements the `ObservableOperator` interface. As per our requirement, we kept the class generic, that is, we specified the `Upstream` type to be generic `T`.

We used an `AtomicInteger` as a `val` property of the class, which should be initialized within the `init` block (as we are declaring and defining the property within the class, it would be automatically initialized within `init` while creating instances of the class). That `AtomicInteger`, `counter` should increment on each emission and should return the emitted value as the serial number of the emission.

Inside the `apply` method, I created and returned an `Observer` instance, which would be used to listen to the `upstream` as described earlier. Basically, every operator passes an `Observer` to `upstream` by which it should receive the events.

Inside that `observer`, whenever we receive any event, we echoed that to the `Observer` downstream (where it is received as a parameter).

Inside the `onNext` event of the `Upstream Observer`, we incremented the `counter`, added it as the `first` element to a `Pair` instance, added the item we received (as a parameter in `onNext`) as the `second` value, and, finally, passed it to the `onNext`—`observer.onNext(Pair(counter.incrementAndGet(),t))` downstream.

So, what now? We created a class that can be used as an operator, but how do we use it? It's easy, take a look at this piece of code:

```
fun main(args: Array<String>) {
  Observable.range(10,20)
   .lift(AddSerialNumber<Int>())
    .subscribeBy (
      onNext = {
        println("Next $it")
      },
```

```
        onError = {
          it.printStackTrace()
        },
        onComplete = {
          println("Completed")
        }
    )
}
```

You just have to create an instance of your operator and pass it to the `lift` operator; that's all you need, we have now created our first operator.

Look at the following output:

```
"C:\Program Files\Java\jdk1.8.0_131\bin\java" ...
Next (1, 10)
Next (2, 11)
Next (3, 12)
Next (4, 13)
Next (5, 14)
Next (6, 15)
Next (7, 16)
Next (8, 17)
Next (9, 18)
Next (10, 19)
Next (11, 20)
Next (12, 21)
Next (13, 22)
Next (14, 23)
Next (15, 24)
Next (16, 25)
Next (17, 26)
Next (18, 27)
Next (19, 28)
Next (20, 29)
Completed

Process finished with exit code 0
```

We have created our first operator, and, frankly, that was super easy. Yes, it seemed a bit confusing at the start, but as we moved forward, it became easier.

As you may have noticed, the `ObservableOperator` interface has only one method, so we can obviously replace the class declaration and everything with just a lambda, as shown here:

```kotlin
fun main(args: Array<String>) {
  listOf("Reactive","Programming","in","Kotlin",
  "by Rivu Chakraborty","Packt")
    .toObservable()
    .lift<Pair<Int,String>> {
      observer ->
      val counter = AtomicInteger()
      object :Observer<String> {
        override fun onSubscribe(d: Disposable) {
        observer.onSubscribe(d)
        }

        override fun onNext(t: String) {
          observer.onNext(Pair(counter.incrementAndGet(), t))
        }

        override fun onComplete() {
          observer.onComplete()
        }

        override fun onError(e: Throwable) {
          observer.onError(e)
        }

      }
    }
    .subscribeBy (
      onNext = {
        println("Next $it")
      },
      onError = {
        it.printStackTrace()
      },
      onComplete = {
        println("Completed")
      }
        )
}
```

In this example, we used a list of `String` to create `Observable` instead of an `Int` range.

The following is the output:

```
"C:\Program Files\Java\jdk1.8.0_131\bin\java" ...
Next (1, Reactive)
Next (2, Programming)
Next (3, in)
Next (4, Kotlin)
Next (5, by Rivu Chakraborty)
Next (6, Packt)
Completed

Process finished with exit code 0
```

The program is almost similar to the previous one, except that we used a lambda and used `Pair<Int, String>` as the type of downstream `Observer`.

As we have gained our grip in creating our custom operators, let's move forward by learning how to create transformers—no, not the autobot like the movie series; they are just RxKotlin transformers. What are they? Let's see.

Composing operators with transformer

So, you have learned how to create custom operators, but think of a situation when you want to create a new operator by combining multiple operators. For instance, I often wanted to combine the functionality of the `subscribeOn` and `observeOn` operators so that all the computations can be pushed to computation threads, and, when the results are ready, we can receive them on the main thread.

Yes, it's possible to get the benefits of both operators by adding both operators one after the other to the chain, as shown here:

```kotlin
fun main(args: Array<String>) {
  Observable.range(1,10)
    .map {
      println("map - ${Thread.currentThread().name} $it")
      it
    }
    .subscribeOn(Schedulers.computation())
    .observeOn(Schedulers.io())
```

```
    .subscribe {
        println("onNext - ${Thread.currentThread().name} $it")
    }

    runBlocking { delay(100) }
}
```

Though you're already aware of the output, the following is the screenshot if you need a refresher:

```
"C:\Program Files\Java\jdk1.8.0_131\bin\java" ...
map - RxComputationThreadPool-1 1
map - RxComputationThreadPool-1 2
map - RxComputationThreadPool-1 3
map - RxComputationThreadPool-1 4
map - RxComputationThreadPool-1 5
map - RxComputationThreadPool-1 6
map - RxComputationThreadPool-1 7
map - RxComputationThreadPool-1 8
map - RxComputationThreadPool-1 9
map - RxComputationThreadPool-1 10
onNext - RxCachedThreadScheduler-1 1
onNext - RxCachedThreadScheduler-1 2
onNext - RxCachedThreadScheduler-1 3
onNext - RxCachedThreadScheduler-1 4
onNext - RxCachedThreadScheduler-1 5
onNext - RxCachedThreadScheduler-1 6
onNext - RxCachedThreadScheduler-1 7
onNext - RxCachedThreadScheduler-1 8
onNext - RxCachedThreadScheduler-1 9
onNext - RxCachedThreadScheduler-1 10

Process finished with exit code 0
```

Now, say we have this combination of the subscribeOn and observeOn operator throughout our project, so we want a shortcut. We want to create our own operator where we would pass the two Scheduler's where we want subscribeOn and observeOn, and everything should work perfectly.

RxKotlin provides the `Transformer` interfaces (`ObservableTransformer` and `FlowableTransformer` are two `Transformer` interfaces) for that purpose. Just like the `operator` interfaces, it has only one method—`apply`. The only difference is that here, instead of `Observers`, you have the `Observable`. So, instead of operating on individual emits and their items, here, you work directly on the source.

Here is the signature of the `ObservableTransformer` interface:

```
interface ObservableTransformer<Upstream, Downstream> {
    /**
    * Applies a function to the upstream Observable
    and returns an ObservableSource with
    * optionally different element type.
    * @param upstream the upstream Observable instance
    * @return the transformed ObservableSource instance
    */
    @NonNull
    fun apply(@NonNull upstream: Observable<Upstream>):
    ObservableSource<Downstream>
}
```

The interface signature is almost the same. Unlike the `apply` method of `ObservableOperator`, here, the `apply` method receives `Upstream Observable` and should return the `Observable` that should be passed to the `Downstream`.

So, back to our topic, the following code block should fulfill our requirements:

```
fun main(args: Array<String>) {
    Observable.range(1,10)
        .map {
            println("map - ${Thread.currentThread().name} $it")
            it
        }
        .compose(SchedulerManager(Schedulers.computation(),
            Schedulers.io()))
            .subscribe {
                println("onNext - ${Thread.currentThread().name} $it")
            }

        runBlocking { delay(100) }
}

class SchedulerManager<T>(val subscribeScheduler:Scheduler,
val    observeScheduler:Scheduler):ObservableTransformer<T,T> {
    override fun apply(upstream: Observable<T>):
    ObservableSource<T> {
        return upstream.subscribeOn(subscribeScheduler)
```

```
            .observeOn(observeScheduler)
      }

  }
```

In the preceding code, we created a class for our requirement—`SchedulerManager`—that would take two `Scheduler` as parameters. The first one is to be passed to the `subscribeOn` operator and the second one is for the `observeOn` operator.

Inside the `apply` method, we returned the `Observable Upstream`, after applying two operators to it.

We are omitting the screenshot of the output, as it is the same as the previous one.

Like the `lift` operator, the `compose` operator can also be implemented using a lambda. Let's have another example where we will transform an `Observable<Int>` to an `Observable<List>`. Here is the code:

```
        fun main(args: Array<String>) {
          Observable.range(1,10)
            .compose<List<Int>> {
                upstream: Observable<Int> ->
                upstream.toList().toObservable()
            }
            .first(listOf())
            .subscribeBy {
                println(it)
            }
        }
```

In the preceding code, we used `upstream.toList().toObservable()` as the `Observable$toList()` operator converts an `Observable<T>` to `Single<List<T>>`, so we need the `toObservable()` operator to convert it back to `Observable`.

Here is the screenshot of the output:

```
"C:\Program Files\Java\jdk1.8.0_131\bin\java" ...
[1, 2, 3, 4, 5, 6, 7, 8, 9, 10]

Process finished with exit code 0
```

Composing multiple operators to create a new one is also super easy in RxKotlin; just add a bit extension function to it to see how things become more delightful.

Summary

This was a short chapter about resource management and custom operators in RxKotlin. You learned how you can (or should) create, use, and dispose resources. You learned to create custom operators. You also learned how to compose multiple operators to create your desired one.

This was the last chapter on the fundamentals of RxKotlin. From the next chapter onward, we will start applying our gained knowledge to real-life scenarios and projects.

In today's app-driven era, writing APIs is a primary requirement; in the next chapter, you will start learning Spring in Kotlin so that you can develop your own API for your projects.

10
Introduction to Web Programming with Spring for Kotlin Developers

Kotlin is a powerful language, and its power increases, even more, when the Spring Framework is used with it. Up until this point, you've learned the concepts of reactive programming and how to apply these concepts to Kotlin. So far, we developed and wrote code that interacts with the console, but that's not what we will do while developing professional apps. We will either build apps that will run on mobile devices or we will build web applications or REST APIs. At least those are the most commonly built professional software solutions.

So, how to build them? How to create RESTful web APIs and Android apps? Let's discover. The last three chapters of this book are dedicated to building REST APIs and Android apps and, most importantly, making them reactive. Spring is such a vast topic that covering it in a single chapter is simply not possible, so we will have two chapters on Spring.

This chapter will start by introducing you to Spring, and, by the end of this chapter, you should be proficient enough to write REST APIs in Kotlin with Spring. We will not add reactive features in this chapter because we don't want to distract you from the concepts and ideas of Spring. We want you to grasp the concepts and knowledge of Spring itself well enough before moving ahead with making them reactive.

In this chapter, we will cover the following topics:

- Introduction to Spring, history, and origin of Spring
- Spring IoC and dependency injection
- Aspect-oriented programming in Spring
- Introduction to Spring Boot
- Building REST APIs with Spring Boot

So, what are we waiting for? Let's get started and get familiar with Spring.

Spring, history, and origin of Spring

What is Spring? We cannot give a short answer. It's really tough to define Spring in a sentence or two. Many people may say Spring is a framework, but this would be also an understatement for Spring, as it may also be called a **framework of frameworks**. Spring provides you with a lot of tools, such as **DI** (**dependency injection**), **IoC** (**Inversion of Control**), and **AOP** (**Aspect-oriented programming**). While we can use Spring in almost any type of Java or Kotlin JVM application, it is most useful while developing web applications on top of the Java EE platform. Before moving into the details of Spring, we should first understand from where and why Spring originated and how it has evolved.

The origin and history of Spring

It has been more than two decades (around 22 years) since Java has been around. For enterprise application development, Java introduced a few technologies that were heavyweight and were very complex enough.

In 2003, Rod Johnson created Spring as an alternative to the heavyweight and complex Enterprise Java Technologies and EJB to make it easy to develop enterprise applications in Java. Being lightweight, flexible, and easy to use, Spring gained popularity soon. Over time, EJB and Java Enterprise Edition (then J2EE) evolved to support POJO-oriented programming models such as Spring. Not only that, arguably inspired by Spring, EJB also started offering AOP, DI, and IoC.

However, Spring never looked back. As EJB and Java EE started including ideas inspired by Spring, Spring started exploring more unconventional and unexplored technology areas, such as Big Data, Cloud Computing, Mobile App Development, and even reactive programming, leaving EJB and Java EE far behind.

During the start of the year, on the month of January 2017, Spring surprised everyone by announcing its support for Kotlin (yes, they announced Kotlin support even before Google) and released a few Kotlin APIs. And, when the power of Kotlin was combined with an already powerful Spring Framework, both got even more powerful. As a reason behind adding Kotlin support, they stated:

> *One of the key strengths of Kotlin is that it provides a very good interoperability with libraries written in Java. But there are ways to go even further and allow writing fully idiomatic Kotlin code when developing your next Spring application. In addition to Spring Framework support for Java 8 that Kotlin applications can leverage like functional web or bean registration APIs, there are additional Kotlin dedicated features that should allow you to reach a new level of productivity.*
> *That's why we are introducing a dedicated Kotlin support in Spring Framework 5.0.*

By Pivotal Spring Team `https://spring.io/blog/2017/01/04/introducing-kotlin-support-in-spring-framework-5-0`.

So, let's start by creating and setting up our Spring project.

Dependency injection and IoC

Inversion of Control (IoC) is a programming technique in which object coupling is bound at runtime by an assembler object and is typically not known at compile time using static analysis. IoC can be achieved using dependency injection. We can say that IoC is the idea and dependency injection is its implementation. Now, what is dependency injection? Let's find out.

Dependency injection is a technique where one component supplies dependencies for another component during the instantiation time. The definition sounds confusing, right? Let's explain it with an example. Consider the following interfaces:

```
interface Employee {
  fun executeTask()
}
interface Task {
  fun execute()
}
```

A common implementation of the preceding program will be as follows.

The `Employee` class is as follows:

```
class RandomEmployee: Employee {
  val task = RandomTask()
  override fun executeTask() {
    task.execute()
  }
}
```

And the `Task` interface is implemented as follows:

```
class RandomTask : Task {
  override fun execute() {
    println("Executing Random Task")
  }
}
```

Then, we will create and use the instance of the `RandomEmployee` class in the `main` method as follows:

```
fun main(args: Array<String>) {
  RandomEmployee().executeTask()
}
```

The `RandomTask` class is a simple class implementing an interface `Task`, which has a function named `execute`. The `RandomEmployee` class on the other hand depends on the `Task` class. Now, what do we mean by depends? By depends, we mean that the output of an instance of `Employee` class is dependent on the `Task` class.

Let's take a look at the following output:

```
"C:\Program Files\Java\jdk1.8.0_131\bin\java" ...
Executing Random Task


Process finished with exit code 0
```

The preceding program would work fine, and actually, it is a text book program. In colleges/institutes, when we learned coding for the first time, we learned the way to initialize variables and/or properties inside constructors or during construction time.

Now, just try to remember what you learned a few chapters earlier. We should test everything we write. Now, take a look at the code again—is this piece of code testable? Or even maintainable? How would you assure that the right *Employee* is given the right *Task*? It's a tightly coupled code.

You should always use coupling concisely. It's true that we cannot achieve much without coupling. Tightly coupled code, on the other hand, makes it difficult to test and maintain.

Rather than letting the objects create their dependencies at the construction time, dependency injection provides objects with their dependencies at creation time with some third-party class. That third-party class will also coordinate with each object in the system. The following diagram shows the general idea behind dependency injection:

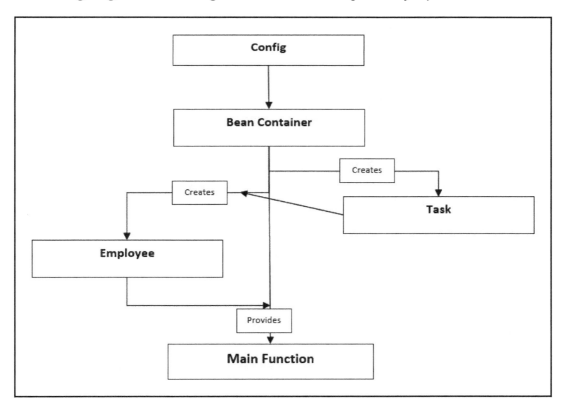

This image clearly depicts the flow of dependency injection. There will be a **Config** class (in Spring, there can be an XML **Config** file or there can be a **Config** class as well) that will create and drive a **Bean Container**. That **Bean Container** will control the creation of beans or POJOs and will pass them where required.

Confused? Let's get our hands-on code and implement the preceding concept. Let's get started with a brand new implementation of the `Employee` interface as follows:

```
class SoftwareDeveloper(val task: ProgrammingTask) : Employee {
  override fun executeTask() {
    task.execute()
  }
}
```

A `SoftwareDeveloper` class can only execute `ProgrammingTask`. Now, take a look at the XML `config` file shown next:

```
<?xml version="1.0" encoding="UTF-8"?>
<beans xmlns="http://www.springframework.org/schema/beans"
    xmlns:xsi="http://www.w3.org/2001/XMLSchema-instance"
    xsi:schemaLocation="http://www.springframework.org/schema/beans
    http://www.springframework.org/schema/beans/spring-beans.xsd">

    <bean id="employee"
    class="com.rivuchk.reactivekotlin.springdi.SoftwareDeveloper">
    <constructor-arg ref="task"/>
    </bean>

    <bean id="task" class="com.rivuchk.reactivekotlin.
    springdi.ProgrammingTask"/>

</beans>
```

The `ProgrammingTask` class, a new implementation of the `Task` interface, looks like as follows:

```
class ProgrammingTask: Task {
    override fun execute() {
        println("Writing Programms")
    }
}
```

This file should be located at `\src\main\resources\META-INF\employee.xml`. Now, let's try to understand the `config` file. We declared each bean using the `bean` tag. Then, we used the `constructor-arg` tag to indicate a constructor argument in that bean.

If you want to pass another object as a `constructor-argref` in a bean, you have to declare that reference object as a bean as well. Alternatively, you can pass `constructor-arg value`, as discussed later in this chapter.

The updated `main` function will look like this:

```
fun main(args: Array<String>) {
    val context = ClassPathXmlApplicationContext(
        "META-INF/spring/employee.xml")//(1)     val employee =
    context.getBean(Employee::class.java)//(2)
    employee.executeTask()
    context.close()//(3)
}
```

Before moving into the details of the preceding program, let's take a look at its output:

```
"C:\Program Files\Java\jdk1.8.0_131
Nov 19, 2017 11:19:49 PM org.spring
INFO: Refreshing org.springframewo
Nov 19, 2017 11:19:49 PM org.spring
INFO: Loading XML bean definitions
Nov 19, 2017 11:19:50 PM org.spring
INFO: Closing org.springframework.c
Writing Programms


Process finished with exit code 0
```

Cropped output of DI with XML Configuration program

The first few red-lined outputs are logs of the Spring Framework. Then, we can spot the output as **Writing Programms**.

Now, let's try to understand the program. The `ClassPathXmlApplicationContext` is the **Bean Container** we mentioned in the figure. It creates and keeps record of all the beans mentioned in the XML file and provides them to us when asked for. The `String` passed in the constructor of `ClassPathXmlApplicationContext` is the relative path to the XML configuration file.

On comment `(2)`, we used `context.getBean()` to get the `Employee` instance. This function takes a class name as a parameter and creates an instance of that class based on the XML configuration.

On comment (3), we closed the context. The context, as a **Bean Container**, always carries the configuration for you, which keeps the memory blocked. In order to clean the memory, we should close the context.

Now, as we have some idea about dependency injection via XML configuration file, we should move toward the annotation-based configuration class and take a look at how it works.

Spring Annotation configuration

Other than XML, we can also define Spring configuration through annotations in a POJO class, which will not be used as a bean. In the previous section, we took Employee task example; let's now take the Student-Assignment example, a similar one. However, this time, we will not use interfaces; instead, we will directly use classes.

So, here is the Assignment class that takes a lambda as a constructor parameter:

```
class Assignment(val task:(String)->Unit) {
  fun performAssignment(assignmentDtl:String) {
    task(assignmentDtl)
  }
}
```

This class takes a lambda as task, to execute it later, inside the performAssignment() method. Here is the Student class that takes Assignment as a property:

```
class Student(val assignment: Assignment) {
  fun completeAssignment(assignmentDtl:String) {
    assignment.performAssignment(assignmentDtl)
  }
}
```

So, Student would depend on its Assignment and an Assignment would depend on its task definition (Lambda). The following diagram describes the dependency flow for this example:

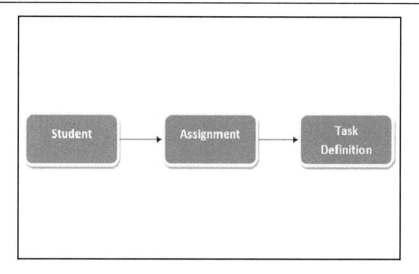

How to depict this dependency flow in code? It's easy with Annotation Config. Here is the
Configuration class that we used:

```
@Configuration
class Configuration {

    @Bean
    fun student() = Student(assignment())

    @Bean
    fun assignment()
       = Assignment { assignmentDtl -> println
       ("Performing Assignment $assignmentDtl") }
}
```

Simple and straightforward, isn't it? The class is annotated with @Configuration, and the
function to return the Student and Assignment beans is annotated with @Bean.

Now, how to use this class? Simple, like the previous one, take a look at the `main` function here:

```kotlin
fun main(args: Array<String>) {
    val context = AnnotationConfigApplicationContext
    (Configuration::class.java)
    val student = context.getBean(Student::class.java)
    student.completeAssignment("One")
    student.completeAssignment("Two")
    student.completeAssignment("Three")

    context.close()
}
```

Instead of `ClassPathXmlApplicationContext`, we used `AnnotationConfigApplicationContext` and passed the `Configuration` class. The rest of the program is the same.

This is the output of the program:

```
"C:\Program Files\Java\jdk1.8.0_131\
Nov 20, 2017 6:06:40 AM org.springfra
INFO: Refreshing org.springframework.
Performing Assignment One
Performing Assignment Two
Performing Assignment Three
Nov 20, 2017 6:06:42 AM org.springfra
INFO: Closing org.springframework.co

Process finished with exit code 0
```

Cropped output of DI with Annotation Configuration program

So, we learned dependency injection with Spring. It's really easy, isn't it? Actually, the Spring Framework makes everything easy; whatever feature they offer, they make it as easy as calling a method from a POJO class. Spring truly utilizes the power of a POJO.

So, as we got our hands on dependency injection, let's move forward with Aspect-oriented programming.

Spring – AOP

Before learning how to implement Aspect-oriented programming with Spring, we should first learn what Aspect-oriented programming is. The definition of Aspect-oriented programming says it is a programming paradigm that aims to increase modularity by allowing the separation of cross-cutting concerns. It does so by adding additional behavior to existing code (an advice) without modifying the code itself.

Now, what did we mean by cross-cutting concerns? Let's explore.

In a real-life project, multiple components play their own role. For example, if we take our previous scenario into account, the Student class itself is a component, similarly there could be a faculty component who would evaluate the student based on his/her performance. So, let's add a faculty to our program.

The Faculty class should be simple enough, with just a method to evaluate a student. Just as follows:

```
class Faculty {
  fun evaluateAssignment() {
    val marks = Random().nextInt(10)
    println("This assignment is evaluated and given $marks points")
  }
}
```

Now, how should the faculty grade a student? He/she must somehow know that the student has completed an assignment. A common implementation of this business logic would be by modifying the Student class, as follows:

```
class Student(val assignment: Assignment,
  val faculty: Faculty) {
    fun completeAssignment(assignmentDtl:String) {
      assignment.performAssignment(assignmentDtl)
      faculty.evaluateAssignment()
    }
  }
```

The Faculty instance will be passed to a Student instance, and, once the student is done with performing the assignment, it will call the Faculty instance and instruct it to evaluate the assignment. However, think again. Is this a proper implementation? Why should a student instruct his/her faculty? It's the faculty's job to evaluate assignments of a student; it just needs to get notified somehow.

That very thing is known as a cross-cutting concern. `Faculty` and `Student` are different components of the program. They shouldn't have direct interaction at the time of the assignment review.

AOP let's implement the same. So, here, the `Student` class will be back to almost its original state:

```
open class Student(public val assignment: Assignment) {
  open public fun completeAssignment(assignmentDtl:String) {
    assignment.performAssignment(assignmentDtl)
  }
}
```

Did you notice the differences in the actual code for the `Student` class in the previous section? Yes, here we added `open` keyword to the class declaration and all the properties and functions of the class. The reason is that, to implement AOP, Spring sub-classes our beans and overrides methods (including getters of our properties). However, with Kotlin, everything is final unless you specify it as open, and that will block Spring AOP to accomplish its purpose. So, in order to make Spring work, we have to mention each property and method as open.

The `main` method will be similar, except that we are back to XML-based configuration. Take a look at the following piece of code:

```
fun main(args: Array<String>) {
  val context = ClassPathXmlApplicationContext(
      "META-INF/spring/student_faculty.xml"
  )
  val student = context.getBean(Student::class.java)
  student.completeAssignment("One")
  student.completeAssignment("Two")
  student.completeAssignment("Three")

  context.close()
}
```

The only file with new things is the configuration file. Take a look at the configuration file here before we explain it:

```
<?xml version="1.0" encoding="UTF-8"?>
<beans xmlns="http://www.springframework.org/schema/beans"
   xmlns:xsi="http://www.w3.org/2001/XMLSchema-instance"
   xmlns:aop="http://www.springframework.org/schema/aop"
   xsi:schemaLocation="http://www.springframework.org/schema/beans
   http://www.springframework.org/schema/beans/spring-beans.xsd
   http://www.springframework.org/schema/aop
```

```
                http://www.springframework.org/schema/aop/spring-aop.xsd">

      <bean id="student" class="com.rivuchk.reactivekotlin.
        springdi.aop_student_assignment.Student">
        <constructor-arg ref="assignment"/>
      </bean>

      <bean id="assignment" class="com.rivuchk.reactivekotlin.springdi.
        aop_student_assignment.Assignment" />

      <bean id="faculty"
      class="com.rivuchk.reactivekotlin.springdi.aop_student_assignment.
      Faculty" /><!--1-->    <aop:config><!--2-->          <aop:aspect
      ref="faculty"><!--3-->              <aop:pointcut
      id="assignment_complete"
      expression="execution(* *.completeAssignment(..))"/><!--4-->
      <aop:after                     pointcut-ref="assignment_complete"
      method="evaluateAssignment" /><!--5-->
      </aop:aspect>
      </aop:config>

      </beans>
```

So, let's explain the configuration. On comment (1), we declared a new bean named faculty, although it really isn't a new thing to you and you may have already expected it. I mentioned it in order to prepare you for the next few lines.

On comment (2), we indicated that the AOP configuration begins. On comment (3), we indicated that this AOP is regarding the Faculty class, as the Faculty class is the class that should be notified.

On comment (4), we declared pointcut. A pointcut is like a bookmark on a method, so whenever that method is called, your class should get notified. The id field denotes the id for that pointcut, so that you can refer to it in your code. The expression field denotes the expression for which we should create the pointcut. Here, with the execution expression, we stated that the pointcut should be on execution of the completeAssignment method.

On comment (5), we declared the method in Faculty class that should get called after the pointcut expression is executed. We can also declare a method to execute before pointcut by using aop:before.

So, now, let's take a look at the following output:

```
"C:\Program Files\Java\jdk1.8.0_131\bin\java" ...
Nov 21, 2017 7:57:05 AM org.springframework.contex
INFO: Refreshing org.springframework.context.suppo
Nov 21, 2017 7:57:05 AM org.springframework.beans.
INFO: Loading XML bean definitions from class path
Nov 21, 2017 7:57:07 AM org.springframework.aop.fr
INFO: Final method [public final com.rivuchk.react
Performing Assignment One
This assignment is evaluated and given 5 points
Performing Assignment Two
This assignment is evaluated and given 0 points
Performing Assignment Three
This assignment is evaluated and given 9 points
Nov 21, 2017 7:57:08 AM org.springframework.contex
INFO: Closing org.springframework.context.support.

Process finished with exit code 0
```

Cropped output of DI with Spring AOP program

As you can see, the `evaluateAssignment` method is called from the `Faculty` class every time we call the `completeAssignment` method, apparently, with no code, but only with configuration.

Introduction to Spring Boot

So, we are now familiar with Spring, especially with Spring DI and AOP. Spring Boot makes a developer's life easier. So far, we've seen how to perform various operations just by using POJO classes and Spring configurations. What would be your reaction if I tell you that we can even minimize this configuration? Will you be shocked? Then brace yourself, because it's true. With Spring Boot, you can get your code ready with minimal configuration and in just a few steps.

So, what is Spring Boot? It is a Spring module that provides **RAD (Rapid application development)** features to the Spring Framework. It is designed to simplify the bootstrapping and development of new Spring applications. The framework takes an opinionated approach to configuration, freeing developers from the requirement to define boilerplate configurations, further reducing your development time.

So, let's get started. If you are using the IntelliJ IDEA Ultimate edition, you can follow these steps to create a Spring Boot application:

1. Start a **New Project**.
2. From the **New Project** dialog, select **Spring Initializr**, define **Project SDK**, and click on **Next**, as shown in the following screenshot:

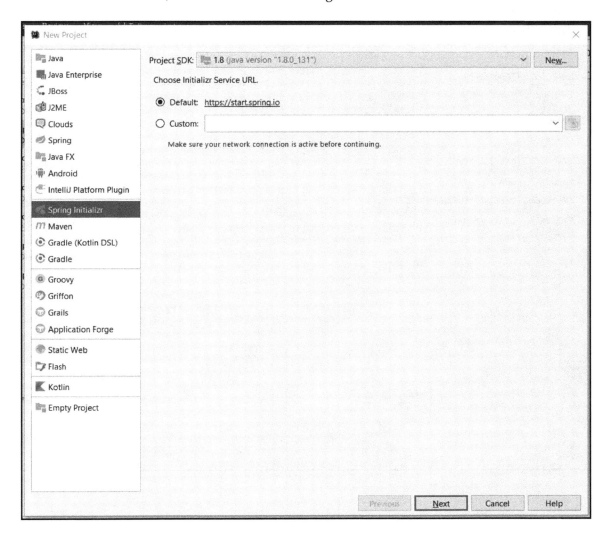

3. On the next screen, define the **Group**, **Artifact**, **Type** (Gradle or Maven), **Language** (**Java/Kotlin**), **Packaging** (**Jar/War**), **Java Version**, **Name**, and root package for the project, as shown in the following screenshot:

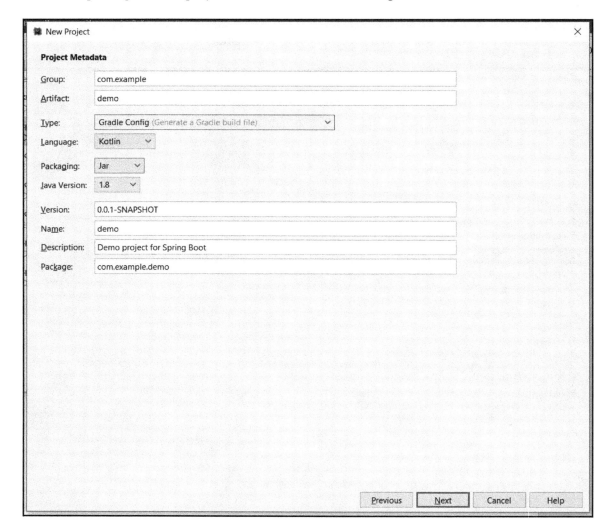

4. The next screen lets you select multiple Spring dependencies. Make sure to set the Spring Boot version to 2.0.0 M6 and above in this screen. For AOP and DI, you need to select **Aspects** under **Core**, as shown in the screenshot:

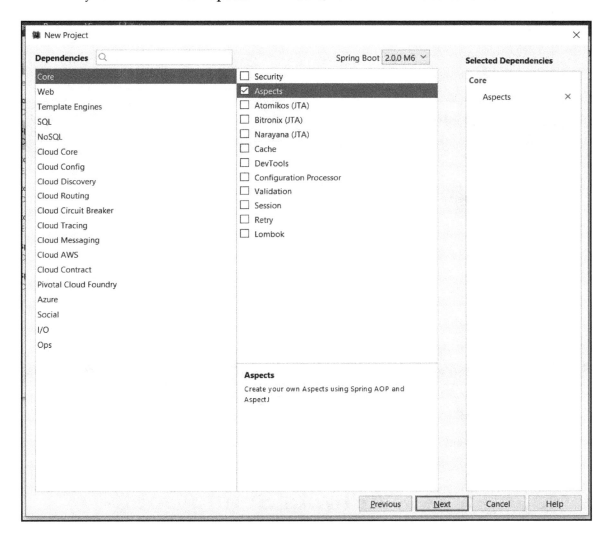

5. Provide **Project name** and **location** and click on **Finish**.

Wasn't it quite easy? Don't get upset if you don't have IntelliJ IDEA Ultimate. Spring Boot is for everyone. Follow these steps to create a new Spring Boot project for whatever IDE you have:

1. Go to `http://start.spring.io/`.
2. Provide the following details, which are similar to IntelliJ IDEA:

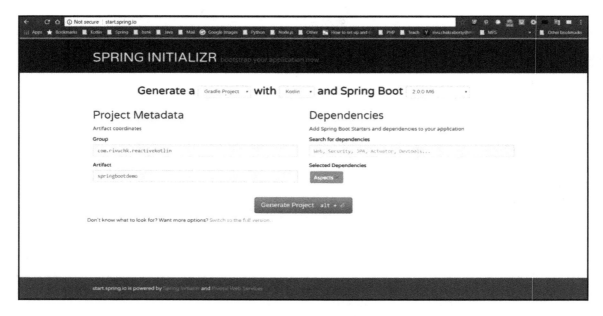

3. Click on **Generate Project**. The project will get downloaded to your machine.

Wasn't it simple enough? Let's try our hands at creating APIs with Spring.

Creating a Rest API with Spring Boot

We've seen the power of Spring and Spring Boot. So, let's use it without any further delay. We will build a RESTful web service that will return a `Todo` object. We will further enhance this project in the next chapter, where we will add `Todo` and fetch a list of `Todo` from the database. We will use JPA and Hibernate along with Spring for that purpose.

When we are done with this example, we should get the following response:

{"id":1,"todoDescription":"TODO Project","todoTargetDate":"31/11/2017","status":"Running"}

Cropped screenshot of browser output

So, let's start by creating a new project. You can use `http://start.spring.io/` or you can use IntelliJ IDEA as well to create a new project.

After you have created the new project, you will see that there's an `Application` class; don't give much focus to it, it's there in almost all Spring Boot applications. We need to create a new class for `Todo`, as follows:

```
data class Todo (
    var id:Int = 0,
    var todoDescription:String,
    var todoTargetDate:String,
    var status:String
)
```

A REST API requires us to create `RestController`, which would be the endpoint for API requests, so here's our `RestController`:

```
@RestController@RequestMapping("/api")
class TodoController {
  @RequestMapping("/get_todo")
  fun getTodo() = Todo(1,"TODO Project","31/11/2017","Running")
}
```

Study this small class carefully. First, we annotated our class with `@RestController` and `@RequestMapping`. The purpose of them is simple `@RestController` denotes that this class will act as a `Controller`, that is, all API requests should pass through this class, `@RequestMapping("/api")` denotes that the URL of this class will have an `/api` suffix after your base URL (note that the URL in the screenshot is `http://127.0.0.1:8080/api/get_todo`). We can skip the second annotation if we want for this class.

Then, we have the `getTodo()` function; the `@RequestMapping` annotation is required for this method as it will define the endpoint. This method is also simple—it just returns a new object of `Todo`, statically created.

What? Are you expecting anything more? Sorry to disappoint you, but we are done with the API. You can just run the project and hit `http://127.0.0.1:8080/api/get_todo` to get the following JSON response:

```
{"id":1,"todoDescription":"TODO
Project","todoTargetDate":"31/11/2017","status":"Running"}
```

Isn't it simple enough?

Summary

In this chapter, you were introduced to Spring with Kotlin. We learned about dependency injection and Aspect-oriented programming. We learned how a simple POJO class can show great power with the help of the Spring Framework. In this chapter, we also learned to create a simple API with Spring.

In the next chapter, we will focus on enhancing our API to a fully functional one with the help of JPA and Hibernate to work with MySQL database. We will also learn to implement reactive programming with Spring.

So, don't wait! Head over to the next chapter right now. Our API is still incomplete.

11

REST APIs with Spring JPA and Hibernate

In the previous chapter, we learned how to create REST APIs with ease. We learned how to leverage the power of Spring, Hibernate, and JPA to create REST APIs with lines of code that can be counted on one hand. Those were powerful REST APIs, but they weren't reactive. This book's primary concern is to teach you how to make everything reactive and to teach you how to create non-blocking apps and APIs.

So, let's move on. Let's make our REST API reactive. Due to the power of Spring, this chapter will be short. We will cover the following topics:

- Spring Boot with JPA and Hibernate
- Reactive programming with Reactor

So, lets get started with the Reactor Framework.

REST API with Spring Boot, Hibernate, and JPA

In the previous chapter, we saw how to create a static RESTful API. We will now learn how to manipulate database records as response to an API request. I've used MySQL as a database in this project.

We will use JPA in this project. You can start a new project and add JPA as one of the dependencies. Alternatively, you can add this to your Gradle dependencies list:

```
compile('org.springframework.boot:spring-boot-starter-data-jpa')
```

> Note: You don't need to put version and artifacts here, it is automatically managed by a Spring Gradle plugin and Spring Boot.

Now, as you added the dependency, you have to add application.properties. Go to resources and add a file named application.properties with the following content:

```
## Spring DATASOURCE (DataSourceAutoConfiguration &
DataSourceProperties)
spring.datasource.url = jdbc:mysql://localhost:3306/tododb
spring.datasource.username = root
spring.datasource.password = password


## Hibernate Properties

# The SQL dialect makes Hibernate generate better
SQL for the chosen database
spring.jpa.properties.hibernate.dialect =
org.hibernate.dialect.MySQL5Dialect

# Hibernate ddl auto (create, create-drop, validate, update)
spring.jpa.hibernate.ddl-auto = update
```

Replace tododb with your database name, root with your database username, and password with your database password. Please note, that you have to create a blank database with the provided database name (in this case, tododb) prior to running this app.

We've added a little modification to the Todo class. Take a look at the following piece of code:

```
@Entity
data class Todo (
  @Id @GeneratedValue(strategy = GenerationType.AUTO)
  var id:Int = 0,

  @get: NotBlank
  var todoDescription:String,

  @get: NotBlank
  var todoTargetDate:String,
```

```
    @get: NotBlank
    var status:String
) {
    constructor():this(
    0,"","",""
    )
    }
```

Yes, we have just added the annotations and a blank constructor, which is required by Spring Data. So, let's take a look at the annotations and their purposes:

@Entity: This defines a new entity in the database, that is, for every class annotated with @Entity, a table in the database will be created.

@Id: This annotation defines the primary key (or composite primary key, if multiple) for a table. The @GeneratedValue annotation denotes that the field value should be autogenerated. JPA has three strategies for ID generation, as described here:

- GenerationType.TABLE: This denotes that the primary keys should be generated with an underlying table to ensure uniqueness, that is, a table with a single column and a single row will be created, which will hold the next primary key value with the column name next_val, and every time a row is inserted in the target table (the table created with our entity), the primary key will be assigned the value of next_val and next_val will be incremented.
- GenerationType.SEQUENCE: This denotes that the primary keys should be generated with an underlying database sequence.
- GenerationType.IDENTITY: This denotes that the primary keys should be generated with an underlying database identity.
- GenerationTypeenum: This also provides an additional option—GenerationType.AUTO, one which denotes that a proper autogeneration strategy should be automatically selected.

The next annotation is @get: NotBlank, which denotes that the field in the table should be not-null.

So, we are done with the changes in our Todo class. We also have to create a Repository interface. Take a look at the following interface:

```
@Repository
interface TodoRepository: JpaRepository<Todo,Int>
```

Yes, that short. The `@Repository` annotation denotes that this interface should be used as a repository (a `DAO` class) for the project. We implemented `JpaRepository` in this interface, which declares methods to manipulate the table. The first generic parameter for this interface is the `Entity` and the second one is for the type of the `ID` field.

We have also created a new class, `ResponseModel`, to structure our response JSON. Find the class definition here:

```
data class ResponseModel (
  val error_code:String,
  val error_message:String,
  val data:List<Todo> = listOf()
) {
    constructor(error_code: String,error_message:
    String,todo: Todo)
    :this(error_code,error_message, listOf(todo))
}
```

This response model contains the `error_code` and `error_message` properties. Let's describe them; if there's an error while processing the API request, `error_code` will hold a non-zero value and `error_message` will hold a message describing that error. The `error_message` property can also hold a generic message.

The `data` property will hold a list of `Todo`, which will be converted to a JSON array in the response JSON. The `data` property is optional, as this response model will be used for all APIs in this project and all APIs may not return a list of `Todo` or even a single `Todo` object (for example the edit, add, and delete Todo APIs do not require to send a `Todo`).

The final part of this API is the `controller` class. Here is the definition:

```
@RestController
@RequestMapping("/api")
class TodoController(private val todoRepository: TodoRepository) {

  @RequestMapping("/get_todo", method =
 arrayOf(RequestMethod.POST))
  fun getTodos() = ResponseModel("0","", todoRepository.findAll())

  @RequestMapping("/add_todo", method =
 arrayOf(RequestMethod.POST))
  fun addTodo(@Valid @RequestBody todo:Todo) =
  ResponseEntity.ok().body(ResponseModel
  ("0","",todoRepository.save(todo)))

  @RequestMapping("/edit_todo", method =
 arrayOf(RequestMethod.POST))
```

```
fun editTodo(@Valid @RequestBody todo:Todo):ResponseModel {
    val optionalTodo = todoRepository.findById(todo.id)
    if(optionalTodo.isPresent) {
        return ResponseModel("0", "Edit
        Successful",todoRepository.save(todo))
    } else {
        return ResponseModel("1", "Invalid Todo ID" )
    }
}
@RequestMapping("/add_todos", method =
arrayOf(RequestMethod.POST))
fun addTodos(@Valid @RequestBody todos:List<Todo>)
        = ResponseEntity.ok().body(ResponseModel
        ("0","",todoRepository.saveAll(todos)))

@RequestMapping("/delete_todo/{id}", method =
arrayOf(RequestMethod.DELETE))
fun deleteTodo(@PathVariable("id") id:Int):ResponseModel {
    val optionalTodo = todoRepository.findById(id)
    if(optionalTodo.isPresent) {
        todoRepository.delete(optionalTodo.get())
        return ResponseModel("0", "Successfully Deleted")
    } else {
        return ResponseModel("1", "Invalid Todo" )
    }
}


}
```

So, apart from the get_todo endpoint, we have added endpoints for add_todo, edit_todo, delete_todo, and add_todos. We will take a closer look at each of them. However, the first focus on the constructor of the TodoController class. It takes a parameter for TodoRepository, which will be injected by the Spring Annotation. We are using that todoRepository property in all our APIs to read/write to and from the database.

Now, take a closer look at the get_todo API. It uses the findAll method of TodoRepository to get all todos from the DB. Here is the JSON response of that API (note this response will vary as per the state of the database and Todo table):

```
{
    "error_code": "0",
    "error_message": "",
    "data": [
        {
            "id": 1,
            "todoDescription": "Trial Edit",
```

```
                "todoTargetDate": "2018/02/28",
                "status": "due"
        },
        {
                "id": 2,
                "todoDescription": "Added 2",
                "todoTargetDate": "2018/02/28",
                "status": "due"
        },
        {
                "id": 3,
                "todoDescription": "Edited 3",
                "todoTargetDate": "2018/02/28",
                "status": "due"
        },
        {
                "id": 4,
                "todoDescription": "Added 4",
                "todoTargetDate": "2018/02/28",
                "status": "due"
        },
        {
                "id": 5,
                "todoDescription": "Added 5",
                "todoTargetDate": "2018/02/28",
                "status": "due"
        },
        {
                "id": 7,
                "todoDescription": "Added 7",
                "todoTargetDate": "2018/02/28",
                "status": "due"
        }
    ]
}
```

The next API is the add_todo API:

```
@RequestMapping("/add_todo", method = arrayOf(RequestMethod.POST))
fun addTodo(@Valid @RequestBody todo:Todo) =
  ResponseEntity.ok().body(ResponseModel
  ("0","",todoRepository.save(todo)))
```

This API takes a `Todo` from the body of a `POST` request, stores it, and returns a success `ResponseModel`. The following Postman screenshot shows the request sent to the API:

In the JSON request, we are sending all details of `Todo` except the ID, as the `id` field will be autogenerated.

The response of the API is as follows:

```
{
  "error_code": "0",
  "error_message": "",
  "data": [
    {
      "id": 8,
      "todoDescription": "Added 8",
      "todoTargetDate": "2018/02/28",
      "status": "due"
    }
  ]
}
```

The `add_todos` API is almost similar to the `add_todo` API, except that here it takes an arbitrary number of `Todos` to be added to the database.

The `delete_todo` API is different than all other APIs in this project. Take a closer look at this API here:

```
@RequestMapping("/delete_todo/{id}", method =
arrayOf(RequestMethod.DELETE))
fun deleteTodo(@PathVariable("id") id:Int):ResponseModel {
  val optionalTodo = todoRepository.findById(id)
  if(optionalTodo.isPresent) {
    todoRepository.delete(optionalTodo.get())
    return ResponseModel("0", "Successfully Deleted")
  } else {
    return ResponseModel("1", "Invalid Todo" )
  }
}
```

This API takes a `DELETE` request in all other APIs other than the `POST` request (reason is simple, it just deletes `Todo`).

It also takes the ID of `todo` in the path variable instead of `RequestBody`; again, simple reason, we just need one field in this API, that is, ID of the `Todo`, to be deleted. So, no need to take an entire JSON as a request body here. Instead, a path variable will be a perfect fit for this API.

An example request to this API will be this URL—`http://localhost:8080/api/delete_todo/7`. The API will check if `Todo` with the specified ID exists, it will delete `Todo` if it exists; otherwise, it will just return an error.

Here are two ideal responses of this API:

```
{
  "error_code": "0",
  "error_message": "Successfully Deleted",
  "data": []
}
```

If `Todo` was found and deleted, you'll get this response:

```
{
  "error_code": "1",
  "error_message": "Invalid Todo",
  "data": []
}
```

If `Todo` with the specified ID is not found.

Now, as we gained some knowledge on Spring, let's get started with **Reactor**, a fourth-generation reactive programming library by **Pivotal**—the custodian for Spring.

Reactive programming with Reactor

Just like the **ReactiveX** Framework, **Reactor** is also a fourth-generation reactive programming library. It allows you to write non-blocking reactive apps. However, it has some significant differences as compared to **ReactiveX**, as listed here:

- Unlike ReactiveX, which supports several platforms and languages (for example, RxSwift for Swift, RxJava for JVM, RxKotlin for Kotlin, RxJS for JavaScript, RxCpp for C++, and so on), Reactor supports only JVM.
- You can use RxJava and RxKotlin, if you have Java 6+. However, to use Reactor, you need Java 8 and above.
- RxJava and RxKotlin doesn't provide any direct integration with Java 8 functional APIs, such as CompletableFuture, Stream, and Duration, which Reactor does.
- If you're planning to implement reactive programming in Android, you have to use RxAndroid, RxJava, and/or RxKotlin (collectively, ReactiveX) or Vert.X, unless you have minimum SDK as Android SDK 26 and above, that too without official support. As reactor project doesn't have official support on Android and it works only on Android SDK 26 and above.

Other than these differences, Reactor and ReactiveX APIs are quite similar, so get started by adding Reactor to your Kotlin project.

Add Reactor to your project

If you're using Gradle, add the following dependency:

```
compile 'io.projectreactor:reactor-core:3.1.1.RELEASE'
```

If you're using Maven, add the following dependency to the POM.xml file:

```
<dependency>
  <groupId>io.projectreactor</groupId>
  <artifactId>reactor-core</artifactId>
  <version>3.1.1.RELEASE</version>
</dependency>
```

You can also download the JAR file from
`http://central.maven.org/maven2/io/projectreactor/reactor-core/3`
`.1.1.RELEASE/reactor-core-3.1.1.RELEASE.jar`.

For more options, check
out `https://mvnrepository.com/artifact/io.projectreactor/reactor-`
`core/3.1.1.RELEASE`.

So, as we're done with adding Reactor Core to our project, let's get started with `Flux` and `Mono`, producers in Reactor.

Understanding Flux and Mono

As I said, Reactor is another fourth-generation Reactive library like ReactiveX. It originally started as a lightweight version of Rx; however, with time, it grew, and today it's almost of the same weight as ReactiveX.

It also has a producer and consumer module, just like Rx. It has `Flux`, similar to `Flowable` and `Mono` as a combination of `Single` and `Maybe`.

Note that when describing `Flux`, I said Flowable, not Observable. You can probably guess the reason. Yes, all Reactor types are backpressure enabled. Basically, all the Reactor types are a direct implementation of the Reactive Streams `Publisher` API.

Flux is a Reactor producer that can emit *N* number of emissions and can terminate successfully or with an error. Similarly, with `Mono`, it may or may not emit single items. So, what are we waiting for? Let's get started with `Flux` and `Mono`.

Consider the following code example:

```
fun main(args: Array<String>) {
  val flux = Flux.just("Item 1","Item 2","Item 3")
  flux.subscribe(object:Consumer<String>{
    override fun accept(item: String) {
        println("Got Next $item")
    }
  })
}
```

The output is as follows:

```
"C:\Program Files\Java\jdk1.8.0_131\bin\java" ...
[DEBUG] (main) Using Console logging
Got Next Item 1
Got Next Item 2
Got Next Item 3

Process finished with exit code 0
```

The output, as well as the program, is quite similar to RxKotlin, isn't it? The only difference is that we are using `Flux` instead of `Flowable`.

So, let's take a Mono example. Take a look at the following example:

```kotlin
fun main(args: Array<String>) {

    val consumer = object : Consumer<String> {//(1)
        override fun accept(item: String) {
            println("Got $item")
        }
    }


    val emptyMono = Mono.empty<String>()//(2)
    emptyMono
        .log()
        .subscribe(consumer)

    val emptyMono2 = Mono.justOrEmpty<String>(null)//(3)
    emptyMono2
        .log()
        .subscribe(consumer)

    val monoWithData = Mono.justOrEmpty<String>("A String")//(4)
    monoWithData
        .log()
        .subscribe(consumer)

    val monoByExtension = "Another String".toMono()//(5)
    monoByExtension
        .log()
        .subscribe(consumer)
}
```

Before we describe the program line by line, let's first focus on the `log` operator in each of the subscriptions. The Reactor Framework understands a developer's need to log things, that's why they provided an operator so that we can have a log of every event within a Flux or Mono.

On comment (1), in this program, we created a `Consumer` instance to use in all the Subscriptions. On comment (2), we created an empty Mono with the `Mono.empty()` factory method. As the name depicts, this factory method creates an empty Mono.

On comment (3), we created another empty `Mono` with `Mono.justOrEmpty()`; this method creates `Mono` with the value passed or creates an empty `Mono` if null is passed as a value.

On comment (4), we created `Mono` with the same factory method, but this time with a `String` value passed.

On comment (5), we created `Mono` with the help of the `toMono` extension function.

Here is the output of the program:

```
[DEBUG] (main) Using Console logging
[ INFO] (main) onSubscribe([Fuseable] Operators.EmptySubscription)
[ INFO] (main) request(unbounded)
[ INFO] (main) onComplete()
[ INFO] (main) onSubscribe([Fuseable] Operators.EmptySubscription)
[ INFO] (main) request(unbounded)
[ INFO] (main) onComplete()
[ INFO] (main) | onSubscribe([Synchronous Fuseable] Operators.ScalarSubscription)
[ INFO] (main) | request(unbounded)
[ INFO] (main) | onNext(A String)
Got A String
[ INFO] (main) | onComplete()
[ INFO] (main) | onSubscribe([Synchronous Fuseable] Operators.ScalarSubscription)
[ INFO] (main) | request(unbounded)
[ INFO] (main) | onNext(Another String)
Got Another String
[ INFO] (main) | onComplete()

Process finished with exit code 0
```

So, as you have learned about Spring and you also learned about reactive programming with Reactor; would you like to do some research yourself and make our API reactive? As a helping gesture, I would like to suggest that you study a little bit about WebFlux. You can also read through *Reactive Programming in Spring 5.0* by *Oleh Dokuka* and *Igor Lozynskyi* (`https://www.packtpub.com/application-development/reactive-programming-spring-50`).

Summary

In this chapter, we learned about creating a REST API quickly with Spring JPA, Hibernate, and Spring Boot. We also learned about Reactor and its use. We created the RESTful API for our project, which we will use in the next chapter while creating the Android app.

The next chapter, which is the last chapter of this book, is about creating an Android App with Kotlin and reactive programming.

You're about to complete this book—complete learning *Reactive Programming in Kotlin*. Just another chapter is ahead. So, turn the page fast.

12
Reactive Kotlin and Android

So, our learning about reactive programming in Kotlin is almost complete. We have arrived at the last, but probably the most important, chapter of this book. Android is probably the biggest platform for Kotlin. During the last Google IO—Google IO 17, Google announced official support for Kotlin and added Kotlin as a first-class citizen of the Android application development. Kotlin is now the only officially supported Android application development language other than Java.

Reactive programming is already there in Android—most of the top libraries in Android support reactiveness. So, it is quite obvious that in a book titled *Reactive Programming in Kotlin*, we must cover Android as well.

Teaching you Android development from scratch is beyond the scope of this book, as it's a vast topic. You can find many books out there if you would like to learn Android development from scratch. This book assumes you have some basic knowledge in Android application development and can work with `RecyclerView`, `Adapter`, `Activity`, Fragment, CardView, AsyncTask, and more. If you are not familiar with any of the topics mentioned, you can read *Expert Android Programming* by *Prajyot Mainkar*.

So, are you wondering what this chapter has for you? Take a look at the following list of the topics we will cover:

- Setting up Kotlin in Android Studio 2.3.3 and 3.0
- Getting started with `ToDoApp` in Android and Kotlin
- API calls with Retrofit 2
- Setting up RxAndroid and RxKotlin
- Using RxKotlin with Retrofit 2
- Developing our app
- A brief introduction to RxBinding

So, let's get started with setting up Kotlin in Android Studio.

Setting up Kotlin in Android Studio

We strongly encourage you to use Android Studio 3.0 for Android development, irrespective of whether you're using Kotlin or not. Android Studio 3.0 is the latest version of Android Studio, with a lot of bug fixes, new features, and improved Gradle build time.

For Android Studio 3.0, you don't need to do any setup to use Kotlin for Android development. You just need to select **Include Kotlin support** while creating a new project. Here is a screenshot for your reference:

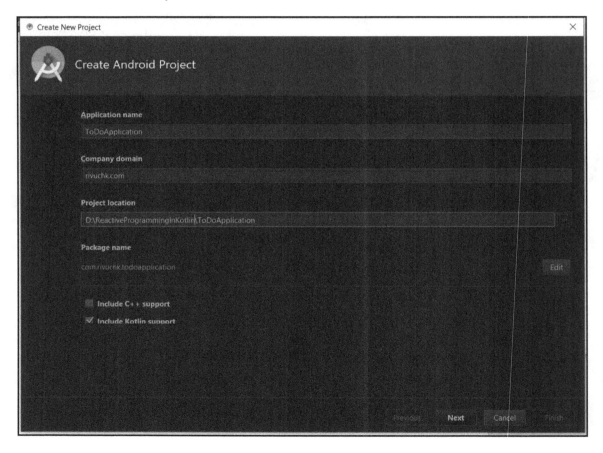

We've highlighted the **Include Kotlin support** section of the Android Studio—**Create Android Project** dialog.

However, if you're using Android Studio 2.3.3, then follow these steps:

1. Go to **Android Studio** | **Settings** | **Plugins**.
2. Search for Kotlin (take a look at the following screenshot) and install that plugin as follows:

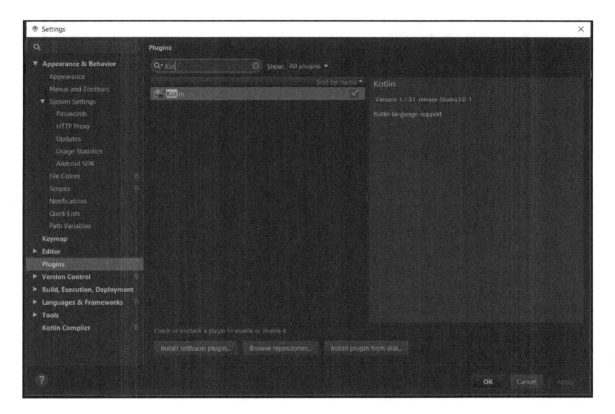

3. Start a new Android project.

4. To apply the Kotlin plugin to the project, open the project level `build.gradle` and modify the content, as shown here:

```
buildscript {
    ext.kotlin_version = '1.1.51'
    repositories {
        jcenter()
    }
    dependencies {
        classpath 'com.android.tools.build:gradle:3.0.0'
        classpath "org.jetbrains.kotlin:kotlin-gradle-plugin:$kotlin_version"

        // NOTE: Do not place your application dependencies here; they belong
        // in the individual module build.gradle files
    }
}
```

5. Open the `build.gradle` in your module (or we might say, app level `build.gradle`) and add the following `dependencies`:

```
compile "org.jetbrains.kotlin:kotlin-stdlib-jre7:$kotlin_version"
```

You are now all set to start writing Kotlin code in Android Studio.

However, before starting with the Kotlin code, let's first review our `build.gradle`. The preceding code that I showed for Android Studio 2.3.3 is valid for Android Studio 3.0 as well, you just don't have to manually add this as Android Studio 3.0 automatically adds it for you. However, what is the purpose of those lines? Let's inspect them.

In the project level `build.gradle` file, the `ext.kotlin_version = "1.1.51"` line creates a variable in Gradle with the name of `kotlin_version`; this variable will hold a `String` value, `1.1.51` (which is the latest version of Kotlin at the time of writing this book). We are writing this in a variable, as this version is required in a number of places in the project level and app level `build.gradle` file. If we declare it once and use it in multiple places, then there will be consistency, and there won't be any chance for human mistakes.

Then, on the same file (project level `build.gradle`), we will add `classpath "org.jetbrains.kotlin:kotlin-gradle-plugin:$kotlin_version"`. This will define a classpath used by Gradle to search for `kotlin-jre` when we add them as a dependency.

Inside the app level `build.gradle` file, we will write `implementation "org.jetbrains.kotlin:kotlin-stdlib-jre7:$kotlin_version"`.

So, let's get started with the Kotlin code. As we mentioned in the previous chapter, we will create a `ToDoApp`. There will be three screens, one for the `ToDo List`, one to create a `ToDo`, and one to edit/delete `ToDo`.

Getting started with ToDoApp on Android

As mentioned earlier, we are using Android Studio 3.0 (stable) for this project. The following screenshot depicts the project structure that we're using:

In this project, we are using package-by features, and I do prefer to use package-by for Android development, mainly for its scalability and maintainability. Also, note that it is best practice to use package-by feature in Android; although, you can obviously use your preferred model. You can read more about the package-by feature at `https://hackernoon.com/package-by-features-not-layers-2d076df1964d`.

Now, let's understand the package structure used in this application. The root package here is `com.rivuchk.todoapplication`, the package for the application, identical with the `applicationId`. The root package contains two classes—`ToDoApp` and `BaseActivity`. The `ToDoApp` class extends `android.app.Application` so that we can have our own implementation of the `Application` class. Now, what is `BaseActivity`? `BaseActivity` is an abstract class created within this project, and all activities in this project should extend `BaseActivity`; so, if we want to implement something throughout all the activities in this project, we can write the code in `BaseActivity` and rest assured that all activities will now implement the same.

Next, we have an `apis` package for the classes and files related to the API calls (we will use Retrofit) and `datamodels` for models (POJO) classes.

We have the `Utils` package for `CommonFunctions` and `Constants` (a singleton `Object` to hold constant variables such as `BASE_URL` and others).

The `addtodo`, `tododetails`, and `todolist` are three feature-based packages. The `todolist` package contains `Activity` and `Adapter` for displaying the list of todos. The `tododetails` package contains the `Activity` responsible to display the details of todo. We will use the same `Activity` to edit as well. The `addtodo` package holds the `Activity` that will be used to accomplish the functionality of adding a todo.

Before starting with the activities and layouts, I want you to take a look inside `BaseActivity` and `ToDoApp`, so here is the code inside the `ToDoApp.kt` file:

```
class ToDoApp:Application() {
  override fun onCreate() {
    super.onCreate()
    instance = this
  }

  companion object {
    var instance:ToDoApp? = null
  }
}
```

A small class indeed; it contains only a `companion object` to provide us with the instance. This class will grow as we move ahead with this chapter. We declared `ToDoApp` as the `application` class for this project in the manifest, as shown here:

```
<application
  android:allowBackup="true"
  android:icon="@mipmap/ic_launcher"
  android:label="@string/app_name"
  android:roundIcon="@mipmap/ic_launcher_round"
  android:supportsRtl="true"
  android:theme="@style/AppTheme"
  android:name=".ToDoApp">

  . . . .
</application>
```

The `BaseActivity` is also now small. As with the `ToDoApp`, it'll also grow over the course of this chapter:

```
abstract class BaseActivity : AppCompatActivity() {
    final override fun onCreate(savedInstanceState: Bundle?) {
      super.onCreate(savedInstanceState)
      onCreateBaseActivity(savedInstanceState)
    }
    abstract fun onCreateBaseActivity(savedInstanceState: Bundle?)
}
```

For now, `BaseActivity` only hides the `onCreate` method from the `Activity` class, and provides a new abstract method—`onCreateBaseActivity`. This class also mandates that we override `onCreateBaseActivity` in child classes so that if there's anything we need to implement inside the `onCreate` method, of all activities, we can do that inside the `onCreate` method of `BaseActivity`, and forget the rest.

So, let's get started with the `todolist`. This package contains all the sources required to display the list of todos. If you look at the previous screenshot carefully, you should notice that the package contains two classes—`TodoListActivity` and `ToDoAdapter`.

So, let's start with the design of `TodoListActivity`; when completed, this `Activity` should look like the following screenshot:

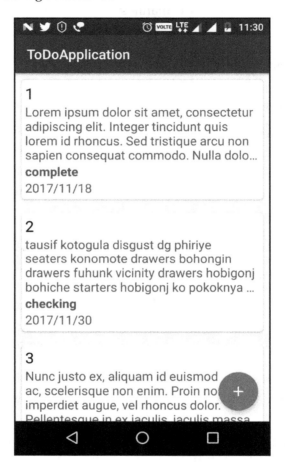

As the screenshot depicts, we will need a `FloatingActionButton` and a `RecyclerView` for this `Activity`, so here is the XML layout for this example—`activity_todo_list.xml`:

```
<?xml version="1.0" encoding="utf-8"?>
<android.support.design.widget.CoordinatorLayout
  xmlns:android="http://schemas.android.com/apk/res/android"
  xmlns:app="http://schemas.android.com/apk/res-auto"
  xmlns:tools="http://schemas.android.com/tools"
  android:layout_width="match_parent"
  android:layout_height="match_parent"
```

```
tools:context="com.rivuchk.todoapplication.
todolist.TodoListActivity">

<android.support.design.widget.AppBarLayout
    android:layout_width="match_parent"
    android:layout_height="wrap_content"
    android:theme="@style/AppTheme.AppBarOverlay">

<android.support.v7.widget.Toolbar
    android:id="@+id/toolbar"
    android:layout_width="match_parent"
    android:layout_height="?attr/actionBarSize"
    android:background="?attr/colorPrimary"
    app:popupTheme="@style/AppTheme.PopupOverlay" />

</android.support.design.widget.AppBarLayout>

<android.support.v7.widget.RecyclerView
    android:id="@+id/rvToDoList"
    android:layout_width="match_parent"
    android:layout_height="match_parent"
    app:layoutManager="LinearLayoutManager"
    android:orientation="vertical"
    app:layout_behavior="@string/appbar_scrolling_view_behavior"/>

<android.support.design.widget.FloatingActionButton
    android:id="@+id/fabAddTodo"
    android:layout_width="wrap_content"
    android:layout_height="wrap_content"
    android:layout_gravity="bottom|end"
    android:layout_margin="@dimen/fab_margin"
    app:srcCompat="@drawable/ic_add" />

</android.support.design.widget.CoordinatorLayout>
```

Take a look at the preceding layout. In the declaration of RecyclerView, we set layoutManager to LinearLayoutManager and orientation to vertical-all from the layout itself, so we would not need to worry about setting it inside the code.

We used a FloatingActionButton to add new todos. We also used AppBarLayout as an action bar.

It's time to move ahead and take a look inside the `onCreateBaseActivity` method of the `TodoListActivity`, as shown here:

```
lateinit var adapter: ToDoAdapter

private val INTENT_EDIT_TODO: Int = 100

private val INTENT_ADD_TODO: Int = 101

override fun onCreateBaseActivity(savedInstanceState: Bundle?) {
  setContentView(R.layout.activity_todo_list)
  setSupportActionBar(toolbar)

  fabAddTodo.setOnClickListener { _ ->
    startActivityForResult(intentFor<AddTodoActivity>
    (), INTENT_ADD_TODO)
  }

  adapter = ToDoAdapter(this, {
   todoItem->
   startActivityForResult(intentFor<TodoDetailsActivity>
   (Pair(Constants.INTENT_TODOITEM, todoItem)), INTENT_EDIT_TODO)
  })
  rvToDoList.adapter = adapter

  fetchTodoList()
}
```

In the preceding program, we created an instance of `ToDoAdapter` to set it as the adapter of `rvToDoList`, the `RecyclerView` where we will display the list of todos. While creating the instance of `ToDoAdapter`, we passed a `lambda`; this `lambda` should be called when an item from the `rvToDoList` is clicked.

We also called a `fetchTodoList()` function at the end of the `onCreateBaseActivity` method. As the name indicates, it is responsible to fetch the todo list from the REST API. We will see the definition and go into the details of this method later, but, for now, let's take a look at `Adapter`:

```
class ToDoAdapter(
  private val context:Context, //(1)
  val onItemClick: (ToDoModel?)->Unit = {}//(2)
  ):RecyclerView.Adapter<ToDoAdapter.ToDoViewHolder>() {
  private val inflater:LayoutInflater =
  LayoutInflater.from(context)//(3)       private val
  todoList:ArrayList<ToDoModel> = arrayListOf()//(4)        fun
  setDataset(list:List<ToDoModel>) {//(5)
    todoList.clear()
```

```
      todoList.addAll(list)
      notifyDataSetChanged()
   }
   override fun getItemCount(): Int = todoList.size

   override fun onBindViewHolder(holder: ToDoViewHolder?,
   position: Int) {
      holder?.bindView(todoList[position])
   }

   override fun onCreateViewHolder
   (parent: ViewGroup?, viewType: Int): ToDoViewHolder {
      return ToDoViewHolder
      (inflater.inflate(R.layout.item_todo,parent,false))
   }

   inner class ToDoViewHolder(itemView:View):
   RecyclerView.ViewHolder(itemView) {
      fun bindView(todoItem:ToDoModel?) {
         with(itemView) {//(6)
            txtID.text = todoItem?.id?.toString()
            txtDesc.text = todoItem?.todoDescription
            txtStatus.text = todoItem?.status
            txtDate.text = todoItem?.todoTargetDate

            onClick {
               this@ToDoAdapter.onItemClick(todoItem)//(7)
            }
         }
      }
   }
}
```

Study the preceding code carefully. It's the complete `ToDoAdapter` class. We took an instance of `context` as a comment (1) constructor parameter. We used that `context` to get an instance of `Inflater`, which in turn was used to inflate the layouts inside the `onCreateViewHolder` method. We created a blank `ArrayList` of `ToDoModel`. We used that list to get item counts of the adapter `getItemCount()` function, and inside the `onBindViewHolder` function, to pass it to the `ViewHolder` instance.

We also took a lambda as a `val` parameter inside the constructor of `ToDoAdapter`—`onItemClick` (comment (2)). That lambda should receive an instance of `ToDoModel` as a parameter and should return unit.

We used that lambda at `bindView` of `ToDoViewHolder`, inside `onClick` (comment `(7)`) of `itemView` (the view for that item in the list). So, whenever we click on an item, the `onItemClick` lambda will be called, which is passed from the `TodoListActivity`.

Now, focus on comment `(5)`—`setDataset()` method. This method is used to assign a new list to the adapter. It will clear the `ArrayList`—`TodoList` and add all items from the passed list to it. This method, `setDataset`, should be called by the `fetchTodoList()` method in `TodoListActivity`. That `fetchTodoList()` method is responsible for fetching the list from the REST API, and it will pass that list to the adapter.

We will look inside the `fetchTodoList()` method later, but let's concentrate on the REST API and Retrofit 2 for API calls.

Retrofit 2 for API calls

Retrofit by Square is one of the most famous and widely used REST clients for Android. It internally uses OkHTTP for HTTP and network calls. The word REST client makes it different from other networking libraries in Android. While most of the networking libraries (Volley, OkHTTP, and others) focus on synchronous/asynchronous requests, prioritization, ordered requests, concurrent/parallel requests, caching, and more. Retrofit gives more attention to making network calls and parsing data more like method calls. It simply turns your HTTP API into a Java interface. And it doesn't even try to solve network problems by itself, but delegates this to OkHTTP internally.

So, how does it transform an HTTP API into a Java interfaces? Retrofit simply uses a converter to serialize/deserialize **POJO (plain old Java object)** classes into/from JSON or XML. Now, what is a converter? Converters are those helper classes that parse JSON/XML for you. A converter generally uses the `Serializable` interface internally to convert to/from JSON/XML and POJO classes (data classes in Kotlin). It being pluggable gives you many choices of converters, such as the following:

- Gson
- Jackson
- Guava
- Moshi
- Java 8 converter
- Wire
- Protobuf
- SimpleXML

We will use Gson for our book. To work with Retrofit, you'll need the following three classes:

- A `Model` class (POJO or data class)
- A class to provide you with the Retrofit client instance with the help of `Retrofit.Builder()`
- An `Interface` that defines possible HTTP operations, including the request type (GET or POST), parameters/request body/query strings, and finally the response type

So, let's get started with the `Model` class.

Before creating the class, we need to know the structure of the JSON response first. We all saw JSON responses in the previous chapter, but, as a quick recap, here is the JSON response for the `GET_TODO_LIST` API:

```
{
  "error_code": 0,
  "error_message": "",
  "data": [
    {
      "id": 1,
      "todoDescription": "Lorem ipsum dolor sit amet, consectetur
       adipiscing elit. Integer tincidunt quis lorem id rhoncus. Sed
       tristique arcu non sapien consequat commodo. Nulla dolor
       tellus, molestie nec ipsum at, eleifend bibendum quam.",
      "todoTargetDate": "2017/11/18",
      "status": "complete"
    }
  ]
}
```

The `error_code` denotes whether there are any errors. If `error_code` is a non-zero value, then there must be an error. If it's zero, then there is no error, and you can proceed with parsing the data.

The `error_message` will contain information for you if there's an error. If the `error_code` is zero, the `error_message` will be blank.

The `data` key will hold a JSON array for the list of todos.

One thing to note here is that `error_code` and `error_message` will be consistent for all APIs in our project, so it will be better if we create a base class for all the APIs, and then we extend that class for each API when required.

This is our `BaseAPIResponse` class:

```
open class BaseAPIResponse (
  @SerializedName("error_code")
  val errorCode:Int,
  @SerializedName("error_message")
  val errorMessage:String): Serializable
```

We have two `val` properties in this class—`errorCode` and `errorMessage`; note the annotations `@SerializedName`. This annotation is used by Gson to declare the serialized name for a property; the serialized name should be the same as the JSON response. You can easily avoid this annotation if you have the same variable name as the JSON response. If the variable name is different, the serialized name is used to match the JSON response.

Let's now move ahead with `GetToDoListAPIResponse`; the following is the class definition:

```
open class GetToDoListAPIResponse(
  errorCode:Int,
  errorMessage:String,
  val data:ArrayList<ToDoModel>
):BaseAPIResponse(errorCode,errorMessage)
```

Here, we skipped the `@Serialized` annotation for `data`, as we are using the same name as the JSON response. The remaining two properties are declared by the `BaseAPIResponse` class.

For data, we are using an `ArrayList` of `ToDoModel`; Gson will take care of the rest to convert a JSON array to an `ArrayList`.

Let's now take a look at the `ToDoModel` class:

```
data class ToDoModel (
  val id:Int,
  var todoDescription:String,
  var todoTargetDate:String,
  var status:String
):Serializable
```

The `builder` class for Retrofit is simple, as shown here:

```
class APIClient {
  private var retrofit: Retrofit? = null
  fun getClient(): Retrofit {
    if(null == retrofit) {

      val client = OkHttpClient.Builder().connectTimeout(3,
```

```
        TimeUnit.MINUTES)
        .writeTimeout(3, TimeUnit.MINUTES)
        .readTimeout(3,
        TimeUnit.MINUTES).addInterceptor(interceptor).build()

        retrofit = Retrofit.Builder()
            .baseUrl(Constants.BASE_URL)
            .addConverterFactory(GsonConverterFactory.create())
            .client(client)
            .build()
        }

        return retrofit!!
        }

        fun getAPIService() =
        getClient().create(APIService::class.java)
    }
```

The `getClient()` function is responsible to create and provide you with a Retrofit client.
The `getAPIService()` function helps you with pairing the Retrofit client with your
defined HTTP operations and create an instance of the interface.

 We used `OkHttpClient` and `Retrofit.Builder()` to create the
`Retrofit` instance. If you're not familiar with them, you may visit
http://www.vogella.com/tutorials/Retrofit/article.html.

Let's now create the interface for the HTTP operations—`APIService`—as follows:

```
interface APIService {
    @POST(Constants.GET_TODO_LIST)
    fun getToDoList(): Call<GetToDoListAPIResponse>

    @FormUrlEncoded
    @POST(Constants.EDIT_TODO)
    fun editTodo(
            @Field("todo_id") todoID:String,
            @Field("todo") todo:String
    ): Call<BaseAPIResponse>

    @FormUrlEncoded
    @POST(Constants.ADD_TODO)
    fun addTodo(@Field("newtodo") todo:String): Call<BaseAPIResponse>
    }
```

We have created API interfaces for all our APIs. Note the return types of the functions. They return a `Call` instance that encapsulates the actual expected response.

Now, what is `Call` instance? And what is the purpose of using it?

The `Call` instance is an invocation of a Retrofit method that sends a request to a webserver and returns a response. Each call yields its own HTTP request and response pair. What to do with the `Call<T>` instance? We have to `enqueue` it with a `Callback<T>` instance.

So, the same pull mechanism, same callback hell. However, we should be reactive, shouldn't we? Let's do that.

RxKotlin with Retrofit

In Android, we can use RxAndroid in addition to RxKotlin for added Android flavors and benefits, and Retrofit supports them as well.

So, let's start by modifying our `build.gradle` in favor of ReactiveX. Add the following dependencies to the app level `build.gradle`:

```
implementation 'com.squareup.retrofit2:adapter-rxjava2:2.3.0 '
implementation 'io.reactivex.rxjava2:rxandroid:2.0.1'
implementation 'io.reactivex.rxjava2:rxkotlin:2.1.0'
```

The first one will provide Retrofit 2 Adapters for RxJava 2, while the following two add RxAndroid and RxKotlin to the project.

 Note that RxKotlin is a wrapper on top of RxJava, so adapters for RxJava 2 will work perfectly with RxKotlin 2.

Now that we have added the dependencies, let's move on by modifying our code to work with `Observable/Flowable` instead of `Call`.

This is the modified `APIClient.kt` file:

```
class APIClient {
    private var retrofit: Retrofit? = null
    enum class LogLevel {
        LOG_NOT_NEEDED,
        LOG_REQ_RES,
        LOG_REQ_RES_BODY_HEADERS,
        LOG_REQ_RES_HEADERS_ONLY
```

```kotlin
}
/**
 * Returns Retrofit builder to create
 * @param logLevel - to print the log of Request-Response
 * @return retrofit
 */
fun getClient(logLevel: Int): Retrofit {

    val interceptor = HttpLoggingInterceptor()
    when(logLevel) {
        LogLevel.LOG_NOT_NEEDED ->
            interceptor.level = HttpLoggingInterceptor.Level.NONE
        LogLevel.LOG_REQ_RES ->
            interceptor.level = HttpLoggingInterceptor.Level.BASIC
        LogLevel.LOG_REQ_RES_BODY_HEADERS ->
            interceptor.level = HttpLoggingInterceptor.Level.BODY
        LogLevel.LOG_REQ_RES_HEADERS_ONLY ->
            interceptor.level =
        HttpLoggingInterceptor.Level.HEADERS
    }

    val client = OkHttpClient.Builder().connectTimeout(3,
    TimeUnit.MINUTES)
        .writeTimeout(3, TimeUnit.MINUTES)
        .readTimeout(3,
        TimeUnit.MINUTES).addInterceptor(interceptor).build()

    if(null == retrofit) {
        retrofit = Retrofit.Builder()
            .baseUrl(Constants.BASE_URL)
            .addConverterFactory(GsonConverterFactory.create())
            .addCallAdapterFactory
            (RxJava2CallAdapterFactory.create())
            .client(client)
            .build()
    }

    return retrofit!!
}

fun getAPIService(logLevel: LogLevel =
LogLevel.LOG_REQ_RES_BODY_HEADERS) =
getClient(logLevel).create(APIService::class.java)
}
```

This time, we added an OkHttp Logging interceptor (`HttpLoggingInterceptor`) along with an RxJava adapter. This OkHttp Logging interceptor will help us log requests and responses. Coming back to the RxJava adapters, look at the highlighted code—we added `RxJava2CallAdapterFactory` as the `CallAdapterFactory` of the Retrofit client.

We will need to modify the `APIService.kt` file as well, to make the functions return `Observable` instead of `Call`, as shown here:

```kotlin
interface APIService {
  @POST(Constants.GET_TODO_LIST)
  fun getToDoList(): Observable<GetToDoListAPIResponse>

  @POST(Constants.EDIT_TODO)
  fun editTodo(
      @Body todo:String
  ): Observable<BaseAPIResponse>

  @POST(Constants.ADD_TODO)
  fun addTodo(@Body todo:String): Observable<BaseAPIResponse>
}
```

All the APIs now return `Observable` instead of `Call`. Finally, we are all set to look inside the `fetchTodoList()` function from `TodoListActivity`.

```kotlin
private fun fetchTodoList() {
  APIClient()
  .getAPIService()
  .getToDoList()
  .subscribeOn(Schedulers.computation())
  .observeOn(AndroidSchedulers.mainThread())
  .subscribeBy(
    onNext = { response ->
                adapter.setDataset(response.data)
              },
    onError = {
                e-> e.printStackTrace()
              }
  )
}
```

The function does a simple task; it subscribes to the API (`Observable` from the API) and sets the data to the adapter when it arrives. You should consider adding logic to check the error code before setting the data here, but for now it works quite well. The screenshot of this activity is already shown at the beginning of this chapter, so we will omit it here.

Making Android events reactive

We have made our API calls reactive, but what about our events? Remember the
`ToDoAdapter`; we took a lambda, used it inside `ToDoViewHolder`, and created and passed
the lambda at `TodoListActivity`. Quite messy. This should be reactive as well, shouldn't
it? So, let's make the events reactive as well.

`Subject` plays an awesome role in making events reactive. As `Subject` is a great
combination of `Observable` and `Observer`, we can use them as `Observer` inside `Adapter`
and as `Observable` inside `Activity`, thus making passing events easy.

So, let's modify the `ToDoAdapter` as follows:

```
class ToDoAdapter(
  private val context:Context, //(1)
  val onClickTodoSubject:Subject<Pair<View,ToDoModel?>>//(2)
):RecyclerView.Adapter<ToDoAdapter.ToDoViewHolder>() {
  private val inflater:LayoutInflater =
  LayoutInflater.from(context)//(3)
  private val todoList:ArrayList<ToDoModel> = arrayListOf()//(4)

  fun setDataset(list:List<ToDoModel>) {//(5)
    todoList.clear()
    todoList.addAll(list)
    notifyDataSetChanged()
  }

  override fun getItemCount(): Int = todoList.size

  override fun onBindViewHolder(holder: ToDoViewHolder?,
  position: Int) {
    holder?.bindView(todoList[position])
  }

  override fun onCreateViewHolder
  (parent: ViewGroup?, viewType: Int): ToDoViewHolder {
    return ToDoViewHolder(inflater.inflate
    (R.layout.item_todo,parent,false))
  }

  inner class ToDoViewHolder(itemView:View):
  RecyclerView.ViewHolder(itemView) {
    fun bindView(todoItem:ToDoModel?) {
      with(itemView) {//(6)
        txtID.text = todoItem?.id?.toString()
        txtDesc.text = todoItem?.todoDescription
```

```
            txtStatus.text = todoItem?.status
            txtDate.text = todoItem?.todoTargetDate

            onClick {
              onClickTodoSubject.onNext(Pair
             (itemView,todoItem))//(7)
            }
          }
        }
      }
    }
```

The adapter looks cleaner now. We've got a `Subject` instance in the constructor, and when the `itemView` is clicked, we call the `onNext` event of the `Subject` and pass both the `itemView` and `ToDoModel` instance with help of `Pair`.

However, it still looks like something is missing. The `onClick` method is still a callback; can't we make it reactive as well? Let's do that.

Introducing RxBinding in Android

To aid us Android developers, Jake Wharton created the RxBinding library, which helps you get Android events in a reactive way. You can find them at `https://github.com/JakeWharton/RxBinding`. Let's get started by adding it to the project.

Add the following dependency to the app level `build.gradle` file:

```
implementation 'com.jakewharton.rxbinding2:rxbinding-kotlin:2.0.0'
```

Then we can replace `onClick` inside `ToDoViewHolder` with the following line of code:

```
itemView.clicks()
.subscribeBy {
    onClickTodoSubject.onNext(Pair(itemView,todoItem))
}
```

It's that easy. However, you're probably thinking, what's the benefit of making them reactive? The implementation here was simple enough, but think of a situation where you've tons of logic. You can easily divide the logic into operators, especially `map` and `filter` could be of great help to you. Not only that, but RxBindings provides you with consistency. For example, when we need to observe text changes on an `EditText`, we generally end up writing lines of code in a `TextWatcher` instance, but if you use RxBindings, it will let you do that as follows:

```
textview.textChanges().subscribeBy {
    changedText->Log.d("Text Changed",changedText)
}
```

Yes, it's really that simple and that easy. RxBinding provides you with a lot more benefits as well. You can take a look at `https://speakerdeck.com/lmller/kotlin-plus-rxbinding-equals` and `http://adavis.info/2017/07/using-rxbinding-with-kotlin-and-rxjava2.html`.

So now, thanks to Jake Wharton, we can make our views and events reactive as well.

Kotlin extensions

At the end of this chapter, I would like to introduce you to the Kotlin extensions. No, not exactly the Kotlin extensions functions, although they are very much related to the Kotlin extension functions. Kotlin extensions is a curated list of the most commonly used extension functions in Android.

For example, if you want an extension function to create a bitmap from a `View/ViewGroup` instance (especially useful while adding Markers in MapFragment), you can copy and paste the following extension function from there:

```
fun View.getBitmap(): Bitmap {
    val bmp = Bitmap.createBitmap(width, height,
    Bitmap.Config.ARGB_8888)
    val canvas = Canvas(bmp)
    draw(canvas)
    canvas.save()
    return bmp
}
```

Or, a more common case, when you need to hide your keyboard, the following extension function will help you:

```
fun Activity.hideSoftKeyboard() {
    if (currentFocus != null) {
        val inputMethodManager = getSystemService(Context
          .INPUT_METHOD_SERVICE) as InputMethodManager
        inputMethodManager.hideSoftInputFromWindow
        (currentFocus!!.windowToken, 0)
    }
}
```

This online listing has a lot more extension functions for you, which are maintained by Ravindra Kumar (Twitter, GitHub—@ravidsrk). So, the next time you need an extension function, take a look at `http://kotlinextensions.com/` before writing your own.

Summary

We are done with the final chapter of the book. In this chapter, we learned how to configure Retrofit for RxKotlin and RxAndroid. We learned how to make our Android views and events as well as our custom views reactive.

We learned how to use RxJava2Adapter for Retrofit and how to use `Subject` for event passing. We also learned how to use RxBindings.

Throughout this book, we tried to go to the depth of reactive programming and cover every possible concept, and we tried to make all our code reactive.

 If you find any questions, or if you get any concerns regarding this book, feel free to drop a email at `rivu.chakraborty6174@gmail.com` and mention `Book Query - Reactive Programming in Kotlin` in the subject line of the email. You can also check out Rivu Chakraborty's website (`http://www.rivuchk.com`) as he regularly posts there about Kotlin, Google Developer Group Kolkata, and Kotlin Kolkata User Group Meetups. He also writes tutorials and blogs there as well as writes introductions to Android Plugins developed by him. Also, when he writes blogs and articles elsewhere, he posts URLs to them on his site.

Thank you for reading this book. Happy reactive programming in Kotlin.

Index

www.ingramcontent.com/pod-product-compliance
Lightning Source LLC
Chambersburg PA
CBHW080624060326

40690CB00021B/4807